IT'S ALL JUST NUTS

IT'S ALL JUST NUTS

Shirley Clayton

Copyright © 2013, Shirley Clayton

All rights reserved. No part of this book may be reproduced, stored, or transmitted by any means—whether auditory, graphic, mechanical, or electronic—without written permission of both publisher and author, except in the case of brief excerpts used in critical articles and reviews. Unauthorized reproduction of any part of this work is illegal and is punishable by law.

ISBN 978-1-300-21320-8

Preface

Life in a British Colony was good. Heavens it was good. From the Middle and Far East to tropical Africa where time virtually stood still. In the early 1900's countless families ventured out to the colonies, pioneering their way thousands of miles to unknown worlds on other continents and the dawning of a new life. This is a gut wrenching life story of such a family. Life, and all its problems was, contrary to popular belief, much the same in these colonies as it was in England, their motherland. It reveals how ephemeral life is; how a lifestyle, safe and secure, can disintegrate like a fleeting mortal wave rolling to shore. Be sure to cherish your life, your family, your circumstances.

It's All Just Nuts *is dedicated to my darling mum and dad, Jilly and Choo-Choo. Without their precious existence in my life this story would not have been possible.*

Choo-Choo was with me during the three months spent writing the book in England, so patient, loving and gracious. My beloved treasure departed this world three years later aged 18 ½ years.

CHAPTER 1

July 1915 Ootacamund, India. Dorothy was far from nervous. Why should she be? She'd travelled on her own through Russia, China and west again to India and she was looking forward to her life with Charles, an officer in the Indian Army. She had known him for three months but little did she know, she didn't know him at all.

Margaret looked at Dorothy. She was quite stunning, a beautiful woman with high cheekbones and full lips, meticulously painted with strawberry red lipstick, accentuating her deep blue eyes.

"Ready Dorothy?" quizzed Margaret whose husband was also an army officer.

"Well, yes, ready as I'll ever be!" Dorothy sounded confident as she stumped out her cigarette in a conch shell, usefully transformed into an ashtray. "Sounds like the car outside. Charles has arranged for Peter to pick us up."

Dorothy closed the windows and shutters in her small room. She had rented a room in a huge old colonial house and was to move into married quarters with Charles after their wedding ceremony. She had packed all of her earthly belongings into an old scuffed leather suitcase that had been her wardrobe through China and India.

She walked to the door and looked back at the smoky room. She stood for a moment and sighed. The car horn sounded outside.

"Come on Dorothy. We'll be late." Margaret sounded anxious.

Dorothy closed the door gently behind her. Her suitcase was heavy and her stiletto heels felt like stilts. Even her legs were feeling like jelly. Don't be mad, she thought to herself. You're getting married to an officer in the army and life can only be wonderful from now on but she hesitated momentarily. Was her sixth sense telling her something else, she thought.

"Thank you Pete." Peter rushed towards Dorothy and took her suitcase from her. "I hope you haven't forgotten yesterdays rehearsal!" Dorothy was out of breath. "You've been a great friend to Charles and we're so grateful to you for agreeing to give me away. My poor father died last year and I know he would have been delighted to have done the honours today."

"I've known Charles for a few years now. I'm really happy for him today. He needs a woman to control him …" Peter stopped short and hurriedly put the suitcase in the boot of the car.

Dorothy thought his comment strange. "What do you mean 'control him'?"

"Oh, ah, nothing really!" Peter tried to make light of Dorothy's forceful questioning.

They drove through narrow streets, twisting and turning through the village and as they turned the last corner the little stone-clad church came into view. It was a pretty little building set amongst leafy trees and neatly manicured lawns.

"We're bang on time." Dorothy sounded confident again. "Maggie, you had better go in before us. Thanks for your help and support."

The church was packed. Charles and Dorothy had agreed on thirty guests and there must have been sixty there. The service was uneventful and they headed to a popular hotel outside the village for the reception. What a reception. It was bigger than Dorothy had anticipated. Charles had ordered the finest French champagne and there were crates and crates of it.

Dorothy nudged Charles. "Charles darling, this is going to cost a fortune!"

"Don't worry my sweet. You're the best thing that's happened in my life and I want to make sure you have nothing but the best."

The champagne and wine flowed freely late into the night and Dorothy was relieved when the guests started to thin out. Her feet were aching. It was shortly before midnight when Charles and Dorothy bid farewell to the last of their guests. Charles had booked the honeymoon suite in the hotel and they gladly headed for their room.

"Thank you my darling. You made me feel like a queen." Dorothy was feeling light headed but was not inebriated enough not to be aware of her sexual feelings.

Charles sat on the bed and took off his shoes. "That was the whole idea. You *are* my queen, the light of my life."

Dorothy and Charles prepared to go to dinner on their second night. She sat on the dressing table stool, richly covered in gold and blue embossed velvet. She looked at

Charles through the mirror as she had a long drink from her beer glass. She placed the glass down gently on the dressing table and continued to screw on her earrings. Charles was ready and was leaning against the windowsill, beer glass in hand.

"Are you ready, my darling?" asked Charles in a relaxed tone.

"I'm almost there." Dorothy had stretched her upper lip to apply her red lipstick, making her voice sound aristocratic. And so it should have. Dorothy was born in England in 1886 to a wealthy family. She had a good education, was well read, an accomplished pianist and singer, and spoke eloquently. In her early twenties she had an arranged marriage to a Belgium Baron in Paris. He was much older than her but died from pneumonia several months after their marriage.

After she was widowed she booked to go on the Titanic's maiden voyage to America in 1912. Fate would not allow her journey on the doomed ship because she changed her mind and in great pioneering spirit headed east on the Trans Siberian Railway to Shanghai. From there she travelled to Canton, then to India where she met Charles, an officer with the Royal Engineers in the British Army. She was a wealthy woman in her own right having inherited her father's estate and the stately fortune from her elderly deceased Baron.

She was a fine woman, dressed immaculately and carried herself well. She certainly *looked* wealthy and although she and Charles had only known each other for three months, they never discussed her financial status.

Dorothy's earrings were in place and she struggled to fasten the matching necklace around her neck. She didn't have to ask Charles to help her.

"I'm starving. I wonder what's on the menu tonight. Shall we wander down to the sitting room?" Charles quizzed her through the mirror.

The passages were wide with high pressed ceilings. Continuous lengths of red and gold carpets adorned the wooden strip floorboards throughout the hotel and leafy tropical pot plants in heavy brass containers crowded the corridors, landings and foyer.

Couples were sparsely seated in the main sitting room and although the atmosphere was humid, a breeze flowed through the French doors opening onto the veranda cooling the air with the assistance of over-head fans flying around at hurricane speed. Dorothy and Charles ordered their Scotch and soda and sat alone in low back red leather chairs, the smell of leather permeating the room.

"Cheers," their crystal glasses clicked together and they sipped the pure spirit. Warmed with the intake of their drinks they went into the dining room and dined like royalty but Dorothy felt unsettled, something wasn't right.

"Let's go on the veranda and cool off." Charles led her outside after dinner.

The hotel was the ideal retreat for a honeymoon, a typical colonial building built specifically for warmer climates with wide verandas that overlooked sweeping green lawns, dotted with fishponds and secluded waterfalls flowing gently over granite rocks. The gardens were particularly attractive in the evenings with strategic lights illuminating the waterfalls, lawns and palm trees. Charles and Dorothy sat arm in arm and took in the scenery, the sound of chirping crickets adding to the tranquillity of the night. Dorothy was anxious, concerned at the cost of their stay. It was a top class hotel and Charles was sparing nothing. He was an army officer yes, but heavens, could his salary cope with such extravagance? She sighed and snuggled down into his chest.

"How about a liqueur?" asked Charles.

"Yes, why not!" said Dorothy as she slid a cigarette into her lengthy cigarette holder.

Charles waved to a nearby waiter. "Can we have two liqueurs please?"

"Certainly sir." The waiter hurried away.

Dorothy blew her cigarette smoke high into the air. "Charles, will you be able to afford our stay here? I'm sure it's going to cost you a fortune."

"Well, yes, I'm sure it won't be that much. Don't you worry about that." Charles didn't sound concerned.

Dorothy sat on the veranda of her new home with a cup of tea in one hand and a cigarette in the other. Although it was 4 o'clock in the afternoon the sun was hot. It felt good and she was as brown as a berry. They had been in the officers married quarters for two months and life was being kind to them. Charles had a batman, Jay, who as an angel. He managed to do so much in a day and was always willing and cheerful. He brought them their early morning tea, prepared breakfast, did the laundry. Ironing Charles' uniform each day seemed so easy for him. The tunics were heavily starched and required ironed without a single crease but somehow he managed. Then there were the other bits and pieces to go with the uniform. The brass buttons, brass badges of rank not to mention the brass buckles on the leather belt and Sam brown. Spit and polish were the order of the day.

Dorothy sat with her eyes shut and heard the familiar scuffle of bare feet. It was Jay.

"Excuse me Mrs Butler. Will you and Mr Butler need anything for dinner?" Dorothy more often than not prepared dinner, usually a light snack, but Jay was always willing to go that extra mile.

"No thank you Jay. Mr Butler should be home in about an hour. I'll prepare dinner."

Jay gave a slight bow turned on his heels and disappeared quickly into the house.

Dorothy lit another cigarette and sighed. Charles had been arriving home late some nights and he assured her he had been catching up on paperwork in the office. It was becoming more regular now. At first it was 9 or 10 o'clock and some nights it was nearly midnight when he'd slink quietly into the house.

She put her cigarette out in a delicately designed pewter ashtray and went into the house. She was happy there but something kept nagging her. She remembered Peter's comments when he took her to the church on her wedding day… "'He needs a woman to control him.'" She kept telling herself not to be concerned about it but it kept coming back to haunt her. What did Pete mean? Dorothy was tempted to speak to Peter but pride prevented it.

7 o'clock. Not another late night she thought. It seemed to be heading that way. Charles smelt of whisky when he

returned from his previous late night out. She pondered as she prepared herself a sandwich in the kitchen. I'm not a fool or a walkover she thought to herself. Why didn't I quiz him that night? He said he'd been at the office yet he smelt of liquor. He wasn't drunk by any means. He was his usual polite, cheerful self. Surely there's not another woman? She'd walk out and kill him. Well, not in that order. She'd kill him first then walk out. She wasn't going to put up with that carry on. Forget it.

She turned on the radio and it crackled into life. Someone was blurting out a news bulletin from London. Very boring she thought. She paced the huge kitchen. Oh heavens, what am I going to do? Her mind was still racing. She wanted to speak to Peter there and then. He lived in the single quarters only a twenty-minute walk away. No. She and Charles had to sort this out themselves without bringing the whole of the barracks into their private life.

It was quarter to twelve and Dorothy had elected to stay up. On previous nights when he had come home late she was in bed and to avoid any disagreements or arguments she had pretended to be asleep. She wanted some answers tonight.

Dorothy was sitting at the head of the oak dining table playing patience, her favourite card game. Patience in more than one way she often thought. She heard a car pull up at the front door. The engine stopped. Silence for a minute and the car door shut. The front door closed. She stared at the door into the sitting room anticipating Charles' appearance.

The dining room light was usually off and Charles sensed Dorothy's presence in the room. He walked slowly to the open door and stopped, Dorothy in his sight.

"Hello." He was nervous. "I'm so sorry I'm late again my darling. Work is just piling up. I'm really letting you down and we're not spending enough time together."

Dorothy had been ready to start the inquisition but suddenly she felt sorry for him. Was he *really* being honest, was he really working late? She'd let things slide this time, but not again.

"I'd like to make this up to you. Can I take you to dinner at the officer's mess tomorrow night?"

Dorothy couldn't bring herself to quiz him, not now. Anyway it was late and she was tired. "Yes my love. That would be great." She held out her hands to him and he walked over to her.

They walked up the steps to the officer's mess. There was a buzz inside. The doorman greeted them and showed them into the sitting room. There was a smell of cigarette and cigar smoke in the large room but that was overpowered by the strong smell of leather from the chairs. Eight ceiling fans spun around fervently as though wilful and determined to clear the smoke from the room. It was cosy and very plush.

Charles led Dorothy to a vacant table near one of the doors leading to the veranda. She sat down and he went to the bar to order their long cold beers, their thirst quenchers in the hot steamy Indian climate. They weren't alone for long when Charles' officer commanding, Sir Edmund Dalhousie and his wife Lady Mary, greeted them and Charles invited them to join their table. He was wondering if he had done the right thing but he had no choice.

"You met wife Dorothy as I recall, a few months ago?" Charles introduced Dorothy.

"Yes of course my dear." Sir Edmund kissed Dorothy's hand and gave her a naughty wink. "It's a pleasure to see you again."

Lady Mary fanned her face with a highly decorated Japanese fan and appeared unconcerned and accustomed to her husband's antics.

"Hello my dear. I trust you're settling in to married life?" Lady Mary sounded genuine. She was known for her sincerity and was always busily involved in charity work with the community.

"Yes. Thank you." Dorothy gave a nervous laugh. It was not the sort of evening Dorothy and Charles had envisaged.

Dorothy saw a couple sitting a short distance away and observed a woman waving in their direction. She saw Charles wave back and he smiled at the woman.

"Who's that?" whispered Dorothy.

Charles was blushing. "Oh just an old friend. Can I get you a drink Sir Edmund, Lady Mary?"

Dorothy was annoyed at Charles fobbing her off. He walked over to the bar and the mystery woman held out her hand and stopped him. Charles kissed the back of her hand, mimicking Sir Edmund's trick. Dorothy couldn't hear what they were saying but Charles only stopped momentarily to talk to her.

Sir Edmund lent back in the wide leather chair. He was a big man, over six feet tall and a big build. He had a ruddy, rugged face. "Tell me Dorothy. What have you been doing since moving into the officers married quarters? I trust you've found plenty to do?"

"Well, actually." Dorothy hesitated, and then thought to hell with it. She remembered she had a mind of her own. "Charles has been working late on and off for a number of weeks and we haven't been able to plan many outings."

"Oh. Hmm." Sir Edmund looked blankly into the room. He looked puzzled and rubbed his chin. "I'm not aware of any staff working excessively late. I'll have to look…"

"Here we are." Charles guided the waiter to their table.

Dorothy was agitated. She hated uncertainty. Blast it she thought. Damn, damn, damn.

They had a superb meal and sat with the Dalhousies. The Scotch flowed freely and the evening went without a hitch. All four were ticking nicely when they bade their farewells well after midnight.

Charles' driver was waiting for them outside the mess and drove them home. Dorothy felt warm and contented and she wasn't thinking about Sir Edmunds comments earlier in the evening.

Two nights had passed. It was 10.30 in the evening and Dorothy was alone. It's happening again, she thought.

"Damn it." she said out loud to herself.

Her thoughts were muddled. Who *was* that woman waving at Charles? Sir Edmund said staff weren't working late. So what the hell was Charles up to? She was fed up. Married for nearly three months and now this. She had to get a straight answer from Charles. She sat in the sitting room gazing into space thinking about that trip she never took on the Titanic and it's ultimate demise into the bowels of the dark cold Atlantic. She was glad of her decision. After all, she'd never have met Charles. She loved him dearly and she knew in her heart of hearts that he cherished her. But just what was he up to? She was miles away when she heard Charles' voice.

"Hello darling."

"Good grief, you gave me a fright. These late nights are really becoming a habit Charles. I think we'd better talk this over as two responsible adults." Dorothy sounded sincere. She found it difficult to sound or feel angry. She wasn't going to leave anything to chance. "Sir Edmund told me the other evening that staff weren't working late, yet you've be telling me you've been working late at the office. What am I to believe?"

Charles took his hands out of his pockets. He thought that looked confrontational and he certainly didn't feel like that inside. "My love, my love, what can I say." He hung his head and walked over to the mantelpiece, his back to Dorothy. He couldn't face her.

Dorothy was almost nervous. What was he going to say?

"The truth is." He stopped and placed both hands on the mantelpiece, looking down at his feet. "Dorothy, I'm in debt. Up to my bloody neck in it." He'd said it. He knew she'd have to know eventually but not this soon into their marriage.

"So? What has that to do with your supposedly 'late nights at the office'?" She sounded almost sarcastic but she wanted the truth.

"I, I um. I've been meeting with some of the chaps in the Sergeant's Mess." He knew he was getting nowhere but found it hard to be straight with Dorothy.

Dorothy sat on the couch. She didn't move or say anything.

Charles was hoping for a prompt from her but it wasn't forthcoming. He felt very uncomfortable. His throat was dry. He walked over to the bar in the corner of the room, still with his back to Dorothy. "Scotch?"

"Yes please." Dorothy wasn't helping him and offered no comment.

He poured two drinks and turned to face Dorothy. She was looking straight at him and had a blank look on her face. He wasn't sure how to read into that. He sighed and walked over to her, handed her a glass and sat down at the far end of the couch.

"I've been gambling. I'm trying to sort out my finances and I hoped that playing poker would solve my problems. It just isn't working and I'm getting deeper and deeper in the crap, to put it bluntly." He sat on the edge of the couch rolling his glass in his hands.

"What do you owe and to who?" Dorothy wasn't convinced.

"Oh I don't know. It's all just piling up."

"For heavens sake Charles, you must know how much you owe your creditors and who are they? This is crazy. You'll have to be straight with me, you know that. If our marriage is going to stay intact we can only be honest with each other. There's no other way."

Charles knew she was right. "I love you more than you'll ever know and I want you to have the very best and I'll go to any length to see that you have the best."

"Don't tell me you've been frequenting the Sergeants Mess. A Major and an engineer at that, and you have to play poker in the Sergeants Mess. For goodness sake

Charles. I bet you Peter is a partner in this too, is he?" Dorothy seemed more concerned about his reputation.

"Well, yes, as a matter of fact Pete is one of the regular four. It's very much a closed shop." Charles felt deflated. He had let down the woman who meant everything to him. "I'm so, so sorry my love. You know what you mean to me and hurting you is the last thing in the world I would want to do."

"How much do you owe?"

Charles didn't answer straight away. He walked over to the window. The lights were not bright on the veranda but they threw a delicate light onto the lawn and date trees in the garden. It looked neat, crisp and green. He needed confidence to continue. He swirled the last bit of whisky in his glass and the crystal tinkled from the ice. He knocked it back and poured himself another Scotch. He poured another for Dorothy and went back to the window. He couldn't face her. He took a deep breath. "Too much. Too damn much."

"How much is 'too much'?" She sounded impartial.

"Four, five thousand pounds". He knew it had to come out eventually.

"That's a lot of money in any man's language. Why in heavens name do you owe so much?"

"Dorothy, I'm an impulsive gambler. I've been gambling for years. I've managed to keep my head above water all these years but things are getting on top of me. I've been borrowing to gamble to pay off the debts and the whole thing is out of control. I owe money to bookies in London as well." He felt like a fool but his problem wasn't new, well not new to him and he wondered how she would react to it.

An 'impulsive gambler.' The words stuck in Dorothy's mind. Surely not, she thought. All of a sudden her wealth felt important to her. Neither of them had discussed finances before. It seemed irrelevant. Money was never important to Dorothy and she presumed Charles felt the same way. Her mind was racing. She didn't want to be dishonest with Charles. No. She needn't be. Not disclosing her wealth is not being 'dishonest' she thought. She's just not telling him. No harm in that.

"Your salary must be a pittance compared to what you owe. You'll never be able to settle that."

"I don't want you to worry about that my love. I'm sure I'll be able to settle it in a few months."

"And how do you propose doing that? Gamble I suppose?"

"I've got myself out of debt before and I'll do it again. I just need a few good hands at poker and I'll be fine." Charles sounded confident, as gamblers usually do.

"No Charles. That's not the answer. You're going to get yourself deeper and deeper into the mire." She wanted to help him. She loved him passionately but she wanted to be careful how she handled it. She was afraid that if he knew her wealth his gambling would continue.

"I have a little money in England, a small inheritance from my father. Let's settle your debts and start afresh. But please Charles, I want you to promise me, promise me faithfully, you'll stop this obsession."

Charles felt terrible but at the same time he knew he was up to his neck in debt and getting out of it this time was going to be hard, if not impossible. "How can I allow you to do that? It's not right. Shall we sleep on it?"

"I don't think we have a choice. If you owe that money, it should be paid and gambling is not going to solve the problem." Dorothy was a level headed woman. "Give me details of what's owed to who and let's get this behind us. Come on, it's late. Let's get to bed."

Chapter 2

Kandi, Ceylon, 1921. Dorothy was heavily pregnant with their second child. Betty, now two, was born in England. Dorothy's life had had so many ups and downs, highs and lows over the last six years that she knew exactly what it was like to be in heaven and the pits of hell. She'd been in both places many times. Her social life had been great but her hardships with Charles had caused her great anguish and mental torment.

Charles' gambling had continued in Ceylon and Dorothy spent many a lonely night in their enormous rambling home in Kandi. Charles was earning a very good salary. He was an engineer by profession and had been seconded into the army during the war. He attested at the rank of Major and was well respected in his profession. The army was in need of professionals after the war and he elected to remain in the army.

His gambling was his downfall. Charles and Dorothy discussed it many times and he always promised to stop. It was like asking him to stop breathing. It was an obsession with him. Every six months or so, she would have to wire her bank in England so she could settle Charles' debts. It was an endless nightmare and the amounts increased. Dorothy couldn't fathom out if Charles was taking advantage of her bailing him out each time or if his problem was seriously getting worse. She feared it was the latter.

She knew Charles loved her and always showed his deepest regrets. His continual habit was seemingly beyond his control and he was taking Dorothy's goodwill for granted. She hadn't used her wealth to finance their living as she was, understandably, terrified that Charles would blow that too. His heart was in the right place and he never queried her financial status. He felt too proud. He wanted to give Dorothy the best of everything and his salary would have seen them through very nicely but his ghastly obsession only put them deeper and deeper in debt.

It was February and Dorothy was expecting her second baby in May. Although they now had a maid and their faithful batman Jay, who came with them when Charles was transferred from India to Ceylon, Dorothy liked to keep busy in the house. She was cutting flowers in the garden as Sir Edmund and Lady Mary were coming for dinner. It was his annual visit to Ceylon and he was to inspect the headquarters and barracks and address the troops. She liked them both and had corresponded with them on a regular basis. She had never mentioned Charles' problem to Sir Edmund and she often wondered if he was aware of it.

As Dorothy pondered, she saw Jay standing on the steps. "Excuse me Mrs Butler. What time will you be eating tonight?"

"Oh. Sir Edmund's arriving at 7.30, so I think 8.30 will be fine, thank you Jay."

Dorothy had cut the flowers just in time. The sky was black in the east and the clouds looked threatening. "We're in for a storm Jay. Could you ask Girlie to close the windows?" Girlie was their maid. Dorothy loved her and she was a gem with Betty. She was a local Indian in her late teens, a strong energetic woman with a round face, which was never without a smile. Her real name was Joyce. Her mother had worked for an English family and her mother chose the name after her employer. She was nicknamed 'Girlie' when she was a baby and the name stuck.

A few large drops of rain fell on Dorothy's arm and the black clouds lit up. About five seconds later there was a clap of thunder and she knew the storm wasn't far away. Many a time she had sat on the veranda alone on summer evenings and watched the storms. She knew so many seconds between the flash of lightning and the sound of thunder meant the storm was that many miles away. Betty clung to Dorothy's skirt. "Come on darling. Let's get inside." Betty ran up the wide wooden steps and Dorothy followed slowly, suddenly aware of the weight she was carrying in her belly.

As Dorothy walked through the hallway she could smell the roast lamb. Good, Jay had started cooking she thought as she went through to the kitchen. She found Girlie peeling the potatoes.

"I think fresh peas and pumpkin would be a nice combination, don't you think Girlie? Don't forget the mint sauce!"

Dorothy got two vases from the cupboard and prepared the flowers on a spare wooden table in the middle of the kitchen.

The darkness set in early that evening, the gaps between the lightning and thunder shortened until a huge crack of thunder shook the house as a flash of lightning lit up the garden and the lights flickered.

"That's all we need tonight." Dorothy spoke to herself.

"It'll probably snow tonight." She heard Charles' voice right behind her. He kissed her on her head.

Dorothy noted his sarcasm. "Yes indeed. If you're home so early tonight, it *will* snow! I presumed you'd be home early tonight anyway. Have a good day?"

The raindrops on the roof became more frequent and seconds later the heavens opened and sounded like an orchestra in full swing, the tin roof accentuating the powerful crescendo. Thunder cracked right over the house again and a lightning flash lit the garden.

Charles had followed Dorothy into the dining room. She wanted to help Girlie lay the table but most if it had been done. Poor Girlie always muddled up the soup and dessertspoons and Dorothy walked around the table moving them into their correct places when she suddenly pulled out a chair and sat down. "Heavens, I feel dizzy."

"You've had a few turns like this recently darling. I think we should call the doctor." Charles sounded very concerned.

"Oh, it's nothing Charles. I'm pregnant. Remember?"

Charles walked up to her and held her head in his hands. "You look very pale. In fact you look a bit *yellow* and pale."

"Don't fuss my darling, I'll be fine. Now let's get ready. Our guests will be here shortly."

"Well even if I say so myself, Jay has excelled himself." Charles concealed a burp in his starched napkin. "Excuse me. Now who's for seconds? Lady Mary?"

"Those roast spuds were beautiful. I won't say no to another one. I'll have to play an extra game of tennis next week!"

Dorothy rang the little bell on the table to summons Girlie. "Sir Edmund?"

"No. No thank you. That was most enjoyable. I'm as full as a pig." Sir Edmund patted his stomach, which was surprisingly flat and muscular for a man of his age and stature.

"Would the ladies like a Port?" Charles walked over to the bar at the end of the dining room.

"I'd love coffee. Shall we have a chat in the sitting room Dorothy and leave these two hunks to enjoy their Port together?" Lady Mary had had a good few glasses of wine and she had to steady herself for a moment when she stood up from the table. "Woo, I've had one too many!" Lady Mary giggled, her speech slightly slurred.

Sir Edmund looked sternly at her over his spectacles. They glanced momentarily at each other and Lady Mary gave him a little wave. His authoritarian look dissolved and broke into a huge grin. "See you in a while. Have yourself a black coffee darling."

There were four coffee cups on the silver tray in the sitting room, Girlie wisely leaving nothing to chance. Dorothy poured their coffee and she sat gingerly in a leather chair.

Charles poured himself and Sir Edmund another Port.

"Charles, I've been hearing various reports over the last year about your…" Sir Edmund stopped. Charles was a personal friend and he hated doing this. But it was his duty, not only to the army but the Empire. Sir Edmund took a deep breath. "Let me get to the point Charles. Your obsession with gambling has people talking in high places in London. I had a wire from the Foreign Office last week asking me to approach you. In a nutshell Charles, you are an embarrassment to the Empire and the army and the whole bloody thing is falling on my shoulders as your commanding officer."

Charles was standing with his hand in one pocket and clutching his glass with the other. He turned to face Sir Edmund and looked down, staring at his feet.

"Damn and blast it. What the hell has London got to do with my personal life? I run a tight ship here Edmund and as you know I take my rank and profession very seriously. What I do in my own time has bugger-all to do with bloody London." Charles was decidedly agitated that his 'cover' had been blown. He thought only he and Dorothy were aware of his obsession.

"I know how you feel Charles. Gambling, when it controls your life, is an illness. It's like alcoholism. Alcoholics drink secretly and clearly you wanted your gambling to remain a secret. The thing…" Sir Edmund was stopped by another outburst from Charles.

"Don't bloody well lecture me. I know what I'm doing damn it."

"You've lost control. My office has several final demands from individuals andcompanies you've borrowed from in London. I'm talking to you as a friend Charles. If this doesn't stop, you'll be kicked out of the bloody army, to put it bluntly. And the boot will come from London. I'll have no control over it. I also understand engineers are needed in Hong Kong. That's between you and me, nothing official." Sir Edmund hesitated. "Heaven knows what you'd get up to there."

Charles was picking the dried wax from the side of a candle on the table. He stared blankly at the candle and only offered a quiet "Hmmm."

They were jolted out of an atmosphere neither were enjoying by Lady Mary shouting from the dining room door. "Edmund, Charles. Dorothy's collapsed. I think she's fainted. I think you should call the doctor."

Charles ran into the sitting room and found Dorothy on the floor, lying in the prone position. He felt her carotid artery. Her pulse was there but weak.

Engineer or no engineer, all army personnel had to learn basic first aid and although he'd never had to use it, his training came in useful.

"I've called Colonel Branch. He'll be here in a few minutes." Sir Edmund knelt down with Charles and they tried to rouse Dorothy.

"I hope she didn't fall on her stomach?" Charles looked worryingly at Lady Mary.

"No Charles. She tried to stand up but fell on her knees and onto her side. I'm quite sure there was no injury to the baby."

Dorothy started to murmur, opened her eyes and placed her hand on her forehead.

"I've got a dreadful headache. What happened?"

"You fainted my sweet. We've called the doctor." Charles placed a cushion under her head. "You were out for a few minutes. Now don't worry."

"You're the one worrying my darling."

"Hello? Can I come in?" Colonel Branch was at the door.

"Yes. Thank you Colonel." Sir Edmund beckoned him in to the room. "The Major's wife fainted and we thought you'd better have a look at her."

Colonel Branch was very tall and thin and wore half rimmed glasses on the end of his nose. His appearance lived up to his nickname 'Twiggy.'

He knelt down next to Dorothy and opened his brown leather bag. He put his stethoscope on her extended belly and listened intently for some time.

"The baby's fine. Now, how are you!" he exclaimed, trying to make light of a tense atmosphere. He placed a thermometer in her mouth and carried on using his stethoscope, listening to Dorothy's chest.

"You're a little yellow." He felt around her liver for some time.

"Yes doctor, I thought that earlier today when she had a dizzy spell and she tried to shrug it off with her pregnancy. What do you think it is?" Charles was still kneeling next to Dorothy.

"Hmm. 102.2. You've got a fever. I'd like to say it's malaria but I'm concerned about your colour. I'll need some blood samples and I'll carry out a few tests. I think we should get you to bed. You must rest. The baby's due in a few months. Now, are you feeling steady enough to stand?" The Colonel was taking control of the situation.

Dorothy managed the long walk down the passage to their bedroom with Charles and the Colonel on either side of her. She walked well but they wanted to be sure she didn't pass out again.

"Let me see Sir Edmund and Lady Mary off. I'm sure they're keen to get away now. I'll be back in a moment doctor." Charles hurried out of the room.

"What's wrong with me doctor? You know I'm fit and strong and I perish the thought of being under the weather. What is it?"

"We'll have a better understanding after I've carried out some blood tests. Now don't worry your pretty little head. I'll take the blood now and give you something to help bring down the fever and help you to sleep. I want you to stay in bed tomorrow."

"I can't stay in bed! I'm just not the type to linger. Ouch, that's a huge needle." She sounded frustrated and annoyed.

"I'll see you in the morning. Just relax and get some sleep." The tall thin slab hurried out of the room and Dorothy heard him talking to Charles in the passage.

It was nearly two months since Twiggy Branch told Dorothy and Charles the news. Dorothy had black water fever. It was thought to be akin to malaria but it affected and enlarged the liver hence the jaundice type symptoms she was experiencing. She continued to have attacks of biliousness and fever. Twiggy visited the house two or three times a week and was concerned about Dorothy's pregnancy.

Dorothy sat on the veranda in the late afternoon sun. The sun was still hot although it was now April and she only had her legs exposed to the sun. She was annoyed that she had no energy. She felt tired although she had done little in the last few months. Colonel Branch's words kept preying on her. 'I must let you know that foetal retardation often occurs in cases of black water fever.' She couldn't get those two words out of her mind. 'Foetal retardation.' It was like a nightmare coming back to haunt her everyday.

Charles had been a tower of strength. He was home straight after work most afternoons. They played chess when Dorothy was up to it or he sat in the chair in the bedroom on her bad days. Her 'bad days' were becoming more frequent and she was often bedridden with fever.

Charles drove slowly up the driveway and parked in front of the house. He saw Dorothy on the veranda and was relieved that she felt well enough to be up. He bundled a newspaper under his arm, pulled his heavy briefcase from the passenger seat and slammed the car door. He stood there and looked up at Dorothy.

"Hello darling." He put his paraphernalia at the top of the steps. "You worry me and I think about you every minute of the day. I spoke to Twiggy today and I suggested you go to London and have the baby there. He was adamant the treatment you're getting here is as good and up to date as it would be in England. How do you feel about it?"

"You know that would cost a small fortune. You really are the last of the big spenders Charles. In any event, I have every confidence in Colonel Branch. Black water fever is a bastard to get rid of and being here or in England wouldn't make the slightest difference. I'm just concerned about the baby but he tells me the heartbeat is strong. You're like a mother hen Charles. I love you for it but please stop worrying. I'll be fine. Thank you Jay." Jay had heard the car arriving and brought them a tray of tea and freshly made sandwiches.

They had had a quiet evening and went to bed early. Charles was a light sleeper and was woken at 4 o'clock with the sound of Dorothy groaning.

"What is it Dorothy?"

"I feel awful. I feel nauseous and my head's spinning. It's terribly hot. Can you put the fan on?" Dorothy's shortly cropped permed hair was saturated with perspiration.

"You've got a fever again. I'm calling the doctor." Charles ran into the hallway wearing only his pyjama shorts.

It was 2am and Dorothy was lying on her back, her torso propped up with half a dozen pillows. Her complexion was decidedly yellow against the crisp white starched sheets. She was in a private room in the local Government hospital in Kandi where all Officers and their families were automatically upgraded to private patient status. Her breathing was shallow and she had been in a semi-conscious state.

Charles was slumped in an armchair next to her bed. He cherished his beloved and was devastated by her illness. She meant everything to him and consequently had been at her bedside for three days since her admission. He would leave for the office at 7.30 each morning and was back at her side before 6 o'clock in evening having showered at home and changed into mufti. Good old Jay routinely placed a freshly ironed uniform in Charles' car. He ate his meals at the Officers Mess. Girlie, their maid and Betty's nanny had been a rock. She and Betty got on like a house on fire and during this upheaval she slept in the spare room in the house, right next to Betty's bedroom.

Charles hadn't slept well for the last few nights, waking frequently to check on Dorothy. Tonight he was extra tired, his head resting on the back of the chair with his mouth open and his raucous snoring was enough to put a herd of elephants to shame. The nightlight on the wall next to Dorothy's bed woke Charles, coupled with confusion in the room.

He had been in such a deep sleep he had been oblivious to Dorothy's screaming. Two nurses were calming her as she tried to get out of the bed. The drip stand supplying saline to Dorothy's arm was lying on the floor.

"Get it out of here. Get that bloody thing out of here. I hate them. Charles." Dorothy was shrieking at the top of her voice. "Charles, help me. Please please kill that thing. They're all over the room now. Charles." Dorothy was screaming and covering her face.

The nurses were having difficulty constraining her. Charles shook Dorothy lightly.

"What is it? What's the matter?"

"Those huge spiders. Look on the wall. Kill them Charles. Quickly."

"Dorothy darling. Listen to me. There are NO spiders in here. I promise. There are none. Believe me. You have been delirious for a few days. It's your fever and you're hallucinating. Believe me darling. There is nothing there. Just lie back and shut your eyes." Charles had to alleviate her fears. She was arachnophobic at the best of times and living in India and Ceylon always posed a real threat of encountering those eight-legged hairy creatures.

The senior night Sister came into the room with a tray covered with a green cloth. She held a small syringe up to the dim light and pushed the plunger with her thumb, expelling the air until a clear liquid squirted momentarily onto the floor. One nurse rolled Dorothy onto her side and in a flash the Sister had inflicted the minute puncture in her rump.

"It's just a mild sedative to calm you down. High fevers can cause hallucinations. Can you see anything on the walls now?"

Dorothy closed her eyes and didn't answer. The nurses had picked up the drip stand and the Sister inserted a fresh needle into the back of Dorothy's hand and checked the saline bag hanging on the stand. It was half empty and she adjusted the drip flow and watched it for a few seconds.

"Everything should be all right now sir. Please push the bell if there are any problems but I'm quite sure she'll sleep now." The Sister and her entourage left the room.

"Phew." Charles rubbed his face and eyes hard with both hands. He leant back in the chair and closed his eyes.

Charles was in his office a few days later, looking at a plan on a drawing board. He wasn't particularly interested in a new bridge development. Well, not at that moment. Too many thoughts were drifting through his mind. A possible transfer. Dorothy's black water fever. Was the baby going to be all right? His gambling problems. "Blood, bloody hell," he said out loud to himself. He was jolted out of his misery by the phone ringing. It was Twiggy Branch.

"Yes, right. Thanks Twiggy. I'll be there right away." Charles placed the receiver gently on its cradle. Dorothy was in labour, three weeks early and they were moving her to a private ward in the maternity wing at the hospital. He sat in his chair for a moment. He didn't want to go to the hospital. There was nothing he could do right now anyway. He knew it. He was afraid.

It was nearly 4.30. Charles decided to call it a day. He drove back to the house and had his usual shower. He had to talk to someone. He explained Dorothy's situation to Jay and Girlie who listened intently and with great concern.

"I'll sleep at the hospital again tonight. Now, madam." Charles got down on his haunches and put Betty on his knee. "Your mother is having a baby so you will have a brother or sister to play with soon. Won't that be great?"

"I thought Mummy was sick? I want to see her Daddy." Betty sounded quiet and inquisitive.

"Well yes, she hasn't been well but she's also having a baby. Children are not allowed to visit in the hospital darling. Mummy will be home soon and we'll all be together. Now let Girlie bath you and I understand you'll be having your favourite scrambled egg and bacon for supper." Charles winked at Jay who beamed down at Betty. He hugged Betty and nudged her towards Girlie. Girlie was a big woman and picked her up with the greatest of ease and sat her on her forearm. "Come on little one, time for your bath."

Charles felt better having spoken to them and especially to Betty. He had been so wrapped up in his visits to the hospital, rushing back and forth between office, house and hospital, little Betty had taken back stage. He had also showered and changed into mufti. Yes, he felt much better.

Charles parked in the car park outside the hospital. He turned off the engine and looked at the hospital. It was only just dark and the lights outside the casualty department lit up the car park. He hated the place. He was reluctant to go in and had to force himself out of the car. He walked through the main doors. The kitchen must have been near the entrance as hideous combined smells of boiled cabbage and disinfectant greeted him. "Institutional cooking," he said to himself. He had no idea where the maternity wing was situated and stopped two nurses to enquire.

It sounded like a good five-minute walk. He was in no hurry. He was really hoping Dorothy would have had the baby by the time he got there. He was concerned about her condition and how she would handle the birth. Twiggy had been confident all would be all right.

He walked up the stairs to the second floor. He saw the notice board 'maternity department' and got a sinking feeling in his stomach. A tough looking woman came out of the office. She looked like a sergeant major, not only in stature and manner, but she had badges plastered all over her chest and epaulettes. She flew down the corridor, her white diamond-shaped headgear trailing behind in the updraft. "Hmmm," Charles said out loud to himself. "Hope she's not attending to Dorothy."

He nearly jumped out of his skin when he felt a hand on his shoulder. He turned around.

"Bloody hell Twiggy, you gave me the fright of my bloody life. How is Dorothy?"

"I've just this minute come out of the delivery room. She had your daughter half an hour ago. Don't worry Charles. She managed very well. She's a strong woman."

Charles put his hands to his face and muffled "Oh thank God for that. I've been beside myself."

"You're looking a bit pale around the gills yourself old boy. Come into the waiting room and I'll arrange for Sister to get you a cup of tea. When Dorothy's settled in her room you can see her, but only briefly Charles. She's very tired."

Twiggy had more news for Charles, not particularly good news. He had to tell him before he saw his new daughter. "Oh Sister, could you arrange for a cup of tea for the Major please? We'll be in the waiting room here." Twiggy lead him into the room.

"Dorothy has been extremely ill the last few months and as I've told you both, foetal retardation is not uncommon in cases of pregnant patients with ….."

"What's wrong with the baby? Blast it, what's wrong?" Charles was envisaging his new baby with two heads or three arms. Even no arms crossed his mind. "What is it?"

"Calm down Charles. It's something minor. Your daughter has no fingers on her right hand. She is perfectly formed in all other respects. A perfect young lass."

"I've got to see them." Charles left the waiting room and stood like a fool in the passage. He realised he didn't know where Dorothy's room was. Twiggy came to his rescue and they walked to the last room in the corridor.

"Just hang on a moment Charles," and Twiggy popped his head around the door. He looked back at Charles, smiled and gave the thumbs up.

Charles' heart was pounding, his mouth dry. Damn it he thought. He should have had a bunch of flowers in his hand. He cleared his throat nervously, and looked around the door. He was surprised. Dorothy was looking good. Her hair was neatly brushed and her lips were as red as cherries. She was propped up in the bed and was holding a little bundle in her arms.

"Hello darling." Charles was nervous. Stupid, he thought. He walked over to her and kissed her on her forehead. He realised Twiggy and the two nurses had left the room. "How are you feeling?"

"Surprisingly well darling." Dorothy didn't want to waste any time. "Do you want to see our little Diana?" and at the same time pulled the shawl back and exposed a tiny little face.

"She's as beautiful as you my love and a true blonde too. I bet you she's got your blue eyes."

Dorothy wanted to tell him more. "Did they tell you about her little hand?" She wanted to show him and she gently removed Diana's right arm from the tightly wrapped shawl. "Isn't it so tiny and beautiful?" Dorothy was smiling at Charles and clearly wasn't concerned with her baby's missing fingers.

"Gosh, yes. Such a tiny hand! She has her thumb though, but so minute. There are little stubs where the fingers should have been."

"The staff said she had a 'deformity' but I don't want to think of it as that. It's just a special little part of our Diana. It's unique to her and special." Dorothy had totally accepted Diana's missing fingers. "Anyway, I think we're very blessed and lucky that it wasn't worse. I had been thinking of all sorts of horrid things the last few months."

Their little love bubble burst when the butch looking Sister with the air of a sergeant major stormed into the room, her head veil still bouncing wildly behind her. A nervous looking young nurse accompanied her.

"Good evening Major. Your wife has had a difficult few hours and we're taking the baby to the nursery so your wife can rest".

Charles wanted to stay with Dorothy as he had done in the other ward. He was sure the 'sergeant major' wouldn't allow it. She was talked about frequently in the Officers Mess and the chaps always said she was a force to be reckoned with. But he thought he would give it a try.

"Ah, Sister. I've been sleeping in the ward with my wife during her illness and I'd like to stay with her…" What he thought would happen, happened. Mrs Tough Cookie didn't hesitate to interrupt.

"Not a chance Major. I run an efficient ward and I'm not having it look like a boarding house. Your good wife will be fine and if there are any problems we will telephone you, which is normal hospital procedure."

Charles was highly annoyed to say the least. He knew he could override her decision but he realised Dorothy was a lot better, better than he thought she'd be and in any event, he wasn't prepared to argue with the old hag.

"I'm delighted you're so much better darling. And well done. Our Diana is beautiful. I'll see you tomorrow."

CHAPTER 3

Hong Kong 1928. Diana was six years old. Betty was eight. They now had a sister, Barbara, who was four. Barbara was born in Hong Kong, shortly after Charles' transfer there. Charles and Dorothy had fallen in love with Kandi and both had been reluctant to move to Hong Kong. Charles' batman, Jay, was able to transfer with Charles. Girlie was their private maid and the girls' nanny and she was happy to go with them to Hong Kong. She loved the girls and was almost part of the family.

Hong Kong had brought them a new life but also new problems. Horse racing was a major sport in the British Colony. But it wasn't just a sport for Charles. It became his life, so much so that his beloved family came second in his life. He wasn't able to control his speculative habit and he knew it and it was ruining him and his family. He spent so much time phoning the bookies that he frequently got behind with his work. He worked late to catch up then couldn't resist the back street gambling houses. Playing poker with the boys in the Sergeants Mess in India and Ceylon was child's play compared to the uncontrollable cancer that was now eating him alive. He would arrive home at 1 or 2am most mornings.

Dorothy gave up waiting for him to come home. They virtually lived separate lives. She continued to finance his cancerous addiction. She had no choice, short of leaving him or worse, divorcing him. He lavished Dorothy with an endless supply of gifts for her and their home. The children had the best clothing available. It was futile asking him to stop.

Charles would use his salary on family necessities and if there was any left over, it went on his nightly escapades. When he ran out of money, he borrowed and borrowed and still borrowed. It became a vicious, uncontrollable merry go round. A never-ending roller coaster.

Dorothy was accustomed to various individuals knocking on their door. It was invariably their last resort. They had reached the end of their patience trying to pin down Charles and thought their safest bet was to find him at home. Many a time he had these men in his study, tempers flared and doors slammed. Like a continual pumping oil well, Dorothy had to bail him out each time. Fortunately the inheritance from Dorothy's father was miraculously elasticised. She knew it wouldn't last forever but Charles was oblivious to it.

Despite their ups and downs Charles and Dorothy had a deep love for each other. Dorothy gave him his dues. He came home late but she knew, she just knew, sixth sense, honesty between them, call it what you will, there was no other woman in Charles' life.

She had made new friends, played tennis and kept a beautiful garden. She kept herself busy. Betty and Diana attended a private English school a few blocks from their house and Dorothy and Girlie took it in turns to do the school runs, which involved a ten minute walk through one of the most affluent leafy suburbs of Hong Kong. The house was perched high on a hill overlooking the harbour with beautiful views day and night.

Charles sat at his office desk. Work was piling up. There were three major surveys in his pending tray, which should have been completed by now. The phone rang. He assumed who it might be and he was right. Someone after their money. He made his usual promises, which were invariably as empty as a colander under a running tap.

"Damn creditors," Charles said to himself. "They should be called predators, more to the bloody point."

He leant back in his chair, his hands behind his head. He knew his life was in a mess. Bookies, horse racing, roulette, all controlling his life. He couldn't damn well stop. It wasn't a game between him and Dorothy either. Charles didn't comprehend the gravity of the situation and was nonchalant, almost oblivious to it at times. It was just Charles, just his way of life. It was Dorothy's elasticised inheritance that kept his creditors at bay and that too had become routine. Being an engineer he should have been aware that elastic, when pulled continuously to capacity, will eventually break. It has to. It's the law of averages.

Charles was brought back to reality when the phone rang. Bookie or predator he thought. He picked it up. "Hello? Ahum. Good afternoon Brigadier." Why the hell, Charles thought to himself, was 'egg on legs' phoning him? The Brigadier never phoned him. They invariably corresponded by letter. "Yes Sir. Certainly. 8.30 tomorrow morning." He put the phone back on its cradle very slowly, deep in thought.

'Egg on legs' was the Commanding Officer for the entire region. He was bestowed with the nickname because of his all too weird shape with his huge waist and skinny short legs, which dangled precariously from his necessarily outsized uniform shorts. He was so wide the local community believed a whole cow was used to make up his leather belt and Sam brown.

Charles pushed himself to take a folder out of his pending tray and he opened a large plan. He couldn't concentrate. It was nearly 4.30 and he wanted to be with Dorothy. All of sudden he didn't want to head downtown for his nightly ritual.

He decided to drive home via the back roads and wanted to avoid the hustle and bustle of down town Hong Kong. He wasn't in the mood to drive cautiously through narrow streets, unruly pedestrians, rickshaws and endless rows of shop stalls. He took the scenic route through affluent suburbia, huge colonial style houses sparsely placed on either side of the roads. Neatly clipped lawns swept down on both sides of the road with colourful hydrangeas and geraniums thoughtfully placed and it looked like a highway to heaven.

Needless to say Dorothy was cautiously surprised to see Charles home at a civilised hour. "Charles you must be sick! What a nice surprise." She didn't intend to be sarcastic. It wasn't in her make up.

They both enjoyed a quiet evening and a game of chess. "Let's sit on the veranda for a while." Dorothy did so on her own most evenings and often wished Charles was with her to enjoy the view. She got up from the chess table and held out her hand to him. "Come," she said quietly.

It was serene and cosy up on the hill. The only sound was the wind rushing through the palm trees in the garden. It was secluded and private with the nearest homestead two hundred yards away. They had uninterrupted views of the harbour, the shoreline demarcated at night by the lights on the junks hugging the shore. Lights flickering from anchored cargo boats near the horizon added to the lustrous vista.

"I could stay here forever." Dorothy leant against Charles on their swing seat.

Charles didn't answer. He was still wondering why the Brigadier wanted to see him. He wasn't in the mood to tell Dorothy. He would, but not now. He never kept anything from her now, even his gambling. She knew all about that.

The sky above them and the garden lit up briefly. A few seconds later thunder rumbled behind the house.

"There's a storm brewing. Shall we hit the hay and listen to the rain on the roof?" Charles put his arm around Dorothy's shoulders and kissed her on her cheek.

Charles was in bed before Dorothy. He watched her sitting at her dressing table. First a cream, then it was wiped off. Then something else and that was wiped off too. Then yet another cream. Then a hairnet to keep the curls in place.

"A thing of beauty is a joy forever," joked Charles.

Dorothy jumped into bed next to him like a five year old. "You never see all this because you're forever dealing out cards or watching those silly balls going aimlessly round and round those roulette wheels or whatever you call them." Dorothy giggled and kissed him briefly.

He grabbed her around the waist and pushed her onto her back. Their sex, when they had it, was still as good as on their wedding night, if not better. They both believed that was the best recipe for a good marriage, coupled with total honesty, in and out of bed. If there wasn't that, something would snap eventually.

The rain pelted down on the tin roof. It was almost deafening. They loved the sound. They lay in each other's arms in the dark, lightning flashes illuminating the room occasionally.

Charles woke early. He immediately had a sinking feeling in his stomach and he knew the impending meeting with the Brigadier woke him, not so much his unusually early night. He brushed his teeth and went into the kitchen to make himself a cup of coffee. He went out onto the veranda and sat on the edge of the swing. The sun was just breaking the horizon, half a red ball sitting on the sea. He sipped his coffee and thought about egg on legs. "What does the fart want?" Charles was at ease talking to himself.

"Who's the fart?" Dorothy stood in her dressing gown with her hands clasped around a cup of coffee and sounded vaguely intrigued in a sleepy way. She sat beside him, also on the edge of the swing, mimicking him.

"Old egg on legs phoned me yesterday and wants to see me at 8.30."

Dorothy knew who he was talking about. "Did he say why?"

"No. No indication. I don't know what the hell it's about." Charles sounded a little anxious.

Deep down they both had a pretty good idea why the Brigadier wanted to see him but neither of them wanted to think about it, let alone talk about it.

The sun had pierced the horizon completely now and globules of water shone on the ruby red bougainvillea flowers, like little eyes looking out to sea. The sun rose by the minute and as it did so the eyes could see further out to sea, calm and glassy after the storm the night before.

"Bye darling. Let me know what his Lordship has to say," Dorothy kissed him through the car window.

Charles drove to the army camp where his office was located. The army headquarters for the Far East was also located in the camp barely a five minute drive from Charles' office. Needless to say the Brigadier was based at army HQ.

Charles went to his office first, to get his mind into gear. He wasn't sure what gear it was in but he wanted to steady his nerves. 8.15. He had better leave.

He stood outside the Brigadiers office. It was 8.25. Charles felt like a schoolboy outside the headmaster's office, waiting for a caning. The old Brigadier was a formidable chap actually. He didn't take crap from anyone and always went by the book. One couldn't fault him. Well, except his shape. Charles grinned to himself.

A Lieutenant came out of a door marked Chief Clerk, right next to the Brigadier's office, bang on 8.30. "Good morning Major. The Brigadier will see you now." He opened the door for Charles. Charles marched in, stood to attention and saluted the very round fat man sitting at a large desk.

"Sir," snapped Charles.

"Sit down Major. This won't take long."

Charles removed his cap and chose to sit in a hard upright chair.

"I'll get to the point Major. This office has received three letters of complaint, final demands actually, in the last week from reputable members of the community. You owe these men an awful lot of money, in fact more than you and I would even earn in an entire year. I had a call from London last week as well. Someone in Hong Kong wrote anonymously to the Minister of Defence complaining about your gambling debts. Whilst we object to anonymous letters, clearly people are agitated and concerned about monies owing to them. We have been aware of your gambling habits. However, we were not aware of the magnitude of your debt. This cannot be tolerated within the army, especially commissioned ranks. What have you to say for yourself Major?"

What could he say? He felt like a caged animal. Snared. Caught. He thought he had been playing his cards close to his chest and wasn't aware old egg on legs had his finger on the pulse. Charles was more than annoyed his creditors had written to HQ.

"I always settle my debts, Sir, and these will be settled as well."

"And how do you propose paying these vast amounts?" The Brigadier was going red in the face.

"Um, my wife has a little money in England and we can arrange payment in a week or so."

"This problem of your stems back a good ten years, to India and Ceylon. You have had previous warnings, duly recorded in your record of service. You're an embarrassment to the army let alone the bloody Empire! You are to be discharged from His Majesty's Services. This directive has come from the Ministry of Defence in London. Your three months notice will commence today. That's all Major."

"Sir, if I settle……..." Charles was plunged into silence.

"You are to be discharged from the army. The chief clerk has the details. That is all, Major."

No point fighting city hall Charles thought to himself. He put on his cap, stood to attention and gave a swift salute.

"Sir" snapped Charles again, did a sharp about turn and marched from the room. He gave the chief clerk's office a wide birth and headed for his car. "Damn it, damn it, damn it," Charles muttered to himself.

Charles went home at 4.30. It was the second night he wasn't interested in going downtown. Whether he went or not, it was too late. The damage was done. He sat in the car outside the house. Who was that bastard who wrote anonymously to London he thought. He sighed. How was he going to tell Dorothy? She loved Hong Kong. So did he. What about the girls? What the hell were they to do? His mind was racing.

He went into the house. He heard chatter and laughter in the kitchen. He stood at the kitchen door and saw his beautiful daughters. All three had their hands in a huge mixing bowl on the table; they were up to their elbows in flour and brown cake mix. Barbara was too small to reach the bowl and was standing on a wooden stool whilst Girlie steadied her. Dorothy was greasing a cake tin.

"My my my. What do we have here? Cordon bleu chefs in the making eh?" Charles smiled at Dorothy.

Dorothy was quick to explain the chaos. "We're making a chocolate cake for Diana's seventh birthday tomorrow. Seven. Can you believe it! How are you darling?"

"I'm parched. I'd love a cup of tea. Can I have a word with you darling?" Charles suddenly felt an urgent need to tell Dorothy what had happened. She was a level headed woman and he drew strength from her.

Dorothy sensed something was wrong. "Girlie, can you carry on and help the girls get the cake into the oven please?"

"Yes Mrs Butler. I'll bring you a tray of tea." Girlie had been their maid for nearly ten years and she too knew something wasn't right.

Dorothy and Charles sat on the veranda where they found sanctuary and peace. It was a muggy afternoon after the storm last evening. The sun had done a one hundred and eighty degree turn since they had sat there in the morning. A huge red ball hung precariously above the horizon falling almost noticeably to its inevitable resting place in the bowels of the ocean. The sky was bright crimson with hints of purple and red with dozens of strips of pink cloud lying horizontally and motionless across the sky and that red ball.

"A red sky at night," were Charles' first words after minutes of silence.

"Is a shepherd's delight," finished Dorothy. Girlie had brought their tray of tea. "Thank you Girlie. A plate of sandwiches too. You're spoiling us. Will you bath the girls and get supper ready?"

"And no chocolate cake until they're finished their supper. We decided to make two, one for pudding tonight and one for the party tomorrow," chuckled Girlie. She had her usual friendly spunk about her.

"What is it Charles? What's wrong? You're home early two nights in a row, which tells me something. I know you too well. What's happened?" Dorothy sounded stern.

"Oh Christ Dorothy. I'm in the crap. Right in it, up to my bloody neck." Charles knew he could talk openly to Dorothy. He relied on her and trusted her explicitly. He was never shy or embarrassed talking to her. "I saw Mr bloody 'egg on legs' this morning. In a nutshell, I've been fired. Kicked out of the army. Three months notice from today. Unemployed and no fixed abode on the 12th August."

Dorothy didn't answer. She didn't really have to. It had happened at last. His gambling had got the better of him and she knew it would happen eventually. They both sat silently for a few minutes. The sun had changed colour and its purple head was slipping behind the earth's bulge, barely visible now in the late spring haze.

"Needless to say Charles, all to do with your gambling." Dorothy made a statement and wasn't questioning him.

"HQ has received three final demands and he tells me some bastard wrote to London – to the Minister of Defence no less, belly aching about my debts. The letter was anonymous apparently. It could have been anyone but I wish I knew who the hell it was. I'd wring his bloody neck." Charles gazed blankly out to sea.

"You've really put your foot in it this time. I suppose I can blame myself in some respects for having fuelled your blasted addiction. What would you have done, had I not kept bailing you out?" Dorothy sounded deflated.

"Probably been behind bars a long time ago." He was fed up and feeling irritable.

Dorothy was feeling far from comfortable. "I suppose I'll have to contact my bank in London and do the necessary *again*. Operation normal. Really Charles, I'm getting just a little fed up with all this. It just goes on and on. It never damn well stops. What's the damage this time?" She seldom lost her rag but she was almost at her wits end with him.

"I don't know. I think it's in the region of £6,000." There was a sense of remorse in his voice.

"What?" Dorothy shouted. Her outburst was involuntary. "You're joking. You must be bloody joking."

"I wish I bloody well was," replied Charles quietly.

"That's it. I've had enough Charles. Enough is enough. You can go to bloody hell." Dorothy stormed into the house like a raging tornado.

The following weeks were rough for both of them. They barely spoke to each other. Charles surprisingly, was home by 5 o'clock every day. He spent his evenings in his study whilst Dorothy played patience in the sitting room. It was their nightly ritual. The children were oblivious to their problems and Dorothy had no intention of mentioning them to her girls. They were far too young.

Dorothy never concentrated on her games of patience. She was quite content to be on her own in the evenings as it gave her time and space to think. She had not spoken to Charles about his mounting debt. Clearly it worried her and she knew in her heart of hearts she would have to settle them. She was intentionally putting off the evil moment. She wanted him to think about it and sweat, which seemed to be working, because she had never seen Charles so quiet and withdrawn. Had he learnt his lesson this time? Never she thought.

He had cost her a small fortune over the years. She knew her father's inheritance was dwindling rapidly and there would be very little left after forking out the £6,000 owing on his latest gambling frenzy. The supposedly bottomless pit was almost empty and Dorothy's stomach turned. What the hell will they do when it *does* run out? She perished the thought and didn't want to think about it but she had to be realistic. They had three girls to bring up and educate and above all she wanted them to enjoy the lifestyle they were accustomed to. She was deep in her thoughts when Charles' voice brought her back to earth with an unpleasant bump. She was enjoying her space and her ability to think her life through.

"Tea, darling?" Charles' voice was almost a whisper. He had a small tray, set with one teacup.

She really wasn't in the mood to talk to him. She was wrapped up in her thoughts and she didn't want to get involved in small talk with him. "Just leave it there." She was abrupt and pointed to a small table next to her.

Charles got the message loud and clear. She certainly wasn't ready to talk to him. "I think I'll be off to bed."

Dorothy didn't answer him. She was devastated. He had ruined his career in the army and he was ruining his family.

Another two gruelling weeks passed and the household was taking on the characteristics of a mortuary. Even Betty and Diana had asked Dorothy what was wrong with their Mummy and Daddy. Girlie and Jay had noticed too but they knew it was not for them to make any comments or ask questions. Dorothy had always been open with Girlie and Girlie wondered why she was not offering an explanation.

Dorothy knew she had to break the ice eventually. Charles wasn't in a position to do it. He knew Dorothy wouldn't budge until she was ready and he had to rely on her to offer the olive branch, if she was willing to do that. Over the past month, Charles had been harassed by his creditors. They had phoned him almost on a daily basis at the office and they were threatening to take legal action. Charles kept stalling by assuring them the money was coming from London. He had no idea if Dorothy had arranged funds from her London account. He knew he had cooked his goose with her and couldn't bring himself to ask her. That would have been the final straw. He had to wait it out.

It was now six weeks before Charles would be out of the army. Time had flown and they had achieved nothing in trying to decide what to do with their lives after that. Their nightly routine was becoming a habit and still little conversation took place between them. Dorothy realised it couldn't go on and she was conditioning herself into talking to Charles again.

As usual, she was in the sitting room after supper with her pack of cards for company. She heard a car drive up to the front of the house and a car door slammed. She heard footsteps come up the wooden steps and onto the veranda. They stopped. She heard a strong knock on the front door. Who the hell is that, she thought.

She knew Charles was in the study next to the sitting room and had obviously heard their unknown visitor arriving as well. She was right as she heard Charles open the study door, walk along the passage and into the hallway. Dorothy heard muffled voices but couldn't hear what was being said. The voices continued for a few minutes then she heard the front door closing. Charles walked back to his study and she heard the door close.

Dorothy played another game of patience. She was itching to know who their visitor was but she couldn't bring herself to talk to Charles. She could be as stubborn as a mule if she wanted to be.

She heard the study door open. Good, she thought, he's made the first move. The sitting room door didn't open. "Damn it. Probably went to the bathroom," Dorothy whispered to herself.

Ten minutes later the sitting room door opened and Charles came in with another peace offering, hoping it would work this time.

"Thank you." Dorothy sounded more amenable than usual and Charles breathed a sigh of relief. "Two cups tonight I see."

Charles gave a nervous short laugh. "Well, yes," he hesitated. "Ever hopeful." He didn't know what else to say and didn't want to fluff his inroads. "Can I be mother?"

"Yes please. Not too much milk for me." Dorothy was finding it a bit easier but she also wanted to know who had been at the door. She couldn't contain her curiosity and she knew Charles would be receptive. "Who was at the door?"

Charles wanted to tell her but he was afraid how she would react. He hesitated for a moment, cautious how to word it. His sense of honesty and forthrightness came to the fore, as was his usual wont with her. "It was the clerk of the civil court." He stopped momentarily. "He served a summons for me to appear in court next week. It's a civil writ. Those three chaps have gone the whole hog, obviously went to their lawyers and are demanding their £6,000." He had mixed feelings. He was glad he had got it off his chest but was terrified how his beloved would react. He loved her and didn't want to lose her.

Dorothy sat silently, both hands clasped around her teacup as she stared uninterested at her hand of cards on the table. She was quiet for a few minutes and Charles was beginning to feel uneasy. He sipped his tea nervously.

Dorothy took a deep breath. She remained quiet for a few moments. "I don't know Charles. What are we going to do?" She knew it was a pointless question. She knew exactly what would happen. "I suppose I will have to foot the bloody bill again." She could feel her blood pressure going through the roof. She knew she had to calm down. Another confrontation wasn't going to solve the problem. "Charles, I am running out of money. I don't know if that makes sense to you. I don't have much left. I'm trying to tell you in plain, simple English. If I pay this I will have very little left and I won't be able to get you out of the muck again." Dorothy remained calm and to the point. She had more to say. "If it ever happens again, I will leave you Charles and I'll go back to England with the girls. I mean it Charles. I won't have you wreck their lives."

Charles felt no relief with her offer. He was devastated that he was hurting the only person he had loved with such passion. They were both silent for a long time.

Dorothy broke the silence again. "I'll wire the bank in the morning. The transfer will take a few days. It should be here before the bloody court date."

Charles took a long time to respond. "Dorothy. You have no idea what you and the girls mean to me. You are my life, my reason for breathing. I'm just heartbroken that I've hurt you. I think you know that. My problem has been an illness I suppose. It's been something I haven't been able to control. This latest incident has scared me. I was afraid of losing you and that's the last thing I want. I promise you I'll do everything in my power to stop."

Dorothy had to drum home her circumstances, which were in her interests as well as his. "I can't reiterate or emphasise this enough. I am running out of money." She said the last sentence slowly and decisively. "I'm going to say it again Charles. I am running out of money. I won't be able to do this again, even if I want to. We will be out on the streets, begging."

Dorothy's bank obliged as they normally did and Charles was able to present a cheque to the clerk of the civil court the day before the court hearing. The case was duly erased from the civil roll and the court file closed.

Another chapter closed in Charles' life thought Dorothy, but she lived in perpetual fear of what he would do next and where it would take their lives.

Girlie put the mail on the kitchen table having collected it from their letterbox at the end of the driveway. Dorothy was in the kitchen concocting a concentrated cool drink for the girls. They loved lemon juice and sugar and iced water when they got home from school.

She noticed a foreign stamp on one of the envelopes and took a closer look. It was from Africa and addressed to Charles. Dorothy was intrigued but wasn't going to open mail addressed to him. She'd have to contain herself until he got home.

True to his word, Charles was home each evening at 5 o'clock and tonight was no exception.

Dorothy greeted him in the passage and wasted no time. She had the letter in her hand. "I'm fascinated by this letter from Africa. Please open it!" She was like a child on Christmas Day.

Charles went into their bedroom and took off his stuffy tunic and put on a cotton shirt and shorts. He joined Dorothy in their favourite spot. "I recognise the writing. I think it's from Sir Edmund." Charles used the end of a teaspoon and opened the letter carefully and lent back on the swing. It was only two pages and didn't take him long. "Hmm. Interesting. Very interesting." There was an air of excitement in his voice.

"What is it? What does he say?" Dorothy sat on a folded leg and jumped up and down on the swing. "Can I read it?"

"Hang on, hang on." Charles sounded happy and held the letter above him out of Dorothy's reach. "You know that Sir Edmund was transferred to Africa from India. Well I wrote to him a few months ago when all this nonsense flared up and asked him if he could put out a few feelers for me on the job front. He gave my credentials to an engineering company and they want me!"

"Let me see, let me see," Dorothy grabbed the letter from Charles. "Oh, he says the company will write to you!

Sounds exciting. Africa! Heavens, what do you think Charles?"

"It will be great. We'll start a new life. There'll be no chance of gambling there! Apparently there are lots of new opportunities and development going on."

Dorothy came down to earth. "I wonder what the schooling will be like for the girls. Oh gosh, we were going to stay in Hong Kong and we were going to rent a house for now."

"Darling, someone here was after my guts. Some bastard stuck a knife in my back when he wrote to London. You know that. As much as we love it, I don't particularly want to go into civilian life here knowing there's a snake out there who might strike again and it could be for another reason. I just don't like the prospect. There are some good schools in Africa, a lot run by missionaries."

"It does sound exciting, doesn't it? Shall we pop a cork tonight?"

Charles was over the moon with Dorothy's excitement.

The house looked like a warehouse. Boxes were piled high, furniture wrapped with cardboard and bound with rope and an air of excitement and expectation abounded. Dorothy, Jay and Girlie hadn't stopped in weeks and Charles did his bit in the evenings as well. The girls never stopped asking questions. They knew they were going to Africa and wanted to know every detail. What would it be like, what would the school be like, what would their new house look like. Their inquisitiveness was endless and invariably Dorothy couldn't give them a decisive answer, not because she didn't want to, but she was as much in the dark as they were. But they all knew it would be a new life and an adventure into the unknown.

Charles had received a letter from his new employer days after receiving the good news from Sir Edmund. The company, based in Nairobi, Kenya had offered to pay for Charles' relocation, including the shipping of their furniture and the fares for the entire family on a ship bound for England. They were to disembark at Mombassa on the East coast of Africa. Charles had successfully negotiated the inclusion of Girlie in the company's package. They had asked her to join them and she agreed, much to the delight of everyone and especially the girls. Girlie was part of the family and they all perished the thought of parting. Jay was to remain at the house and was to be batman to the army officer replacing Charles. Jay had been with him from India days and there was an air of sadness around. He had elected to take the day off on the day they left and said he would head for downtown Hong Kong to try and take his mind off their departure.

It was the 12th August, the day Charles and Dorothy dreaded and a day they thought would never happen. Charles was being discharged from the army. The ship taking them to their new life was leaving Hong Kong on the 16th August and the army had allowed them to remain in their government house until they left. Charles didn't have a penny to his name but of course they were accustomed to that. Their relocation was funded totally by his new employer. Charles had arranged for the finance clerk at HQ to forward his final salary cheque to his new company. Every little helped.

Charles and Dorothy were cautiously excited on the day of their departure. Their last night in the house had been quiet – and empty. They rattled around and their footsteps echoed throughout the house, their furniture already despatched to the ship. The army quartermaster had loaned them camp beds and bedding for their last few nights. They cooked on a small paraffin stove also On His Majesty's Service.

Betty, Diana and Barbara were immaculately dressed as was Girlie. They were waiting on the veranda for over two hours before their taxi was due. There was lots of chatter and laughter and they seemed unconcerned at leaving the house that had been home to them for so long, the thoughts of the ship and a new continent were far more important now.

Dorothy and Charles did a systematic check through each room in the house to ensure everything was clean and that they had left nothing behind. They went outside to join the children and Girlie. Their timing was spot on as the taxi arrived minutes later. Their furniture was to accompany them on the ship and they hoped they would travel with it overland to Nairobi. But that was weeks away and they wanted to spend time together on the ship, relax and take in the sun.

The ship dwarfed them as they made their way along the quay, the smell of the sea, fish and oil culminating into customary dockside smells. It was a British mail ship and made regular journeys between the Far East and England carrying passengers and cargo. Charles saw a large notice on a building near the ship, marked Customs and Immigration.

"Come on darling. Let's clear customs and immigration." Charles showed his family into the building, and with all the paper work in order, led his team to the side of the ship and elected to go up first. Charles had a suitcase in each hand and walked up the gangplank, which swayed slightly as the family followed eagerly behind. Girlie took up the rear and she too was weighed down with a suitcase in each hand.

A member of the crew showed them to their cabins. They had been allocated three cabins, all next door to each other as they had requested. A major debate had already taken place some weeks ago between the girls and Girlie and there had been a consensus on the sleeping arrangements. Betty and Diana would be together and Barbara would share with Girlie.

"I'm delighted we've got outside cabins," said Dorothy as she peeped out of the porthole.

"Yes. I was quite sure we'd be given an inner cabin. The new boss is obviously a generous old fellow. Anyway, one gets quite claustrophobic in those inner cabins. Shall we go on deck?"

"Let's check on the girls." Dorothy went into the cabin next to theirs and Betty and Diana had their heads at the porthole both trying to look out at the same time. The cabin looked cosy and more than adequate for the girls. Charles checked the porthole was permanently sealed. Good, he thought to himself. There was an inter-leading door between the girls' cabins, which was ideal. It was probably designed as a family suite and of course Girlie would be able to keep an eye on them.

"That's an ideal set up. Are you happy with your cabin Barbara, Girlie? They're rather fun and cosy aren't they?" Dorothy was very happy the girls were nearby.

"Come on everyone. We're going on deck. I feel as though I'm in a harem with all these women around me." Charles smacked Dorothy on her rump.

The girls ran along the corridor like a herd of wild animals and Girlie had to rein them in. They stood on the deck and watched the quayside workers doing last minute chores. Everyone must have been on board as a crane lifted the gangplank away from the side of the ship. The quayside was full of family and friends saying their goodbyes to the passengers.

"There's the Blue Peter." Charles looked up on one of the masts near a funnel stack where the flag had been hoisted.

"What's the Blue Peter?" asked Diana.

"It's the name of the flag a ship flies shortly before setting sail," said Charles.

The ropes were released from the quay and two tugs stood by, one either end of the ship, ready to guide her out of her bay. There was a long hoot and the ship shuddered, a strong solid shudder as the starboard propeller was thrown into action.

The gap between the quayside and the side of the ship widened and the railings started to vibrate. A small stream of black smoke now rose from the chimneystack as the tug near the bows started to position herself and nudge the huge ship further away from the quay, until she was facing the vast ocean. The port propeller was activated, joining its partner and the water swirled like a boiling witches cauldron and the shuddering intensified as smoke thickened from the funnel stack.

Diana clung to her mother's hand and Dorothy felt her little hand in hers. She grasped it with both hands and gave it a loving rub. She loved Diana and her little deformed hand. They were all so accustomed to it now no one noticed it. Dorothy felt tears welling in her eyes and she was grateful for Diana and her safe birth despite her own grave illness those seven long years ago.

The bows sliced effortlessly through the turquoise water, which looked greener on some days than others. Then there would be patches of deep blue then green as though an undecided artist had swept his brush across a canvas. The ship rolled gently as she steamed westwards towards Africa, the throb of the engines monotonous yet giving a sense of adventure and purpose.

On the second last day of their trip, Dorothy and Charles were woken as usual by the cabin porter with their morning tray of tea. There was something different that morning. The porter was anxious and spoke decisively and quickly.

"Captain tells us we're heading into a tropical storm. The sea's pretty rough out there this morning." The porter was holding the tray with great concentration as he tried to steady himself in the doorway of their cabin. "You had better keep a hold of the tray sir or it will end up on the floor." He put the tray on a chest of drawers next to Charles' bed and couldn't let go until Charles held the tray. From their bed they could see the ship was rolling; one minute they saw the sea from their porthole and the next minute blue sky.

Dorothy decided the girls should get dressed and get on deck. Dorothy and Charles had travelled on ships before, albeit on their own and before they had met, aware that the best thing to do when the sea is rough is to get on deck to avoid bouts of seasickness.

Dorothy dressed and went into Betty and Diana's cabin to find Girlie had taken the bull by the horns and had told the girls to dress. All four were in the one cabin, Betty looking decidedly pale and they looked nervously at Dorothy.

"The sea looks rough today Mrs Butler. What do you want us to do?" Girlie was looking for support.

"This is exciting Mummy. Can we go up and look at the sea?" Diana was sitting on the bunk, which was probably the safest place to be. The others were holding on to bits of fixed furniture as the ship rolled from side to side.

"It will be better if we all go on deck. We'll feel better up there."

Dorothy led the gang out of the cabin and along the corridor. They were flung in unison from one side of the corridor to the other and stopped on occasions, feet strategically apart to steady themselves. They felt more comfortable as they climbed the steps at the end of the corridor, able to cling to the rails. Then up another set of steps, then another until they could smell the sea air.

There was very little blue sky now and thick black clouds had gathered around them, with huge cumulus clouds towering tens of thousands of feet above the sea. The weather had certainly changed and the wind was reacting to the brewing storm as it churned the sea, like an orchestra responding to its conductor. It had started raining ahead of the ship and the blanket of rain hung like a massive grey blind pulled down from the black turbulent clouds swirling above. It looked threatening and ominous and as the ship rolled and pitched, sailors ran around the deck collecting chairs that had been flung in all directions.

It was too rough to remain on deck and passengers had gathered in the lounges on deck, protected from the weather by thick glass. Dorothy and Charles headed for one of the lounges, the children and Girlie herded together. A senior officer clad in a white uniform with volumes of gold braid on his epaulette was addressing the passengers.

"The Captain is not concerned about the storm. We have encountered much worse but it is obviously of concern to you and we would like to alleviate any of your worries. The storm is at its peak now and we do not anticipate it getting any worse. Breakfast is now being served and those with strong stomachs are requested to make their way to the dining room."

The passengers appreciated his joke and there was spontaneous laughter and clapping. About twenty passengers took up his offer including Charles' brood, Dorothy and Girlie. They all had a strong constitution and they weren't going to allow the storm get the better of them.

They dillydallied over breakfast as there wasn't much else to do with the decks out of bounds during the storm. An hour and a half was spent in the dining room and they noticed the rolling and pitching of the ship had subsided. With stomachs full of cereal, fruit, eggs, bacon and toast and copious cups of coffee, they ventured up on deck again.

A pleasant transformation confronted them. The grey mass of rain and towering cumulus clouds were on the horizon behind the ship and numerous wisps of cirrus hung high in the sky above them. A few miles ahead, almost as though a rubber had been swept across the sky, the line of cirrus stopped and blue sky beckoned. They stood on the deck and watched the sea. The colour varied from dark blue behind them where the storm was petering out to tropical blue beyond the bows where the suns rays had found their way beyond the cirrus cloud. Dorothy wondered if it was a good omen and would it mean a bright new life in Africa. She was brought back to earth when Charles slipped his arm around her waist.

"Penny for your thoughts," Charles whispered in her ear.

"Oh, they're priceless. Not for sale. We arrive in Africa tomorrow. The time has flown by. I hope someone's there to meet us."

"Everything was confirmed, and they're aware of our arrival date. Everything will fall into place," Charles reassured her.

CHAPTER 4

Nairobi, Kenya. 1928. They had been in Kenya for nearly four months. It was magical, absolute bliss, heaven on earth. Charles had turned over a new leaf and had remained true to his word and avoided the pestilent habit that had dominated their lives. Dorothy was elated and thought it was nothing short of miraculous. He had an extremely good salary, much more than he had earned in the army and his new boss John Harvey, director of the engineering company, did everything possible to ensure their comfort. Dorothy got back to her tennis and was heavily involved with charity work with Lady Mary. Sir Edmund was transferred to Kenya a few years earlier from India. He was again appointed Commanding Officer for the region and he and Lady Mary were well settled.

Charles had a company house in an affluent suburb on the outskirts of Nairobi. As with all their previous houses it was a rambling residence with the standard tropical veranda to cool and protect the house from the savage African sun. The house was enhanced by a manageable sized garden caringly maintained by the gardener, Sixpence and Dorothy. Sixpence and the three girls put the wooden crates from their journey to good use and constructed a superb tree house high in an acacia tree in the back garden, with windows tastefully curtained by Girlie from old dresses. Old corrugated iron sheets made a perfect roof and Charles erected a rope ladder enabling the girls to clamber up and down the tree like a troop of monkeys.

The company had a huge amount of work on its books. Kenya was a new British Colony and new ventures and businesses were springing up in the country. Houses, factories, buildings, bridges and railways were mushrooming everywhere and Dorothy and Charles were sure their future was secured for many years ahead.

Christmas Day was weeks away. The girls, Girlie and Dorothy decorated the tree in the sitting room after Dorothy and Sixpence had scoured the area and had found a healthy branch which they hack-sawed off the main trunk of a fir tree. They found an old paint tin in the garage, a left over from the previous tenants, filled it with sand and rocks and the tree stood very elegantly next to the fireplace. The girls took it in turns placing colourful balls on the tree. They had wrapped old matchboxes with colourful paper and tied them like parcels leaving a loop, enabling them to hang on the branches. Despite the intricate way the boxes were tied and looped, Diana managed to do her bit with her one and a half hands. It never ceased to amaze Girlie how she managed to tie the tiniest of bows and reef knots using her thumb and the little soft bump in place of her forefinger. They placed strips of white cotton material on top of the branches, and with a stretch of the imagination resembled a dusting of snow.

"Necessity is the mother of invention. That looks beautiful. First class. Well done everyone." Charles stood in the sitting room doorway admiring the tree.

"It looks good, doesn't it?" Dorothy stood back to admire their handy work. "Now, we've been mixing the Christmas cake. We waited for you to come home so we can all have a wish before putting it in the oven." Dorothy took him by the hand and they went into the kitchen followed by the troop, trailing behind like a row of monkeys. She removed the damp cloth from the bowl of cake mix and they took it in turns to stir the mixture with a big wooden spoon, each making a secret wish as they did so.

"That will take a good four hours to cook. Now everyone...." Dorothy was stopped by the girls.

"Don't slam the doors or the cake will sink," said Diana and Barbara in unison as though mimicking Dorothy. They all knew the routine.

Christmas Day was very much a family day, but they invited their old friends Sir Edmund and Lady Mary, as their children were now grown up and living in England. Dorothy and Girlie did most of the cooking with help from Diana, who was the most domesticated of the girls and loved cooking.

Charles was very busy at work. He impressed everyone he came into contact with, including other engineering companies and local government authorities. He was able to maintain fairly regular office hours and he and Dorothy enjoyed an excellent relationship.

Dorothy on the other hand enjoyed working with Girlie in the house and spent a lot of time designing various parts of the garden with new shrubs, flowerbeds and rock gardens. She worked well with Sixpence who also contributed to new ideas. She played tennis once a week and gave her time in the local community. The children attended a missionary school nearby and life was good, very good. Dorothy would never have dreamt that their lives could have changed for the better.

Charles was to attend a meeting in John Harvey's office. He knew nothing about it but knew some high-powered businessmen were attending. Charles arrived at Harvey's office fifteen minutes before the appointed time, at Harvey's request. Charles knocked on the door.

"Come in," was the muffled response.

Charles opened the door and went in. "Hello Mr Harvey."

"I would like to fill you in before the clients arrive, Charles. These chaps represent a consortium and they've asked us to prepare a plan for local government. They're keen to have a racecourse built in Nairobi. I'd like you to give them your views."

"Yes certainly." Charles was oblivious to the ramifications of such a project and merely thought of it as a challenge.

Four men attended the meeting with Harvey and Charles. They had produced a rough plan of their proposals, desired location, buildings required and length and shape of the course. It was agreed Charles would approach the local planning office prior to a full survey, to establish their willingness for such a project.

Charles wasted no time in seeing the local planning officer. The proposed site was available for use and was suitably positioned in relation to other projects already submitted to the planning office.

"We've been given the green light," Charles informed Harvey a few weeks later.

"Excellent. Can you get the land and course surveyed and in the meantime I'll inform our clients and they can give us a comprehensive idea of the buildings and stables they require. Let's go for it. This is going to be a great recreational sport for the local community."

The months passed. Everything was running smoothly in Charles' household but not in Charles and Dorothy's secret thoughts. Dorothy was well aware of the new racecourse being built and both of them never broached the subject, purposely. Deep down Dorothy was terrified of what might happen and Charles tried to put his worrying thoughts at the back of his mind. He knew it would never happen again. It just couldn't.

Charles had to tell Dorothy about the official opening. "We've been invited to the official opening of the race course next week. It's going to be quite an event apparently and the Governor will be attending."

"I don't care if the King himself attends," Dorothy sounded purposely disinterested.

"What do you mean?" asked Charles.

"It means I'm not going."

"You can't not go, darling. We've both been invited and it'll look pretty stupid if I go on my own." Charles was concerned.

"Tell them I'm sick," replied Dorothy.

"Be realistic. You are really taking this too far. It will be quite alright." Charles wanted to convince her.

"I told you Charles, I am *not* going. Subject closed." She was adamant.

Charles knew better than to get into an argument with his beloved. "You are worrying unnecessarily but if you don't want to go I can't force you but I will have to go. Harvey will expect me to be there."

Charles did go on his own. Dorothy didn't want to be part of his old habit, as though she condoned it.

The weeks ahead were gruelling for Dorothy. The horseracing had started and she heard from Sixpence and Girlie that it was drawing big crowds. She was always quietly delighted when she heard Charles' car in the driveway every afternoon. He was never late.

For several months he arrived home after work and he helped the children with their homework. Dorothy and Charles kept much to themselves and were not great party goers. They enjoyed each other's company and played chess most evenings. There was nothing fragile about their relationship.

It happened one evening, months after the racecourse had opened. Dorothy couldn't believe it. She thought she was dreaming and pinched herself. No, she thought. No, no no. Something must have happened to delay him. The girls were old enough now to ask questions.

"Where's Daddy? It's nearly 9 o'clock," queried Betty.

"He probably had a late meeting. I'm sure he'll be home soon," hoped Dorothy. "You girls had better get ready for bed. You've got school in the morning."

Dorothy wanted to face this on her own. She was accustomed to it. It was after 11 o'clock before Charles came home. He locked up the house but couldn't find Dorothy in the sitting room. He went into their bedroom and found Dorothy in bed, reading. He greeted her nervously "Hello love. Sorry I'm late." He didn't offer an explanation.

"Hello," said Dorothy. She slammed her book closed, turned off her bedside light and slid down under the blanket.

The next night arrived all too soon. It was 10.30 when Charles came home. She and Charles ignored each other the following morning. She was feeling devastated. Were her worst fears looming into reality? She wasn't going to allow a repeat of their weeks and weeks of silence in those dark days in Hong Kong. She decided she was going to wait up for him that night and get to the bottom of his recent late nights.

11 o'clock, then 11.30. No sign of Charles. She heard his car at 11.45. She had to confront him. She had no choice. She stood in the middle of the passage, her arms folded. She was ready for battle, or was she? Her heart was pounding. Charles walked into the passage from the hall and he stopped in his tracks when he saw the woman he loved, poised for a fight.

"Let's go in the sitting room." She walked straight in to the sitting room and stood at the door. Charles followed her like a lamb to the slaughter. She slammed the door in an attempt to condition herself into a rage. She had to bump up her adrenalin. "What's going on?" She sounded stern, sterner than Charles had ever heard her.

"What can I say? I think you know what's happened." There was a dull tone in his voice.

"I'm not a bloody clairvoyant. Well?" She wanted to hear it from him.

"I owe money but it's not out of control."

"I knew it. I knew it would happen. It was too bloody good to be true. You were fine for over three years. It was that blasted racecourse. You've been betting, lost and now you're gambling to pay your debts, right?" Dorothy's anger had a tinge of sarcasm. She wasn't finished. "I've told you before and I'll tell you again. I do *not* have any more money to bail you out Charles. *It is finished*," she screamed at the top of her voice. Dorothy was shaking. Not only had her temper got the better of her, she was afraid. Very afraid. She broke down and sobbed into her hands. Charles placed his hand on her shoulder to console her. She knew she had to control herself. "Leave me alone." Dorothy was swift to move away from Charles.

Charles felt empty inside as though his life, his whole world had been pulled away from under him. "Oh heavens, darling."

"Don't darling me. If you don't stop we're going to be destitute." She wanted to know how much debt he was in. She knew she couldn't help him any more. He had drained her London account. These dreadful fears added to her anger and frustration. "Let me see your recent bank statements."

"I don't know what that will achieve." He knew there were only a few pounds in the account.

"Let me see them Charles." Dorothy was not going to let up. It involved the whole family.

Charles knew he couldn't win. He went into his study, retrieved a file from a filing cabinet and returned to the sitting room. "It's getting very late. Shall we look at this tomorrow?"

Dorothy ignored him and took the file from him. She sat in a chair with the file on her lap and paged through it slowly. "Hum, at least you keep your filing up to date," snarled Dorothy. She had to remain focused, remain angry. She was thinking of their three girls and they needed educating. If Charles lost his job now they would be up the creek without a paddle. There was a lot at stake. "You've written out four cheques for quite substantial amounts recently. You had actually been saving some money Charles and it's gone, boom. Account empty. Who were the beneficiaries?" Dorothy felt like a private detective but she had no choice.

"It's all gambling related. You know that Dorothy. I just had a flutter when the racing started and it'll stop."

"It *won't* stop Charles and we both know it. You are head of this household and supposedly the breadwinner and I have never interfered with your salary or handled the family accounts. That has always been your department." Dorothy knew she had to take hold of the family finances. She continued. "I want you to ask Harvey to pay your salary in cash every month and I want you to close your bank account." Dorothy was firm and her anger had left her.

"That's ridiculous," replied Charles.

"It is not for heavens sake. We'll keep an eye on the finances together and keep the money locked away in your study. We'll keep a petty cash book of sorts. I don't want you writing out cheques willy-nilly to pay your bloody debts. You have a family to think about." Dorothy was worn out.

"We've always agreed on everything Dorothy but I draw the line there and in any event, I don't want to raise Harvey's suspicions. It's out of the question." Charles sounded determined.

"Fine. Do it your way. Carry on in your own sweet way and don't come crying to me when you get final demands and all the bloody rest of it. I've had it Charles." Dorothy stormed out of the sitting room.

The following months tested Charles and Dorothy's resolve. They muddled through each day, each week and managed to converse on daily matters. Charles was home late most evenings. Dorothy was invariably in bed and asleep when he returned home. She would receive phone calls in the evenings from men asking for Charles. It was a strain on their marriage and it was as though they had reached a stalemate. She had virtually washed her hands of his addiction. Whatever she did, it didn't help him and it was as though she was living on death row. The girls fortunately had been busy with school and their activities and they had joined the Girl Guides. Dorothy had confided in Betty and Diana as she thought them old enough to understand but they weren't able to grasp the gravity of the situation.

Dorothy was waiting for the inevitable. It happened, as she feared, at about 8 o'clock one evening. As she recalled, they had had an unwelcome visitor at their house in Hong Kong at about the same time in the evening. It seemed like a lifetime away.

A civil court official was looking for Charles to serve a summons. Dorothy was drained and at her lowest. She asked the official if she could see the summons and she scanned her eyes over the legal jargon until her eyes focused on what she had been looking for – a figure. £2,000. She told him he would be home much later and if he wanted to return after 11 o'clock, he would probably find him at home.

That was no small amount of money. Dorothy felt sick. Sick because she no longer had financial freedom. She wasn't able to help Charles or her family and she felt like a caged animal.

Dorothy saw the summons on Charles' chest of draws in the bedroom the next morning. He had not tried to conceal it from her. She pretended she hadn't seen it. He had got himself into the mess and he could get himself out of it she thought. She knew the hearing was two days away and there was nothing, nothing she could do to help him.

The girls had just left for school and Charles and Dorothy were in the dining room. He wanted to tell her about the summons he'd received the night before. He had always meant well and was always honest with Dorothy. He trusted her explicitly and somehow he still drew strength from her. But he knew, they all knew, his addiction was a grey, secret part of his life over which he had no control.

"I received a summons last night. I have to appear in court the day after tomorrow." Charles' voice was bland.

"I know. The court official was looking for you earlier......." Dorothy was cut short with Charles snapping at her.

"Why didn't you let me know," demanded Charles.

"For Pete's sake Charles, what a stupid comment. How the hell could I? You never tell me where you are at night, probably in some sleazy filthy bar or gambling room." Dorothy was enraged. "You can go to bloody hell." She stormed out of the dining room and into the back garden.

Charles had to appear in court. They just didn't have the finances to settle his debt. The plaintiff's lawyer and the court agreed that Charles should pay off the debt. It wasn't going to be easy and because of the size of the debt, he would have to pay almost half his monthly salary to the clerk of the civil court for over two years. It was either that or prison and if it was the latter, the plaintiff would never have seen his money.

Dorothy believed it was the beginning of the end. Although Charles was earning a good salary, halving it was going to impact on their living. They reluctantly had to release Sixpence from service. He had been with them since they arrived in Nairobi and he was a first class gardener. They were able to find other employment for him which helped Dorothy's sense of guilt. They could barely afford to keep on Girlie but she was part of the family and it would be virtually impossible asking her to leave. After paying the girls school fees and Girlie's wage, there was hardly enough left over for food. It was unsustainable.

Dorothy could turn her hand to most things. In a moment of weakness and panic she telephoned Sir Edmund and asked to see him. She didn't know who else to turn to. She arranged to meet him early one afternoon at his office at army headquarters. She walked to his office, about three miles from the house. She didn't want to tell Charles, not yet anyway, so he couldn't drive her there and the cost of a taxi was out of the question. The afternoon sun was always piercingly hot. She took shortcuts where she could, footpaths through areas of bush and her feet and shoes were full of dust by the time she arrived at headquarters feeling dirty and sweaty.

"Hello Dorothy. Come in. This is a surprise." Sir Edmund was always firm but cheerful.

"Hello Sir Edmund. Thank you for seeing me." Dorothy wanted to get to the point. "Charles will probably kill me for having seen you but my hands are tied. Charles had a civil writ against him a few weeks ago and the court instructed half his salary be paid to the plaintiff, which will take a few years to settle." Dorothy stopped for a moment.

"Dear, dear, dear. I thought Charles had stopped all that nonsense. I am sorry my dear," Sir Edmund was sincere.

"I'm not asking for any favours but I wanted to ask you if there is any work available for me in the army, in a civilian capacity of course." She stopped again and was wondering if she was doing the right thing but necessity forced her to continue. "I'm happy to do anything that's available."

"What a co-incidence. I was speaking to the quartermaster this morning and he's in need of staff – sorting out kit and that sort of thing you know. How does that sound?"

"Gosh Sir Edmund, I wasn't holding out much hope. That would be fantastic!" Dorothy was quite ecstatic.

"Leave it with me and I'll phone you in a day or two. I'm sorry about Charles. If you don't mind me saying Dorothy, he's his own worst enemy. I really thought he had overcome his problem. I'll give you a ring." Sir Edmund opened the door for Dorothy.

Dorothy didn't tell Charles of her secret meeting with Sir Edmund and would only tell him if she got the job. She was sure she would get it. She busied herself in the house and garden for the next two days. She had very mixed feelings. She wanted to be happy with the prospects of the job yet deep down she knew it was not the answer. Charles' cessation of gambling was the only long term solution to their problems. She was pleased at the thought of having her own income and she would at least be able to put a meal on the table each day. Day three dawned and Dorothy was sure she'd hear from Sir Edmund. She wanted to tell Charles about her meeting but knew she had to wait for confirmation.

Day three came and went without a call from Sir Edmund. Surely it wouldn't have taken him that long to sort out a simple job for her at the quartermaster's office? She wondered if he had forgotten. Should she phone him?

It was late afternoon on the fourth day. Dorothy was in the garden clad in a pair of long khaki shorts and a sleeveless top. Although accustomed to the heat she was perspiring from the stifling humidity compounded by her activity in the garden. Her hands and her old sandals were covered in mud from digging a new flowerbed, the muddy surrounds exacerbated by the sprinkler on the lawn. She found contentment working in the garden, surreptitiously venting her frustration and indignation on her strenuous labour.

She heard Girlie call from the house "Phone call for you Mrs Butler."

Dorothy stabbed the fork into the lawn and ran across the garden and into the house. She wiped her muddy hands on her shorts and picked up the receiver. "Hello," she said anxiously. She was quite sure it would be Sir Edmund with good news.

"Hello Dorothy." Sir Edmund's voice was bold. "I'm sorry I didn't come back to you sooner. I've been making some enquiries and I'm afraid we can't take you on."

Dorothy wanted to know every detail and quizzed him "What enquiries did you make Sir Edmund? What's wrong?"

"I can't go into detail but His Majesty's Forces can't employ staff or staff whose family or acquaintances might bring the Forces into disrepute. I'm very sorry Dorothy. I must go by the book." He sounded genuinely concerned but at the same time firm, which made Dorothy realise she had no hope in trying to convince Sir Edmund otherwise.

"Oh gosh. Oh no," said Dorothy. "I was quite sure I'd get the job. Thank you anyway Sir Edmund." She felt totally deflated and she could feel tears of frustration bubbling inside her as she replaced the receiver.

She walked slowly back to her fork in the garden, worn out and dejected. It was jutting out of the ground, lifeless, like a medieval pale through the heart of a worrier and resembling her life, broken and torn apart by the man who had brought her such love and happiness. She sat on the lawn near her excavations. The lawn was wet and she felt the moisture oozing through her shorts. She didn't care. She heard movement behind her.

"What's the matter Mummy?" It was barefooted Diana in her shorts. She picked up a loose granite stone from a nearby rockery and sat on it next to her mother.

"Oh everything darling. Don't tell Daddy but I tried to get a job the other day and it fell through." Dorothy knew she could confide in her girls.

"Why do you have to get a job?"

"You know the situation. I told you Daddy owes a lot of money. He has to pay it back and we don't have much money left over every month. We'll manage somehow. We'll have to. Now, you're filthy dirty and it's bath time now."

"Just half an hour longer Mummy. I've been in the tree house with Betty and Barbara and we're doing our homework there." Diana didn't really understand the problems that were looming ahead for the family.

"I've told you girls before, I don't want you doing home work up there. You can't write properly in there. Bath in half an hour please." Dorothy got up and got back to her flowerbed and Diana ran off towards the back of the house. Dorothy tried not to think of their problems but they were like indelible black clouds hanging over her.

Charles gave a cheque each month to the clerk of the court and brought home the balance of his salary in cash. They paid Girlie and the school in cash each month and the rest went on food. Dorothy had to cut back to stretch out their money. The girls had one glass of milk a day instead of two or three. Eggs were rationed. They had meat once a week now. It frightened Dorothy tremendously, they had never been in that situation before but she and Charles muddled through for three months. They were too distressed to discuss finances but Dorothy knew she had to talk to him. He was coming home late again and that wasn't a good sign.

It was like a repetitive nightmare. She decided to wait up for him one night but it seemed so pointless.

"Charles, we have to talk. We can barely keep our heads above water and you're gambling again, aren't you?"

"I'm only trying to get us out of this mess. I'll bring us out of it," said Charles.

"You know very well you're wasting your time *and* money. I can't take this any more. I don't want someone knocking on the door again demanding money." Dorothy had run out of energy. "Do you owe money to anyone Charles?"

"No darling. I'm managing alright," Charles lied. He had never lied to Dorothy before. He couldn't help himself and he hated doing it. "I'm being very careful and I don't want you to worry." Charles' debts were mounting again and he was desperately trying to stop spiralling into a bottomless pit.

"I don't believe you, I know you're lying. I'm telling you now Charles. We are going to end up destitute, out on the bloody street." She was feeling tearful again but she wasn't going to breakdown in front of him. She was a strong proud woman and she was annoyed that her tearfulness was becoming more and more frequent. Dorothy knew she shouldn't have broached the subject. It was always futile and left her more upset than when she started.

Dorothy had to give up her tennis and resign from the club. She couldn't afford the membership fees. She told her fellow players she had a problem with her knee and her doctor had told her to rest, unable to tell them the real reason.

She had been doing a lot of sewing, making dresses and shorts for the girls. They lived in shorts and were little tomboys. Dorothy was at her machine one night burning the midnight oil and there was still no sign of Charles. It was four months since he had appeared in court and he had been coming home late most nights but he was always home before midnight. It became part of Dorothy's roller coaster life and it was taking a toll on her health. She was run down and losing weight. She had notable bags under her eyes and she knew she felt and looked a wreck.

It was 12.15am when Dorothy went to bed. She dozed on and off and she felt exhausted when the alarm clock went off at 5.45. Charles' side of the bed was neat and tidy. She knew he hadn't come home, as she had been awake more than she had dozed. She felt sick in the stomach. Now she was worried and wondered if he had been involved in an accident. She tried to dispel that; she was sure the police would have notified her.

She decided to phone the hospital anyway. She slipped on her shorts and a cotton shirt and ran barefoot through to Charles' study and dialled the hospital casualty. There was only one government hospital in the town. She gave them his name and told them of her concern but they assured her he hadn't been admitted.

Where the hell was he, she thought to herself. She would phone the police. They would know if anything had happened. She phoned the central charge office and told the Sergeant he had not come home last night and asked if there had been any reports of an accident or some mishap. The Sergeant asked her to hold on. Dorothy was standing next to the desk in Charles' study, tapping a brass container with a pencil.

"Hello," came the Sergeants voice down the phone. "We have a man by that name detained here."

"What do you mean detained? What has happened?" queried Dorothy.

"Detained in our cells ma'am but I'm not allowed to supply information over the phone. You'll have to come down to the charge office for any information." The Sergeant sounded formal.

"Thank you." Dorothy put the phone down. "Oh shit," she said quietly to herself and as she turned around she saw Betty, Diana and Barbara standing in the doorway of the study. They were in their blue and white polka-dot school uniforms, white ankle socks and brown shoes. They appeared dejected, frightened, distinctly fragile. The girls were losing weight, they looked emaciated, their thin little arms and legs dangling like feeble sticks from their uniforms. "Oh my darlings." She held her girls in her arms and hugged them, devastated and suddenly aware of their desperate situation. They responded in a silent embrace, their arms around her like an entangled octopus.

Barbara spoke first "What's wrong Mummy?"

"Where's Daddy?" Betty asked.

"Daddy's at the police station." Dorothy wanted to be honest with them but didn't say he was in jail. She wanted confirmation of that. "I'm going down there now. You all get off to school and I'll see you this afternoon."

"Is he in jail?" Betty asked. They all knew their father had been in court before and owned money to someone.

"I bet he is," said Diana.

"Just keep this under your hats please, as you always have. It's a family problem and we'll sort it out. Now, *off you go, go on. School!*" Dorothy hugged her girls again. Somehow they gave her confidence and she was glad she could talk to them.

Dorothy dressed and made herself respectable. She rushed back into the study and phoned for a taxi. The police station was on the other side of the town and she didn't want to waste time walking there.

The taxi stopped outside the charge office. It cost her a fortune, so she thought, and the money could have been better spent feeding the girls. She walked up the steps and to the wooden counter. A Sergeant approached her and she spoke to him.

"I phoned here earlier and I understand Charles Butler has been detained. Can you tell me what has happened?"

"Are you related to him ma'am?" Dorothy recognised the Sergeant's voice from her earlier call.

"Well, yes." Dorothy hesitated for a moment. "He's my husband. Can you tell me why he's detained please?" Dorothy spoke quietly and decisively.

"We had a complaint of fraud ma'am. He made out a cheque to someone and the bank was unable to honour it. He had insufficient funds in his account." The Sergeant had a folder on the counter in front of him.

"What happens now?" asked Dorothy.

"He'll be taken before a magistrate this morning. He'll be given the opportunity to plead guilty or not guilty. The magistrate will decide whether to sentence him or remand the case. I'm sorry ma'am." The Sergeant noticed Dorothy's anguish.

"I don't believe this." Dorothy held her head down. "Can I see him?"

"Not now, but he'll be taken to the courts shortly and you can see him there." As the Sergeant spoke she saw Charles being led along a corridor towards the charge office. She couldn't believe what she saw. He was barefoot, his hair was dishevelled and he had dark stubble on his face. He was led into a room before reaching the charge office. Dorothy waited at the counter. He had to come out. She was right. He had his shoes on now but his hair was still a mess and he was unshaven. His smart blazer with brass buttons and his old regimental badge on the pocket, check shirt and bow tie looked incongruous. A Sergeant and Constable led him into the charge office and he saw Dorothy and stopped. Their eyes met and mirrored their mutual feelings of deep depression and helplessness. Neither of them spoke and the police officers sensed their passion and desperation. They led him passed Dorothy to a waiting police truck outside.

The Sergeant behind the counter broke the silence. "The magistrates court is a ten minute walk from here ma'am, on the corner of.........."

Dorothy interrupted him. "Yes, I know. Thank you." Her voice was shaking. She walked to the court and tried to shake off her depression. A car pulled up alongside her and an elderly woman offered her a lift but she declined, wanting to be on her own to think.

She saw the cream coloured two storey building ahead, the main entrance evidenced by the Union Jack and a coat of arms above the double wooden doors. She didn't hesitate climbing the wide sweeping steps into the building.

The walk had done her good and she felt a bit better. She walked along the corridor and saw a sign marked 'Prosecutors Office' above a doorway. A good a place as any, thought Dorothy. She went into the office and asked a young woman if she knew of Charles' case. The woman took a sheet of paper from a wire filing basket on her desk, indicating his name was on the court roll in court number two.

The courtroom was massive with wooden panelled walls. The prisoner's dock stood ominously in the centre of the courtroom with the magistrate's bench at the front of the court with a high-backed maroon coloured leather chair. A row of tables for use by the prosecutor and defence council separated the bench and the dock. Several wooden benches were placed neatly at the back of the court and Dorothy sat down. She felt anxious and uncomfortable. A policeman paced the courtroom with a pen in one hand and piece of paper in the other.

A tall scrawny individual clutching a pile of folders swept passed her and into the courtroom, his long black gown flowing precariously behind him. The room was buzzing with activity and a loud knock on the door behind the magistrate's bench brought the court to order.

The man in black bellowed out loudly. "Silence in court."

The door opened and a venerable looking character displaying bushy white sideburns and an unruly shaggy moustache of similar shade, glided into the courtroom and flung his black gown into the air behind him as he sat down behind the bench. Dorothy wondered where Charles was.

"Case one on the roll your Worship. It is requested the accused be further remanded in custody for a week," requested the prosecutor.

"Well where is the prisoner Mr Prosecutor?" The magistrate was abrupt.

The prosecutor looked behind him and went bright red. The prisoner's dock was empty.

"I'm sorry your Worship. Bear with me." The prosecutor peered down the stairs in the prisoner's dock. "Warder, can we have the prisoner for case one," shouted the prosecutor. The prisoner appeared a second later and was pushed up the stairs by a prison warder behind him. The prisoner stood in the dock with the warder next to him.

"Why a further remand?" The magistrate was addressing the prosecutor.

"The police require more time to investigate the case. They feel the prisoner may interfere with witnesses and request he be remanded in custody your Worship."

"Right, right." The magistrate looked at the prisoner and asked his name.

"You are remanded until 14th of this month in this court," The magistrate was looking at the prisoner in the dock. "Next," snapped the magistrate.

"Case two your Worship. This matter may be for plea or remand." The prosecutor looked down the stairs into the holding cells and saw Charles climbing the stairs. He stood in the prisoners dock with a warder next to him. "Allow me to approach the prisoner your Worship." The prosecutor turned to Charles. "How do you plead to the charge of fraud against you?"

"Well, I'm not sure." Charles was nervous.

"Did you issue a cheque with insufficient funds to meet it?" asked the prosecutor.

"Yes sir," replied Charles.

"You have the opportunity to plead guilty or not guilty. If you wish you may appoint a lawyer to act on your behalf," explained the prosecutor.

"No, I just want to get it over with please," answered Charles.

"Your Worship, the accused wishes to plead guilty to the charge of fraud. May I read the indictment to him?"

"Yes, yes Mr Prosecutor. Get on with it." The magistrate was frustrated at the delay.

The prosecutor read the charge to Charles. It was quite audible at the back of the court and Dorothy could hear everything. Charles had fraudulently issued a cheque for £3,000 to a man named in the indictment, knowing he did not have the funds to meet it.

"How do you plead?"

"Guilty sir." Charles answered quietly.

"How much is in your account?" the magistrate asked Charles.

"About £10 sir," answered Charles.

"What is your monthly salary?" the magistrate continued to quiz Charles.

"£200 a month sir."

"Why did you issue the cheque knowing it wouldn't be honoured by your bank?" asked the magistrate.

"The complainant kept asking me for the money and I gave him the cheque to stop him worrying me," explained Charles

"Did you know it was wrong, that it was fraud?" asked the magistrate.

"Yes sir. It was a stupid decision on my part. I'm sorry," answered Charles.

"Anything else Mr Prosecutor?" asked the magistrate.

"No your Worship."

"This court finds you guilty as charged. The court will take into account your co-operation with the police and this court when passing sentence. Any previous convictions Mr Prosecutor?" asked the magistrate.

"I'd like to ask for a weeks remand to allow police to check for previous convictions your Worship. I have no objection to the accused being remanded out of custody but in view of the amount involved, it is requested the accused surrender his passport to the clerk of court and report once a day to the police," requested the prosecutor.

"Charles Butler. You are remanded to the 14th of this month in this court for sentence. You are to surrender your passport to the clerk of the court by 4 o'clock today and report to the police once a day, commencing tomorrow," explained the magistrate.

Do you understand?"

"Yes sir," answered Charles. The prison warder opened the dock door and allowed Charles out. He was free to go for the time being. He walked to be back of the court and saw Dorothy. She got up and walked out of the court with him. Both were silent. They walked to the entrance of the courts and stood at the top of the steps in the sun.

"Where's your car?" asked Dorothy bluntly.

"At the office," said Charles.

"Where did the police arrest you?" Dorothy's voice had no tone.

"At the office," said Charles.

"So Harvey knows about this?" asked Dorothy.

"Yes," replied Charles.

They were both nervous and embarrassed at their new experience and just got on with the basics.

"The office is a ten minute walk from here. I want to see Harvey and gauge his reaction." Charles was to the point. "I'll have to get my passport here this afternoon."

They walked to Charles' office in silence. It was nearly 10 o'clock and the sun was burning already. The town was alive with cars, cyclists and pedestrians. They reached the office and Charles suggested Dorothy waited outside. She stood in the shade of a tree in the car park near the office.

Charles went straight to Harvey's office and knocked on the door. He knew he had to get it over with eventually. It's now or never he thought.

"Come in." He heard Harvey's voice.

Charles tried to smooth his hair with his hands. "Oh damn it," he said to himself having remembered he hadn't shaved. "Shit," he said out loud. "Too late." He opened Harvey's door and braced himself. "Good morning sir."

Harvey had a sullen face. He glanced at Charles, got up from his desk and stood at the window with his back to him. His fists rested on a table under the window, his knuckles taut. The silence was deafening.

"Sir," Charles cleared his throat nervously, "I must apologise for what happened yesterday."

Harvey remained silent. He was thinking. Charles was an exceptionally good engineer and he got on with him. Nairobi was a small town and rumours spread like wild fire. If he retained Charles, it would not do the company image any good. An engineer with a criminal record, and fraud at that. Harvey was weighing all the pros and cons.

Harvey broke the icy silence. "Charles, I'm the managing director of this company. The chairman and directors are based in London as you know." He still had his back to Charles. He felt an element of remorse but his hands were tied. "I have no alternative but to inform the board and they would expect me to take the necessary action. I'm sorry Charles."

"What are you saying, sir?" Charles couldn't come to grips with it.

"You know damn well what I'm saying. Do I have to spell it out for you?" It was clear Harvey regretted his decision.

"Could I not be given a warning sir?" Charles was desperate.

"It's no good Charles." Harvey plucked up the courage to turn around. "The company's reputation is at stake. Fraud is not to be taken lightly. It's a crime of dishonesty. Your dismissal takes effect from today. My hands are tied." Harvey walked around his desk and opened the door. "Please leave the car keys with my secretary. I'll write to you regarding the house and your final salary."

Charles left the office and made no further comment. He walked out of the building and saw Dorothy waiting under the tree. His throat was tight and he felt light headed.

"Let's walk back to the house," said Charles.

"Where's the car?" Dorothy feared the worst.

Charles didn't answer and they started walking along the pavement.

"Well?" asked Dorothy.

"I've been fired." Charles had said it. He felt his head spinning and he was sweating.

He couldn't think straight. He was cursing himself in his mind.

Dorothy didn't answer. She knew disaster had struck. She feared it all those years ago in India, then Ceylon and then Hong Kong. Their life, as they knew it, had been whipped from under their feet. She felt as though her soul had been torn apart by a pride of marauding lions.

Girlie was in the kitchen when they arrived home. Dorothy made a pot of tea and sat at the table in the kitchen. She poured two cups. "Please give that to Mr Butler, wherever he is." Dorothy sounded exhausted. She lit a cigarette and exhaled the smoke forcefully in front of her. Only her second one today she thought. She had managed to cut down. She stared blankly at the kitchen cupboard, her elbows on the table and held the teacup in both hands.

Charles stood at the kitchen door. "I'm taking my passport down to the court."

Dorothy ignored him and sipped her tea. Girlie was preparing vegetables at the sink.

"What's wrong Mrs Butler?" Girlie was concerned. She never asked questions but she knew something was seriously wrong.

"Mr Butler has lost his job Girlie." She had known her long enough to be honest with her. "The police arrested him yesterday for fraud. He wrote out a cheque for someone, which he knew he couldn't honour. It's all a crazy nightmare." Her safety valve gave way and she started crying.

"Oh no, Mrs Butler." Girlie sat in the empty chair next to Dorothy and put her arm around her shoulder. "I would never have thought he would do that."

"Neither did I," said Dorothy. She reached for a tissue in her pocket and blew her nose. It sounded like a foghorn.

"What will happen now?" queried Girlie.

"I have no idea. I really, really have no idea Girlie. I don't want to think about it." Dorothy covered her face with her hands.

Charles received a letter a few days later from Harvey. They had to vacate their company house in six weeks, by 31st March. He felt a sense of relief as he read the letter but it only lasted a few seconds. What then he asked himself. Everything was coming to a head. He owed around £5,000. Charles sat at his desk in his study his thoughts turbulent, muddled. He knew he couldn't pay that, not now. He had to think straight. He had to appear in court in a few days for sentence on the fraud charge. Would he be given time to pay he thought. How could he pay? He had better look for new employment. Nothing was falling into place. There was one huge insurmountable hurdle after another.

"Silence in court," blurted the prosecutor, which summonsed the magistrate into the courtroom. "Your Worship, can we attend to the first case on the roll."

A policeman was standing near the prisoner's dock and made the ritual triple call for the accused. "Charles Butler, Charles Butler, Charles Butler."

Charles was sitting at the back of the court with Dorothy. He stood up and walked uncertainly towards the dock.

"Stand in the dock," said the policeman.

"State your full names," said the prosecutor.

"Charles Butler sir," said Charles.

"Your Worship. The accused has no previous convictions for fraud or dishonesty," said the prosecutor. "It is requested the court passes sentence."

The magistrate wriggled in his chair and cleared his throat. "This is a serious case before the court. The court has accepted your plea of guilty. You wilfully, unlawfully and with fraudulent intent issued a cheque for £3,000 to the complainant. He presented it to the bank but your bank was not able to honour the payment as you had insufficient funds in your account. On your own admission you have a mere £10 in your account and earn £200 a month. Clearly you had no intention of paying the complainant. The court views this very seriously. Do you have anything to say in mitigation before I pass sentence?"

Charles stood up in the dock. His family and life were on the line. "Your Worship," said Charles, mimicking the prosecutor's court lingo. "I lost my job last week because of this case. I owe the clerk of the civil court about £2000 in another case. I would like the opportunity to seek new employment so I can settle these debts. My family and I have to be out of our company house at the end of March." Charles stopped for a moment and coughed nervously. His voice was shaking. "I'm asking the court to be lenient with me and allow me to look after my family. That is all."

The magistrate wrote down Charles' mitigation in a barely legible scrawl.

"You say you owe nearly £2000 in a civil suit. This court has no jurisdiction over civil matters but has taken cognisance of your admission." The magistrate stopped briefly, looking back through his notes. He cleared his throat again and looked directly at Charles. "This court takes into account your co-operation with the police and the court. You have committed a serious offence and the amount involved is quite substantial. You should have thought about your family before getting yourself into debt and the consequences of this crime. You have been a menace to society and it is hoped your sentence will put you on the right path." The magistrate stopped again momentarily and fidgeted with the papers before him. "This court sentences you to 12 months imprisonment with hard labour, 6 months of which is suspended for 3 years on condition you do not commit a crime of dishonesty within those 3 years. Do you understand?"

"Yes sir." Charles felt like a caged animal. There was little he could say or do.

The prison warder standing outside the dock moved swiftly. He entered the dock and took Charles by the upper arm. "Down to the holding cells," said the warder.

"Can I speak to my wife?" asked Charles.

"No," snapped the warder. "There are visiting hours at the prison."

Charles started his descent into the cells under the court. He turned his head as he disappeared into the pits of hell and just caught a glimpse of Dorothy standing alone and anxious at the back of the court. His heart pounded. His sorrow was indescribable and he wanted to hold and be with the woman he loved so much.

Dorothy had a feeling of utter despair. She was looking for support but court officials ignored her. They were accustomed to this sort of thing every day. She wanted to speak to Charles and managed to attract the attention of the prison warder in the courtroom. He came over to her and he explained she could only see him at the prison between 10am and 12pm and 3pm and 5pm each day. She left the court and wasted no time getting home.

Fortunately the girls were still at school. She had some very hard decisions to make and needed Girlie's support. "Girlie, come and sit with me." She was hanging out the washing in the back garden and came in quickly to be with Dorothy. "Girlie I have to be level headed for the girls. Now listen. Mr Butler has been sent to prison for 6 months…"

Girlie interrupted but was hardly surprised. "Oh no, Mrs Butler."

Dorothy contained herself. "We have to be out of this house in five weeks. We have no money and no income now. I just don't know where we'll go. Girlie, I hate to have to say this, but I won't be able to employ you from next week. I'll help you find a new job."

"Mrs Butler, I knew all this would happen and I think you did too but perhaps you couldn't accept it or believe it. I was able to look at it from the outside. I made some enquiries on my own last week. Can I tell you?"

"What have you been up to?" There was a sound of hope in Dorothy's voice. "Shall we have a cup of tea? Perhaps we need something stronger!" giggled Dorothy. She scratched in her bag for a cigarette and lit up. "What enquiries did you make?"

Girlie turned on the kettle. "I've been speaking to a farmer at Max's grocery store for the last few weeks. She shops there frequently. She told me her maid is pregnant and wants to return to her rural home and she asked me to look for a maid for her."

"How long have you known her?" asked Dorothy.

"Oh, I've seen her many times and we always greet each other and chat. Her name is Mrs Jenkins. Do you know her?" quizzed Girlie as she poured the water in the teapot. She went on. "Anyway, I told her yesterday that I might be available, but Mrs Butler, I'll only leave when you're ready."

"Don't be silly Girlie. You have your life to think about. As we're talking, I'm wondering if this Mrs Jenkins might have a little cottage, even a cow shed, for me and the girls on her farm." Dorothy joked at her latter suggestion but deep down she was panicking.

"Are you serious?" asked Girlie.

"Girlie I couldn't be more serious. I have to find somewhere to live. And to top it all, I can't afford to pay rent. I just don't believe this."

"Would you like me to ask her if she has anywhere for you to stay?" asked Girlie.

"Yes, of course. Will you be able to see her today?" Dorothy was desperate.

"I'll go to Max's at 3 o'clock. She's usually there mid afternoon," promised Girlie.

It was a week since Charles received his sentence. Dorothy hadn't been to see him in prison. She didn't want to see him in there, talking to him behind bars. She had so much to think about she didn't know if she was coming or going. Girlie had managed to see Mrs Jenkins at Max's last week and she arranged with Girlie that she'd call on Dorothy at 12 noon today.

Dorothy spent a lot of time with Girlie who was always positive and gave her support.

"I hope Mrs Jenkins hasn't forgotten." Dorothy looked at the clock on the kitchen wall. It was 12.20pm and as she spoke they heard a vehicle at the front of the house. "Come with me," said Dorothy and took Girlie by the hand. They reached the hallway and saw a short plump woman on the veranda. She wore a dirty torn pair of khaki shorts and a khaki shirt in equally poor state of repair with epaulettes and two pockets on the chest. An old cracked leather belt was pulled tightly around her waist, seemingly having the purpose of not only holding up her shorts but pulling in an extended belly as well. She had an old pair of sandals on her dusty feet with toenails that were in need of a farrier's hoof rasp.

"Hello, I'm Dorothy Butler."

"Hello, I'm Esther Jenkins." The round woman had an accent Dorothy couldn't quite detect. She held out her hand and shook Dorothy's hand vigorously.

Dorothy felt like a fool now asking this strange woman for accommodation but she knew she had no choice. "I believe you might have somewhere for us to stay?" asked Dorothy.

The plump woman wasted no time. "I have two old but well built grass huts on the farm. They were part of the original farmhouse. You're welcome to have a look at them."

Dorothy couldn't say no. "Do you have time to show us now?"

"Of course. We're about 5 miles from here. I'll give you direction."

"Um, I don't have a car. Could you take us there please?" Dorothy hated being dependent on anyone.

"Jump in," said Esther and walked to her Ford truck.

Dorothy locked the house and she and Girlie squeezed into the cab of the one-ton truck. Esther walked to the front of the truck and cranked the engine. The engine splattered and the truck rattled into life.

They drove out of Nairobi town and turned off onto a bush road. The truck shuddered over the rough track. After a mile or so, they turned on to narrow dusty strips, with long brown elephant grass on either side. The truck bulldozed the grass in the middle of the strips as Esther sped towards a dwelling house. She drove a few hundred yards behind it and stopped the truck in a cloud of dust outside two grass huts.

"Here we are," said Esther. "We used to store drums of molasses in them until we built those barns over there." Esther pointed to a group of buildings a distance away. "Have a look." She clambered out of the truck and opened the door of one hut and went in.

Dorothy and Girlie followed in silence. They knew what each other were thinking. Basic wasn't the word. It was a small room, barely 30 feet square with a door and a window. The other hut, right next door, was exactly the same. They were made of thatched grass and a mixture of dried mud and cement were used to plaster the floor and walls. An old wooden framed window had four filthy windowpanes in it. The hut smelt musty and was quite dark inside.

Esther spoke. "Girlie told me you needed somewhere to stay where you didn't have to pay rent. It's none of my business but can I ask why you want to do this?" Esther was quite forthright.

Dorothy had to be straight with her. "My husband has a serious problem with gambling. It's an addiction. He borrowed some money from someone and gave him a cheque he couldn't honour. He's lost his job and is serving 6 months now." Dorothy felt as though she was dreaming. It was an unbelievable nightmare. "We have to be out of the company house by the end March."

"You're welcome to use these huts. You won't have to pay rent but you'll have to be self sufficient." Esther was disinterested with Dorothy's horror story and offered no words of sympathy. "Oh, the toilet is behind the huts. It's only a long drop but it'll do."

"Long drop?" queried Dorothy.

"Yes. Come I'll show you." Esther showed her a small grass hut. It had a rickety wooden door about to fall off its hinge and it creaked as she opened it. "There," she said.

Dorothy peered cautiously inside. There was a large wooden box-like structure about knee height with a hole in it. "Oh," said Dorothy. "Is *that* the toilet?" she asked unbelievingly.

"Yes. The hole below the seat is 15 feet deep. It's quite adequate," said Esther, unconcerned

Good grief, Dorothy thought to herself. "Thank you," Dorothy said politely. It was the last place on earth she wanted. She wanted to run away from the place, run as fast as she could but she had to accept it as a new home for her and the girls. "I believe you may want to employ Girlie?" Dorothy changed the subject.

"Yes. I'll show you your accommodation." Esther was a woman of few words. There was a long building about 50 yards from the barns. They consisted of staff rooms, toilets, showers and a kitchen. It was not what Girlie had been accustomed to but it was a roof over her head and a job. "Everybody happy?" asked Esther. "I'll probably see Girlie at Max's and she can tell me when you're ready to move."

CHAPTER 5

Dorothy had to clear out the house and sell most of their belongings. There was only room for one single bed in each hut and a couple of chairs. She would take her carpets and a few pots and pans. There was just no room for anything. Dorothy placed an advert. in Max's window. They had a steady stream of buyers over a week and she managed to sell everything that needed selling. The money she had from the sale of the furniture and their bits and pieces would help feed them for a few months she thought. She was worn out mentally and physically. The thought of those huts being her new home was taking its toll on her morale. The end of the school term was drawing near and Dorothy had told the girls that they would have to leave school. She just didn't have the money for their school fees.

The 31st March arrived. Girlie had arranged for Esther to collect them with their goods and chattels. Betty, Diana and Barbara were very quiet as was Dorothy and Girlie. Their beds, chairs, carpets, suitcases and cardboard boxes were on the veranda. The house was empty.

A strange car arrived in the driveway. A man got out and approached Dorothy.

"Hello. Mr Harvey has asked me to collect the keys to the house," said the strange man.

"Oh, of course," said Dorothy. She had forgotten the phone call from Harvey earlier in the week. "Would you like to go over the house with me?" she asked politely.

"Yes, why not," said Harvey's factotum.

Dorothy entered each room systematically. She also wanted to be sure they had not left anything behind. The girls and Girlie had done a superb job cleaning the empty rooms. Their footsteps on the wooden strip floorboards echoed in the rooms and gave an eerie, lonely feeling. They went back onto the veranda and Dorothy handed the man the house keys and allowed him to lock the front door.

"Thank you," he said and left hastily for his car.

The front garden was like a bus station. He had no sooner left when Esther drove in to the garden in her dented, dusty rattletrap. Her Ford was relatively new but had become a workhorse on her farm and its hard life was starting to show signs of wear and tear.

"Everyone ready I see," said Esther. She opened the tailgate at the back of the truck. "Now, can we get the beds in first." The woman of few words didn't greet them.

It took them a good half hour to load the truck. They planned it to enable the girls to have a place to sit. It was piled high and Dorothy had wisely kept some rope from the garden shed, in anticipation of having to tie everything down. The garden fork, spade and an old hosepipe were the last things to go in and they had difficulty finding a place to put them. Dorothy and Girlie sat in the cab and the girls sat huddled in the little holes they had reserved amongst their tangled belongings, all they had left of their shredded lives. The girls hadn't seen their new abode and had relied on Dorothy's description. They weren't looking forward to it.

It was nearly midday by the time they had unloaded the truck. Esther drove off having said little to them. The five of them stood next to their furniture. They had hardly spoken all day.

"Mummy we can't stay here," said Betty and Barbara agreed. They looked inside the huts. "It's terrible."

"It's the best Mummy can do for us. Anyway, it's all Daddy's fault." Diana sounded supportive. "Let's put the carpets inside then they'll look better."

It was a case of a square peg in a round hole but they manoeuvred and folded the carpets until the floors were totally covered. It looked better already. Then the beds went in, then a chest of drawers and a table in each hut. Dorothy kept the old kitchen curtains and they fitted with a few adjustments.

"I think they look very nice now." Dorothy tried to convince the girls. "What do you think?"

Diana was still positive. "They're all right Mummy. It's not your fault."

"Now girls. How about putting your Girl Guide knowledge to work!" Dorothy wanted to make light of everything. "Let's make a fire and have a cup of tea." There was a large acacia tree near the huts and Esther had told them to make use of a pile of cut wood under the tree. Barbara gathered some big granite stones lying around the area.

"Let's make the fire around the back of the huts then the smoke won't go in the doors," suggested Betty.

They made a neat cooking area with the stones. An old piece of wire gauze leaning up against the barn was ideal for placing over the fire. In no time Diana had raging flames and added pieces of wood to it and the kettle was filled from a nearby standpipe. Luckily they brought five canvas deck chairs and they placed them under the acacia tree. The pantry consisted of three large cardboard boxes and Dorothy scratched around for the tea, sugar and powdered milk.

Tea poured, Dorothy collapsed in a deck chair and sipped the tea. "Hmm, it tastes different, nicely different."

"Anything cooked on a fire tastes different, even stews or vegetables," said Diana. They had learnt some bush craft as Girl Guides and Diana was a particularly good cook. "We've got a bit of meat from the house. I'll cook it for supper tonight before it goes off."

They all had their tea. Betty, Diana and Barbara went for a walk to familiarise themselves with the area. Dorothy poured herself another cup of tea. She hadn't had a cigarette all day and she was dying for one. She took the box from her shorts pocket but it barely resembled a box. The cigarettes had been squashed but were still intact. She poked a dry piece of elephant grass on the embers and it ignited into a flame. She lit her cigarette and threw the burning grass onto the fire. She sat back in her chair and pulled heavily on her cigarette. She closed her eyes and felt unexpectedly at peace. Perhaps she had resigned herself to this very unusual situation they were in. She drew on her cigarette and sipped her smoky flavoured tea. Her feeling of peace slowly melted and was replaced with fear, almost panic that welled up inside her. The money she had would last about two months she thought. All they had to buy was food and she had to be very conservative with it.

"Mummy," called Diana. "We remembered a Girl Guide trick. If Mrs Jenkins can let us have some thin wire gauze, we can make a fridge."

"That sounds funny. How will you do that?"
"We'll show you."

Diana was preparing their first meal in the bush. She cut the meat into squares and diced an onion. The fat from the meat was sizzling in a black enamel pot on the fire. The cooking oil ran out weeks ago and was regarded a 'luxury' in their household. She put the onion and meat into the rendered fat and stirred it. She allowed it to brown then added some water and popped the lid on the pot. She washed some cabbage leaves and left them on the table under the tree. It was getting dark but her eyes adjusted as dusk slipped into darkness.

She sat in a chair by the fire. The other three were also sitting near the fire, gazing silently at the embers. A gust of wind blew and sparks and smoke flew into the air then settled down again.

"How long will we be here?" asked Barbara.

"I don't know darling. We're very lucky Mrs Jenkins has allowed us to stay here. Daddy won't be out of jail for three or four months," said Dorothy.

"What will happen when he comes out?" quizzed Barbara again.

"We'll have to wait and see but for now we'll have to take each day as it comes." Dorothy tried to sound positive for the girls but felt emptiness inside. "How are you doing with the supper darling?" Dorothy asked Diana.

Diana poked the meat in the pot then put the mound of cabbage leaves in the juice in the pot. "Another ten minutes and we can eat," she said.

Dorothy found the plates in a cardboard box and stacked them on the table with the knives and forks. Diana took the big black pot to the table and spooned out the stew equally onto the four waiting plates. "There you are. Eat up before it gets cold." Diana took a plate and knife and fork to her mother, then got her own. Betty and Barbara helped themselves.

"Hmmm. Bon appetit," said Dorothy.

"What?" asked Betty.

"Nothing."

Their first meal was surprisingly good and as Diana had rightly said, it had a special flavour, a smoky campfire taste. Although they were still hungry, there were no second helpings. They were used to that. It was nearly 9 o'clock by the time they'd washed the dishes and put everything away. Their whole routine was different and everything a challenge. Washing the dishes was a challenge. They had to heat the water on the fire, then take it to a bowl on the table. There was nowhere to bath, not even a shower. Esther had not allowed them to use the staff ablutions. The girls had found an old but clean five-gallon tin near the barn and that was all they could use to wash themselves. Sleeping arrangements had been sorted out. Betty and Barbara were to share one bed and Dorothy and Diana the other.

"I think we had better get to bed. It's been a long day," said Dorothy. She kissed and hugged Betty and Barbara and ensured they were safely in their hut then joined Diana. It was strange, all so strange. Dorothy lay awake for hours with so much churning over in her thoughts. Charles had been in prison for six weeks and she hadn't been to see him. It wasn't that she didn't love him.

She knew it would upset her. But she had had so much on her plate, selling up, deciding what to keep, what to sell, consoling the girls, visiting their headmistress at the school. It was endless. Their future, especially the uncertainty, made her stomach turn.

Three days passed. Dorothy was thinking more and more about Charles, now that she had little to do. It was a long way in to town but the girls had found out that local buses used the main road quite frequently. She had to see him and tell him what was happening.

She told the girls to remain on the farm and she left early in the morning and started the two mile hike to the main road. There were no bus stops. It was rural Africa and she just hoped a bus would pass. It was a good three miles into town and she decided to start walking. There was bush on either side of the road and she could see the odd homestead in the distance. It was spring and the grass and bush were brown after a dry winter. The rains fell in summer in Kenya, between April and August. Wild game was not uncommon on the outskirts of Nairobi, although buck, warthog and the like were the most common. Dorothy hoped she wouldn't encounter a hyena or even worse, a lion. The bush along the edge of the road was thick in places and she peered into it hoping not to see any movement. She had walked for about ten minutes on the main road and was beginning to think she was stupid walking on her own, when she heard the rumble of a vehicle in the distance. She looked back and saw a car approaching. She continued walking but decided to wave it down. Dorothy realised she might be lucky when she heard the car slowing down. It stopped next to her and the middle-aged man in a suit asked her if she wanted a lift. She was grateful for the offer and he dropped her in the centre of Nairobi. She had no idea where the prison was and she wasn't going to ask the man in the suit.

That wasn't too bad she thought. She stood outside the town hall. Who could she ask for directions to the prison? She didn't fancy asking anyone such a question. She had a brainwave, she'd ask at the Magistrate's court. Dorothy was given concise directions and found out it was not far from the road leading out to the farm. It would be easier for her next visit. She had plenty of time before visiting hour at 10 o'clock and she strolled in the direction of the prison.

A large high white wall topped with barbed wire loomed ahead of her. Sentry towers were on the two corners she could see from the road. Massive medieval looking wooden doors with a small pedestrian door within it seemed to be the only access to the prison. About twelve people had gathered outside the closed doors and Dorothy joined them. A prisoner warder opened the small door and they were allowed in after giving the name of the prisoner they were visiting. Dorothy's turn came.

"I've come to see Charles Butler."

The warder summonsed her in. She stood in a small courtyard with the other visitors. The warder locked the door with a mass of keys on a large metal ring. He walked into an office and everyone followed, clearly accustomed to the routine. They followed him down a long narrow passage with prison bars along its length that looked out onto a small courtyard. A few minutes later, men clad in long white shorts and baggy shirts filed into the courtyard and they greeted their visitors through the bars. There was no sign of Charles. She peered anxiously at the door the men had come through. Then a man appeared at the door and stood in the courtyard. She wasn't sure if it was Charles. He looked drawn and skeletal with a shaved head. His shoulders were rounded like a broken man and he was barefoot. His eyes were sunken as were his cheeks and he stared blankly at the visitors. It *was* him she thought.

"Charles," she whispered loudly.

He ignored her and stood still with a blank gaze.

"Charles!" Dorothy called out.

He moved his head and looked towards Dorothy.

"Charles," she called again and waved her arm through the bars.

Charles' expression changed for a moment from blank to confused then he ran towards Dorothy with short uncertain steps, his bare feet scuffing the stone floor. He put both arms through the bars and squeezed her like an orang-utan. He held her so tightly against the bars she could hardly breathe and the side of her face was squashed into the iron that separated them.

"Charles darling, I can't breathe!" she joked.

"My sweet, where have you been? Oh how I've missed you. I've been so worried about you." He was sobbing like a child.

They talked and talked for two hours and the time flew by. Dorothy walked out of the wooden door of the prison. The midday sun was beating down and she took a floppy khaki hat and a pair of sunglasses out of her bag and decided to go straight back to the farm but stopped at a small grocery store. They had no food at the huts other than the remains of a cabbage. Maize meal goes a long way

It's All Just Nuts

she thought. It was ground maize and cooked up like porridge. It was nutritious and was served with meat and gravy and vegetables. The little butchery in the store was selling soup bones at a special price. She couldn't resist them. What about a loaf of bread? Yes she thought. She'd spoil them. She reached the main road and started walking in the direction of the farm, hoping again for a lift or a rural bus the girls had spoken about. The sun was burning her bare arms. A few cars passed but didn't stop. She heard the sound of a vehicle behind her. Good, she thought. It was a bus. Dorothy waved it down and it stopped for her. The roof looked like a junkyard with chairs, bags of food, ploughs, wheelbarrows and other paraphernalia. The bus was packed with passengers. She told the driver she wanted to travel for about three miles and she would tell him where to stop.

She stood near the front of the bus next to a wizened old woman in an isle seat. She had a beehive shaped basket on her lap and Dorothy noticed it was full of chirping chicks.

That's a good idea she thought. The woman spoke broken English and after a little sales talk agreed to sell four to Dorothy. She put them in her hat attracting laughter from the other passengers. The bus neared the turn off to the farm and Dorothy tapped the driver on the shoulder. She walked along the dusty road to the farm hoping her money was well spent. Her arms were full with her purchases and the five pound bag of maize meal.

"Hello everyone." Dorothy heard hammering behind the huts. Diana was hammering thin wire gauze onto a wooden frame. Five other gauzed frames lay next to her. "What are you up to?"

"We're making a fridge," said Diana.

"We learnt how to make them in Girl Guides," added Barbara. "Just as well we brought Daddy's tool box. We've used the hammer and saw and used some nails."

"Where did you get the gauze and wood?"

"We asked Mrs Jenkins. It's old mosquito gauze she'd used on windows and doors. Did you see Daddy?" Diana didn't stop her hammering.

"Well I'm confused. You'll have to show me how it works. Yes, he's fine and was very happy to see me. He's lost a lot of weight though," said Dorothy.

"We all have," said Betty. "Something's moving in your hat!" she exclaimed.

"I bought these from a woman on the bus. Look." Dorothy knelt down and put her floppy hat on the ground. Four yellow chicks scurried out chirping and trotting around in the dusty grass.

"Oh great!" said Barbara. "We can have roast chicken."

"Well hopefully we'll get some eggs and offspring from them before they go in the pot," joked Dorothy.

The embers in the fire were still glowing from their morning tea. Dorothy brought it alive and put the kettle on the fire. By late afternoon the girls' fridge was finished. It stood about two feet off the ground on wooden legs. The box-shaped structure on the legs measured about 2 feet square and consisted of a double layer of gauze on all four sides and on the top and bottom of the box. They had packed pieces of charcoal between the layers of gauze leaving no gaps. There had been mounds of burnt wood near a rubbish dump and they had picked out the best pieces. The door was bound several times on one side with baling wire and it served, only just, as a hinge.

The girls had instructed Dorothy not to look at their work of art until it was finished. She promised not to and had a good excuse sit under the acacia tree with her back to the activity and shut her eyes. She had almost dozed off when Diana asked her to stand up. Dorothy obliged and Diana put her hands over Dorothy's eyes feeling Diana's little hand over her right eye.

"OK, you can look!" said Diana excitedly and took her hands away.

"Well I never. A thing of beauty is a joy forever!" laughed Dorothy. "Goodness, is *that* a fridge?"

"Yes," said all three girls together.

"And it works," said Betty.

"Well we don't have anything to put in it yet," said Diana.

"Yes we do." Dorothy went into her hut and brought out a plastic bag. "I did a bit of shopping this morning. Here, let's put these soup bones and a loaf of bread in our new fridge. We'll see in a few hours if they're still cool!"

They had survived another day in their strange existence. They had finished supper and washed the dishes. A regular routine was falling into place. They sat by the fire as it hissed and crackled and Barbara threw a log on the dwindling flames. The African sky was particularly dark and enhanced the star-studded canopy above. Chirping crickets in the nearby bush gave an air of mystery to the night and the croaking frogs signalled the end of spring and the heralding of the first rains of summer.

The soup bones had survived very well in their newfound fridge. They were an economical buy as they had a meal each day from them for a week. Their one meal a day was supper and each night it was the same. The stewed soup bones made gravy, which they had with cabbage and posho. Dorothy was managing to stretch out the money they had. They prepared a vegetable garden with Esther's blessings. The farm had an excellent underground water supply and was pumped into corrugated iron tanks by strategically placed windmills. Dorothy had had the foresight to bring their hosepipe from the house and Esther had allowed them to use as much water as they wanted for their veggie garden. The girls brought bucket loads of kraal manure from the cattle pens and forked it into the watered beds. They were ready for seeds.

It was a week since Dorothy had seen Charles. They were out of soup bones and Dorothy was keen to get some seeds for their new beds. She decided to kill two birds with one stone, visit Charles and do her necessary shopping.

They had been living in the huts for almost four months. Charles would be out of prison in six weeks. Dorothy's money had run out. She had been conservative with it and it lasted surprisingly well she thought. Their vegetables were growing well, the summer rains far more beneficial than their hand watering. They had tomatoes, beans, onions, cabbage and potatoes. The chickens were producing eggs and they now had six additional chickens.

The girls had made friends with the labourers' children on the farm and improved their Swahili so they were almost fluent, although their Nairobi gardener

Sixpence had taught them a lot of the local language. They also introduced them to posho, made like a stiff porridge from crushed maize. They'd eat it with their fingers and learnt to make it into a small ball then push their thumb into the middle to make an indentation to scoop up gravy. They'd nibble around the edges of the ball careful not to breach the gravy hole.

The girls would swap the vegetables with mangos, guavas and gooseberries, which the other children got from a nearby farm. They loved eating mangos that were messy and sticky but juicy and sweet. The hairy pips were put to good use and when lathered with soap, were useful for washing.

It hadn't rained for a few weeks but the rains were like that in Africa. There would be a deluge then nothing for weeks on end. Dorothy had attached their hosepipe to the nearby standpipe and was busy watering the vegetable garden when she saw Esther appear from the direction of her house. She seldom paid a visit.

"Hello Esther."

"Hello," said Esther. "Your husband must be due for release soon." She was to the point as usual.

"Yes. He'll be out in a month." Dorothy wondered if her question was leading anywhere.

"What do you propose doing when he's out?"

"Well," Dorothy hesitated and was beginning to feel uneasy. "We're not sure. We're hoping he'll be able to find another job."

"You're welcome to stay here until you find somewhere else. You're vegetable garden's doing well."

"Thank you," Dorothy was relieved. "I'll send the girls over later with some pickings. Anything in particular you'd like?" They often took vegetables to Esther, which she appreciated.

"No, anything you send over is put to good use. Thank you. I wanted to tell you Girlie left about a month ago. She said she'd found a job in town." The plump woman left without saying anything further.

Dorothy was devastated. She hadn't seen her for a while but wasn't overly concerned. Why, she wondered, did she go without saying goodbye? After all those years of being together? Perhaps she just didn't want to say goodbye.

Diana had become chief cook and enjoyed preparing the meals. They hadn't had any meat for some months other than soup bones.

"Mummy, can we eat a chicken?" Diana was preparing the evening meal.

"Oh dear. I was wondering when one of you would suggest that. Do you *really* want to do that?"

"Yes of course. A few of them aren't laying now anyway. Can we? Please?" pleaded Diana.

"Let's think about it tomorrow."

Tomorrow arrived too soon for Dorothy. Diana may have had a deformed hand but there was nothing wrong with her mind or memory.

"Can we have a chicken for supper tonight?" asked Diana. "Betty said she'd kill it for us."

"Oh alright. I'm sure it'll be very nice," said Dorothy.

"Woopie." Diana ran into Betty and Barbara's hut and told them the good news.

It's All Just Nuts

The sun was high and execution time was nigh and duties had been allocated. Barbara was the youngest and fastest and would catch the doomed chicken. Betty was the oldest and meanest and would perform the execution. Diana would remain in the galley and Dorothy? She'd be referee on the sidelines.

The clucking started and Barbara headed towards the doomed lady. The clucking intensified. Barbara held out her arms and her bony tanned legs moved faster and faster. She neared the marked feathered woman and the clucking changed to shrieks. Wings flapped, feathers and grass flew and Barbara rugby-dived the fleeing bird. She got it. Its wings beat her on the face and head and she tucked the condemned bird under her arm, curtailing its onslaught.

"Your turn," said Barbara and handed the bird to Betty.

"Hmm," said Betty. "The moment of truth. Not sure if I want to do this." She had a large kitchen knife in her hand and walked up to a big granite rock not far from the fire. "The quickness of the hand deceives the eye," and she sliced off the chickens head on the rock. Betty screamed and dropped the knife and the chicken and ran towards Diana and Barbara. "Oh, that was terrible," said Betty, squirming.

"Look, look," screamed Barbara. The headless chicken was running around in circles, blood dripping from the hole in the top of its neck.

"Just look away girls. It's just muscular reflexes. It will stop in a minute." Dorothy was right as it collapsed in no time.

"Who's going to skin it?" asked Diana.

"Not me," said Barbara. "You can do it Betty. You're the biggest and ugliest."

"Why do I have to do all the dirty work? I want the biggest helping then. We'd better boil some water."

"You don't skin a chicken darling, you de-feather it," Dorothy corrected Diana.

They hadn't had anything so tasty for several months and they ate in silence, savouring every mouthful.

"That was absolutely delicious," said Dorothy as she nibbled and sucked a drumstick. "You're a good little cook my darling. Thank you."

"Yeah, thanks. Really tasty," concurred Betty.

"Hmmm," came Barbara's approval as she licked every last drop on her plate.

"We should have had this for Daddy's homecoming," said Dorothy.

Diana giggled. "We'll have another one!"

Charles' release day arrived and they'd arranged between them on Dorothy's last visit weeks earlier, that she'd collect him. She left the girls early in the morning and started her long trek to the prison. She had no alternative now but to walk, her small amount of savings exhausted. A few cars passed her on the main road but they didn't stop. She arrived at the prison at 10.30, later than she had anticipated. The wooden doors were closed and there was no one in sight. She knocked on the door using the metal knocker. She thought no one would hear but she heard footsteps on the other side of the door. The wooden slat slid back on the peephole in the door.

"Yes?" came a voice from the face in the peephole.

"I've come to see my husband Charles Butler. He's due for release today."

The slat slammed shut and she heard the bolts sliding on the smaller door. It opened and a warder beckoned her in.

"Thank you," said Dorothy.

"Come with me," said the warder. The warder took her to an office off the courtyard. "Wait here," he said.

She waited, and waited and waited. It was 11.30 and she wondered if the warder had forgotten her. Another fifteen minutes passed when she heard footsteps, then keys unlocking the door to the office. It opened and Charles came sheepishly through the door. His hair had grown into a short crew cut. He was wearing a dark blue suit, white shirt and his army regimental tie. His clothes hung on him, his eyes were sunken and lifeless and Dorothy responded to his nervous smile They hugged each other.

"Come on," barked the warder. He led them to the little wooden door at the entrance and opened it. "Off you go."

They both said "thank you" simultaneously.

They walked in silence for a few minutes. "It's good to be out," said Charles. "Where are we going?"

"To the farm and the huts. The girls are waiting to see you. We'll have to walk."

"That's alright," said Charles. He took off his jacket and slung it over his shoulder.

It was mid afternoon by the time they arrived at the huts. The girls saw them on the dust road and ran to greet them.

"Daddy we've missed you." Betty hugged Charles for a long time with Diana and Barbara queuing nearby.

"My darlings, my darlings. I'm so, so sorry." There were tears in his eyes.

"Come." Diana didn't want to see him crying. "We've got the kettle on."

It was dusk and they all sat around the fire. The girls had been busy during the day and another non-productive chicken had been decapitated and the smell of it cooking in the pot had their juices running. They were having pot roasted potatoes, beans and gravy with their beautifully basted chicken.

"It's unbelievable what you've done. The veggie garden, the chickens and of course the home made fridge. I'm so proud of you all. The huts are cosy and homely. You've done wonders my darling." Charles held Dorothy's hand and kissed her on the cheek. No one mentioned why they were there and the cause of the total upheaval in their lives. It was too sensitive to even think about right now.

The sleeping arrangements were reorganised. Dorothy and Charles were to have one hut and the three girls shared the other. In their innovative fashion, they had made a camp bed of sorts for Diana. They had cut the rubber tube of an old car tyre into thick strips and nailed them to a low, wooden framed bed. The hammock type strips were padded with layer upon layer of thatching grass they had gathered in the bush and that was covered with a blanket. A tight squeeze but it fitted into Betty and Barbara's hut.

Charles lay with his arm around Dorothy. He had dreamt of this moment for months. They had a lot to talk about but they lay quietly, silently respecting each other's thoughts. He was up before dawn accustomed to prison routine. He slipped out of bed so not to disturb Dorothy. He had never set a fire in his life but Diana had the necessary dry grass and chips of wood neatly stacked with the large logs. Flames were leaping into the air in no time, he added logs to the fire and placed the blackened tatty enamel kettle over the flames. He'd make everyone a cup of tea and also use the hot water to shave.

He sat on a granite stone near the fire. The wild birds were getting noisier as the eastern sky lightened. The smell of the bush, the grass and the odd whiff of smoke were pleasing to Charles. He poured boiling water into his enamel shaving-mug and left the kettle balancing on a rock next to the fire. Too early for tea he thought. The put his mirror on the large granite rock and propped it up with a log of wood. The cooing doves signalled the sunrise, the yellow eastern sky brightening and mingling with a silver glow. The Starlings started their chorus. The bush was coming alive.

He was still shaving when Dorothy came out of the hut in her usual khaki shorts, cotton shirt and sandals. She poked the fire and put the kettle on the wire gauze. The trees were making long eerie shadows across the bush now as the sun glided above the treetops. Charles used the towel over his shoulder to wipe the excess soap from his face and greeted Dorothy.

"Hello darling."

"Hi," she replied sleepily. "What's on the agenda for today?"

"Well, I thought I'd go to town and look for a job. There're a few engineering firms around."

"Yes, alright. What's happened to that civil case? Remember, you were paying half your salary to the clerk of the civil court? What happened about that?"

"Oh heavens, yes," replied Charles. "I don't know why it slipped my mind. I was served with a civil summons a few weeks ago. Blast, I'd forgotten. It's in my jacket pocket," said Charles and disappeared into the hut. He appeared minutes later with a piece of paper in his hand. "Bloody hell. Next week. I've got to appear in the civil court. Oh hell Dorothy. I'm sick of this."

"Whose fault is that?" Dorothy poked the fire, disinterested. That roller-coaster ride hadn't stopped. "I don't know what to say Charles. This whole thing is a nightmare. You haven't got two pennies to rub together and you still owe money. I just give up."

Charles walked to town every day and came back each day, dejected and empty-handed. He had approached dozens of people and companies. It seemed to be a case of not what you know but who you know. He couldn't mention Harvey. They'd want to know why he left there. He was in a no win situation. Charles didn't approach Sir Edmund. That would have been a waste of time seeing he couldn't or wasn't able to help Dorothy.

Dorothy accompanied him to court for the civil hearing. He still owed around £1500 on his first debt. Dorothy was convinced he would be sent to prison again. They were half an hour early for the hearing and they both sat in the back of the courtroom listening to other cases.

Charles' heart sank when the court orderly called his name. He stood in the dock while the prosecutor scratched through the files on his desk. He found the file and read through a document.

"If I may approach the bench, your Worship," said the prosecutor.

"Yes Mr Prosecutor. What is it?" asked the magistrate.

The prosecutor handed a document to the magistrate. He was frowning as he read it. "Right thank you." The magistrate looked at Charles. "Are you Charles Butler?"

"Yes sir."

"The plaintiff in this case, Roger McMinn, has withdrawn the civil suit against you. This court duly withdraws the case. You are free to go."

Charles thought he was hearing things. "Do you mean I don't owe Mr McMinn anything now?"

"That's correct Mr Butler."

Charles continued to stand in the dock. He didn't know what to do.

"You can go now," said the court orderly.

Dorothy accompanied him out of the courtroom. "The devil looks after his own so they say. It's unbelievable." She wasn't excited, just relieved.

"Unbelievable isn't the word. It's a miracle," said Charles. "What worries me is the £3000 I borrowed from Ted Jones, you know, the fraud case. I'm wondering if he's going to make a civil claim for that."

"You're a pain Charles, a real pain in the posterior." Dorothy was so fed up with him.

"I don't want it hanging over my head. Tell you what; Ted's office is not far from here. I want to see him."

"What will that achieve? You can't pay him anyway."

"I just want to see what he intends doing, that's all. Come, let's go."

Dorothy waited outside the building and Charles went inside to see Ted. He knew where his office was and climbed the stairs to the first floor and walked half way along a passage. He hoped he was there. He knocked and heard Ted telling him to come in. Good, he thought.

"Hello Ted," said Charles.

"Huh, well I'm damned. I thought they'd locked you up," said Ted.

"I served six months."

"You should've served six bloody years, you bastard."

"I'm sorry Ted, I'm really sorry. I've lost my job and I don't know when I can re-pay you." Charles was genuinely concerned.

"I know damn well I'll never see my money. It's history, a bad debt. I'm glad you rotted in prison but it should've been longer. You're a fucking thief. Get out of my office. I don't want to see your bloody face again." Ted was red in the face. He opened the door, "Out, get out."

"I'm sorry Ted. Thank you." Charles made a hasty exit.

Charles joined Dorothy downstairs. "This is my lucky day. He doesn't want to see me again."

"What do you mean?"

"He's laughed it off as a bad debt," said Charles.

"So you don't owe anything and you don't have any money. Hey-ho, we're back to square one I suppose." Dorothy was far from excited.

"Well at least the slate's wiped clean."

"Yes, wiped clean with a dirty cloth. It still leaves a mark Charles. Let's go home, if we can call it home."

Weeks passed and Charles walked to town each day job hunting but came home empty handed. The girls continued to amuse themselves and had made a swing, tied in the branches of their acacia tree. They'd leap off the granite rock, swing high in the air and the rope would twist and shorten then unravel in a dizzy spin.

Dorothy would attend to the vegetable garden and do mundane chores like washing and ironing. She had a huge heavy iron with a hinged lid and was designed to take red-hot coals. It worked perfectly and the ironing was done on the carpeted floor in her hut. The routine frustrated Dorothy knowing their lives couldn't go on like that forever. She thought more and more about the only option that would get them out of the squalid lifestyle they were living. Would it change their lives for the better she kept asking herself over and over again. She knew she had to do it.

They were all at their lowest ebb and they retired to their huts early one evening, earlier than usual as Dorothy wanted to tell Charles her plan.

"You do know we can't carry on living like this." She started the conversation. "I think we should all go to England. You're not going to find work here."

"All well and good but we can't pay for a bus fare Dorothy, let alone travel to England."

Dorothy was quiet for a while. She had kept this a secret all through their marriage and hadn't told anyone but she had no choice now. "I have a piece of jewellery given to me by my late husband, the Belgium Baron. I had it valued in Hong Kong years ago and it will get us to England with some change."

"Huh, and you let me go to prison?" snorted Charles.

"Don't speak like that. I'm not going to spend my entire life bailing you out of your bloody debts. I have the girls to think about. You are bloody selfish Charles, bloody, bloody selfish." Dorothy was shouting at him and had lost her temper completely. She was in no mood to be anywhere near him. "Damn you, you make me sick." She stormed out of the hut slamming the rickety door behind her but it made insufficient noise to vent her anger. She put all her force behind it again and slammed it so hard against the frame that it flew back and hung on one hinge. The girls had heard every word and they wondered where all this would lead.

Dorothy spent the night in a deck chair outside. The night was humid but she stoked the fire, the flames and sparks her only companion for the night. Although tired, she only dozed off after midnight and was woken by the sound of Charles putting the kettle on the fire.

She wasted no time and left for town with the necklace she hoped would change their lives. As she recalled, the jeweller in Hong Kong had valued it at £4000. She was sure it had been under valued as the four diamonds were very big. She went straight to a jewellery shop and a little man came to the counter from the back of the shop.

"Good morning. I want to sell this necklace. Would you be interested and what would you give me for it." Dorothy took the necklace out of a black drawstring bag and handed it to the man. He swung the magnifying glass over his eye from a gadget on his head and studied the necklace.

"Hmm, impressive. I'll need to weigh the diamonds. Could you hold on a moment?" The little man went behind a glass partition and she saw him fiddling with her prize possession. He returned and said, "This is a fine piece of jewellery madam. I can offer you £5,000 for it."

Dorothy didn't hesitate and accepted the man's offer. He was surprised at her request for cash but obliged after drawing cash from his bank. She wanted to jump for joy. She needed to think for a moment and went to a tearoom above a departmental store.

She realised what a rough life they were living as she drank her tea out of a fine china teacup again, with starched linen on the table. They had nothing to keep them in Kenya now. She was going to book their trip back to England.

She went straight to a travel agency in Nairobi. A mail ship was leaving Mombassa for England in ten days. The next one was in two months. She made the booking including their train journey to the coast. It was done, decision made. They were leaving for England in ten days. She had a lot of change, which gave her a sense of security. Dorothy walked back to the huts. She had enough change for a few trips to England but she'd learnt what it was like to be without any money and taught her to be conservative with finances.

The ten days flew by. They said their farewells to Esther and left all the bits and pieces they weren't able to take, including their well established vegetable garden. The farm labourers had become good friends and the girls had played many games with their children and the girls were going to miss their new friends.

The ship sailed early afternoon. The girls nattered continuously which made up for Dorothy's and Charles' silence. They stayed on deck for hours leaning on the portside rails as the ship ploughed through the Indian Ocean, north along the African coast that would take them past Aden, through the Red Sea and the narrow Suez Canal and they couldn't help but reminisce.

Diana recalled the years in their big house in Nairobi and Girlie. Girlie used to tease them with stories about the Masai, the fierce tribe that drifted across Kenya with their cattle. They were *told* they were fierce but they later learnt from the children on the farm that they were quite harmless and liked to keep to themselves leading a nomadic life. Girlie had given the impression they were terrifying bogeymen. When the girls were naughty Girlie would threaten to call the Masai and have them taken away in sacks. Diana was terrified some nights, lying in her bed in the dark, thinking an old Masai man was under her bed. The fear was so real to her she'd take a huge leap off her bed, so he wouldn't catch her legs and Diana recalled how she made a mad dash down the passage to Dorothy's room. Dorothy was a poor sleeper and no matter when Diana sped to her, she would be awake, reading. She would hear Diana coming and had her bedclothes turned back ready for her to leap in beside her.

Barbara remembered the short holiday they took to Jinja on the shores of Lake Victoria in Uganda. Their bedroom was a hut and she recalled how they lay awake listening to something grunting and scraping the walls of their round hut. They had thought it was elephants and she remembered how Dorothy had told them it was hippos coming up from the lake at night and scraping the mud off their huge bodies.

The coast was almost on the horizon now and the African sun was setting, a huge red ball balancing majestically in the dusty haze above a silent, enchanting continent. Yes, they were going to miss Africa.

CHAPTER 6

London 1930. Dorothy knew London well and she found them a comfortable hotel. The girls were used to the freedom of running wild in Africa and were frustrated being confined to a hotel room. They were not permitted in the lounges and dining room and had their meals in the children's dining room.

Their boredom led them to a new game, devised by Betty. They got the pillows off their beds and slung them over the banister. They'd climbed on, then slide down swiftly to the hotel foyer with screams of delight and to the astonishment of the manager and guests.. The game was short-lived, as was their stay at the respectable hotel. They were called little monsters by the hotel staff.

They moved to another hotel and Dorothy employed a governess for the girls for a few months. Her name was Olive and she took the girls on frequent walks in the parks and squares. The girls didn't particularly like Olive and led her on a merry dance. They gave her the slip in a square one day and dragged a few park benches together and made a 'den'.

An irate park keeper approached them. "Eh, what ya think ya doin'?" he shouted.

The girls looked at him blankly, turned to each other and broke into Swahili and said,

"Shenzi sana kabesa."*   * Roughly translated as 'nasty piece of work.'
"You little savages," was the keeper's response.

The girls laughed and ran off, leaving the man to straighten the benches. They continued to play in the square and enjoyed climbing the trees, reminding them of their carefree days in Africa. They returned to the hotel dirty but happy.

Charles was away a lot and had a job with the railways. Dorothy was able to give them a bit of pocket money and they handled money for the first time in their lives. They would buy marshmallow fish and liquorice strips, always their favourites. As the year progressed they moved from hotels to boarding houses and the girls were aware that their financial position was changing dramatically and there seemed to be no money for anything. Dorothy was keeping the upper hand with Charles and was receiving his pay each month. She had to rely on his fervent promises to her that he wouldn't borrow or get into debt. He drifted in and out of work, doing contract work here and there. His salary kept a roof over their heads.

Winter arrived and the girls had few toys with them, only the ones they had brought with them from Kenya. They had snakes and ladders, ludo, tiddlywinks and cards that kept them occupied and out of mischief. They did go for walks and were fascinated by a well-muffled figure cooking chestnuts on top of a charcoal brazier. The girls were allowed to buy a few and warmed their gloved hands around them. It was a far cry from Africa.

Dorothy woke the girls one night in the boarding house. She was excited and took them onto the balcony of her room. "Look," she said and pointed into the sky.

They saw a beautiful silver cigar-shaped object sailing silently overhead.

"Look at it carefully, it's an airship. You might never see one like it again." They watched as it slowly went out of sight.

Dorothy had some sad new for them the next day. "Remember the airship last night. It was called the R101 and it was on its maiden voyage. It crashed in France today and killed everyone onboard."

"What's a maiden voyage?" asked Barbara.

"It means it was it's first voyage."

Dorothy recalled her decision not to go on the Titanic's maiden voyage and wondered if she made the wrong choice.

Christmas was very quiet but they were together. Charles had work but spent the holidays with the family. A box of Plasticine kept them occupied for hours. They wasted no time and started making African villages with little huts; minute native figures in colourful 'clothes,' round three legged cooking pots, pestle and mortars, a woman complete with child on her back crushing maize for the posho. It was quite an achievement and depicted a typical African village. It sent a heart-felt message to Dorothy and Charles that they longed for Africa and wanted to go home.

Things didn't improve in 1932. Dorothy was clearly not happy in London and neither were the girls.

"Mummy, can't we go back to Africa?" asked Barbara one day.

"I think we all want to go back darling. Daddy is getting work, sometimes part time work, but he isn't happy here either."

"Is he in debt again?" quizzed Betty openly. They knew all about the problems before.

"No, he's not," said Dorothy. "He gives me his pay each month and he promised me faithfully he'd behave himself."

"Have we got enough money to go back?" asked Diana.

"We'll have to see," replied Dorothy. She didn't want to go into detail with them.

Dorothy knew they had to return to Africa – somehow.

Charles returned home in February, having completed a two-month contract. He was concerned that the family were not happy in England. "How do you feel about returning to Africa darling?"

"You know we all want to go back," said Dorothy. "Africa's a big place. Where are we going to go?"

"I've been thinking about South Africa, possibly Cape Town as a steppingstone. There's a lot of work there and in the Colonies. There'll be lots of advertisements for jobs in the major newspapers."

"We've managed to save a bit which has been a miracle but it won't get us to Cape Town", said Dorothy. They had never discussed the sale of her necklace in Nairobi. Charles had been all too aware of his antics and was embarrassed, even ashamed to ask Dorothy what she sold it for. Dorothy on the other hand, although she liked to be straight with Charles, never told him in fear he'd go off the rails again. She was concerned, above all else, for the welfare of the girls. It was an unwritten law between them. "I'll make enquiries tomorrow and find out what it would cost."

They talked for hours into the night. The girls heard the discussions behind their bedroom door. They had no idea what it was about but felt sure it had to be something exciting.

Charles took the girls for a walk the next day and Dorothy headed off on her own, well able to handle the family affairs. She went from travel agent to travel agent all offering different prices on passenger liners travelling to all the continents. They all varied but she found one that excited her. She could easily manage the fares and she returned to the boarding house with a bounce in her step.

Charles returned with the girls after dark. Dorothy was excited but tried to contain herself until she had agreed with Charles and made the final decision to go. They ate supper earlier than usual and the girls were herded off to play in their room.

Charles had noticed something different about Dorothy, an aura he couldn't explain but he knew it was something good. "Did you make any headway today?" he asked.

"Yes, I think I found a good bargain." She was keen to tell him. "There's a passenger-carrying cargo ship leaving Tilbury next week for Cape Town. The agent agreed to hold five bookings until tomorrow. He said there weren't many left."

"That sounds wonderful!" Charles seldom found moments of excitement. "Now," he was more controlled, "The million dollar question. Can we afford it?"

"We'll use your savings and I'll be able to scrape the balance together," Dorothy lied. She didn't feel guilty either. She just wasn't telling him the size of her nest egg. It was to remain in the family 'vault' and only she had the key.

They all went with Dorothy to the travel agent. The girls were ecstatic and were dancing and jumping all over the pavement, speaking fluent Swahili to each other much to the horror of local pedestrians. Dorothy treated them to tea and cakes at a very nice tearoom. They were so excited Dorothy and Charles could hardly contain them.

"Stop it now," said Dorothy. "Try and behave like ladies, if that's possible. We're only going to Africa!" Dorothy was as excited as they were.

They set sail a week later, along the English Channel, through the Bay of Biscay and into the Atlantic.

CHAPTER 7

The ship anchored briefly off Tenerife in the Canary Islands where they experienced the narrow winding cobbled streets, the tiers of white buildings and masses of people in their flowing colourful robes. Their marrow warmed to the suns rays extending beyond the delectably near tropic of cancer.

As they sailed further south the weather changed and it became colder, the sea rougher and the little cargo ship pitched and rolled in the South Atlantic Ocean, the girls thinking the journey would never end. They were still sleeping early one morning in their box-like cabin when Dorothy came in.

Come," she said excitedly. "I've got something to show you."

The girls clambered up the narrow metal steps onto the deck.

"Look over there, land, and there's Table Mountain!"

They had arrived at the tip of Africa, a long way from the equator and the tropical heat they knew so much but nevertheless it was Africa.

They stayed in a modest hotel in Cape Town. Charles was out each day scouring the newspapers for work either in South Africa or the Colonies in the North.

"I thought I'd have found something by now."

"We've only been here a week Charles. I'm sure something will materialise." Dorothy had to be positive.

She was right. Charles read through the vacancies columns of three papers the next day and something caught his eye.

"Here we are. The Shire Highlands Railways are looking for surveyors. Contract work in *Nyasaland!* How about that?"

"The girls would probably like it. Yes, why not? Where do you write?"

"Let me see. Oh, Johannesburg. They must have a head office there, that's useful."

Charles read the small print at the end of the advertisement. "Interviews in Johannesburg *and* Cape Town. That's great. Shall we go for it?"

"*You* go for it! Start writing and get it posted chop-chop." Dorothy had spoken.

It all happened at lightning speed. Charles attended the interview in Cape Town ten days later and was accepted for the post. The family were on the move again. Dorothy was relieved when Charles told her the company would be paying for the re-location. She was keen to hang on to that nest egg for dire emergencies and she had learnt those came around with immense regularity.

The journey took them through the majestic rugged mountains around Paarl in the Cape, the steam train chugging effortlessly in and out of the shadows of the mountains. There was a sense of serenity about it and Dorothy enjoyed the dining car with the silver service, the white starched linen and fine wines, no doubt from the famous vineyards in the area. This was the life she knew. She recalled the high life in London in her early twenties, her marriage to the Belgium Baron and subsequent life in Paris; her journey on the Trans Siberian Railway all those years ago.

"Cheers darling. Here's to happy days." Charles raised his wine glass.

"Happy days," said Dorothy, their glasses clicking. "This is magical. I could live like this forever."

"I hope I can do that for you. I've caused you a lot of heart-ache over the years and it's hurt me as much, I can assure you."

"You've kept your nose clean for a year Charles. It proves you *can* do it. Keep it up my darling."

The family were allocated two compartments in the first class section. The girls had a four-bunk compartment and there were arguments over the two top bunks. Betty and Diana were the oldest and won the argument. Dorothy and Charles had a coupe right next door.

The steam train went through the highveld, the wide-open plains of Southern Africa. They would stop at dusty sidings and watch the Africans holding up their wares at the windows and bartering with passengers. It was nearly winter in Southern Africa. The nights were cold but day after day the skies were cloudless and blue, the sun warm. They travelled northeast into Portuguese Territory and to their final destination on that train journey, the town of Chinde in Tete province. Chinde was a small town on the southern shores of the mighty Zambezi River that flowed into the Indian Ocean and they had to cross the great river to reach Nyasaland situated north of the river.

There was no station at Chinde and they disembarked onto red earth and the girls ran along the side of the train to see the huge Garrett engine still hissing and puffing at the head of the train. There were plenty of willing African porters who took their luggage to the paddle steamer tied up at the nearby jetty on the river.

"You didn't tell us we're going on this?" Betty was excited.

"You don't know *everything*, although you all think you do sometimes," joked Dorothy. "Nyasaland is up country on the other side of the river. They're taking us up the river in the steamer to a place called Tete and then on *another* train to Limbe."

"Everyone aboard," shouted a man with a white cap. The engines were turning over gently and smoke drifted slowly from the chimneystack. The passengers sat on benches on the low deck, luggage piled in a confined area. African men were strategically positioned on either side of the steamer with their long bamboo poles at the ready in the event of hitting sand banks.

The ropes were thrown aboard and as the gurgling diesel engines burst into a purring crescendo the wooden paddle wheel at the rear of the steamer came to life. The paddle churned the muddy river water and they moved away slowly from the jetty, the start of their long journey up the Zambezi to Tete on the northern shores.

The steamer ran into sand banks many times on the trip, the Africans pushing it free with their bamboo poles as they sang lustily, a throbbing chant keeping in time with the thrusting poles. They were an impressive sight, naked to the waist, their strong muscled backs bending to the task. They saw groups of hippo, their dome-shaped heads and massive snouts jutting out of the water like silent statues, only the involuntary flicking of their ears bringing them to life. The girls were over the moon. This was the life they loved.

They reached Tete at dusk with plenty of bustling and shouting all around, the train waiting to take passengers to Limbe. Charles pointed out the engraved name on the train windows. "See that. 'Shire Highlands Railways!' That's interesting."

The train arrived in Limbe late into the night. There was a yawning sense of deliverance, the real smells and sounds of Africa. Everyone making a din, voices jabbering in the darkness with lanterns bobbing about nearby and in the shadowy bush. They all felt so at home. Someone was there to meet them and they drove to their rented house.

The next six months flew by. They were well settled in their large rambling old house, with veranda's all around and gauze to keep the insects out. There was no electricity but paraffin lamps were everywhere. It was luxury compared to their huts in Nairobi. The garden was huge with vegetable gardens and an array of trees for the girls to climb.

The girls attended a convent school run by nuns from different nationalities. Their education had been sadly neglected and they had difficulty catching up. Charles was very busy with his engineering and survey work, which was done locally enabling him to be with the family until a temporary transfer came up.

"Dorothy, I've got to move to Blantyre for about six months. The company has a contact up there. I'll be staying in a small cottage on Mr Ramsey's property."

"Oh, Mr Ramsey no less! *The* big boss! I'm sure not may employees can boast about that. When are you going?"

"In about ten days but that has to be confirmed. I'll be driving up with my equipment. Will you be alright on your own with the girls?"

"That's a silly question Charles. My concern is you. Things have been fine since we left Kenya and I don't want you going off the rails again."

"For heavens sake Dorothy. I'll be fine."

"Charles, I'm going with you."

"This is a short company contract and the family is not expected to tag along. In any event, the cottage is probably very small and not suitable for you. I doubt Mr Ramsey would be expecting you."

"I don't care. I'm *not* going to sit here for six months, wondering what you are up to. Forget it Charles. I'm coming and that's that. The cottage can't be worse than those huts in Kenya."

"Please Dorothy. Be reasonable. Anyway, what about the girls?"

"There are boarding facilities at the convent and the girls can board for the six months.

We just cannot afford to have our lives ruined again with your gambling. You'll be on your own up there, you'll get bored at night and before you know it you'll be with the boys. Either I come with you or I'm going back to South Africa with the girls."

Dorothy arranged with the Mother Superior at the convent that the girls board for six months. They were excited at the prospect but concerned their freedom would be curtailed but they knew it couldn't be worse than the boarding houses in London.

"Come on girls. Jump in." Dorothy was taking them to school that day, with their suitcases of clothing ready to start their six months of boarding.

"This is like going to prison for six months," said Barbara.

"Yes, we're following in father's footsteps," joked Diana.

"Enough of that," snapped Dorothy as she drove her three hooligans down the driveway. All three sat in the back seat to avoid the arguments as to who would sit in the front. They wore their uniforms and big floppy hats, their luggage piled high in the front seat and the boot.

Dorothy saw them settled in to the one and only dormitory with a few other girls. She hugged them individually and promised to collect them for the school holidays. She drove away from the convent feeling empty. They had never been separated before and she smiled nervously when she wondered how they would behave. It would be good clean fun she thought and no doubt the nuns would keep them under control.

Dorothy and Charles spent their last night in the house in Limbe. It was like a morgue without the girls. Charles loaded the pickup in the morning with his survey equipment.

Their journey to Blantyre was on narrow dust roads with changing scenery. They drove through miles of fertile land, grassy plains as far as the eye could see, dotted with small African settlements depicted by groups of grass huts. They went through forests and past rushing streams. Local Africans walked along the road, some carrying wood or buckets of maize on their heads whilst others herding goats and cattle. The wide-open spaces gave a sense of peace and freedom. Dorothy often felt torn between the culture and fine life she had been accustomed to and to this vast, serene, wild continent, her senses kept drawing her to the latter.

They arrived in Blantyre late in the afternoon. They stopped outside a shop in the dusty streets of the town and asked the Indian storekeeper for directions to Mr Ramsey's house. It was said everyone knew where the 'railway boss' lived. Sure enough, the little round Indian man gave them detailed directions in his broken English, to the 'very very big house' on the 'mountain.' Their pick-up struggled up a steep driveway and they saw the massive house looming out of the dusk. It was a beautiful Dutch gabled design with huge double wooden doors and natural wood shutters on the windows. The lawn went right up to the house with flowerbeds and shrubs of various shapes and sizes dotted over the extensive lawns.

"This is bliss," said Dorothy. "Shall we park in the tradesmen's entrance?" she chuckled. She used the knocker on the wooden doors. "Does this remind you of something?" teased Dorothy.

Charles nudged her on her arm with his elbow. "Don't rub it in."

A tall thin African dressed in a white starched uniform answered the door and they asked for Mr Ramsey. He beckoned them in and told them to wait in the hallway. The walls were packed with mounted animal heads, no doubt trophies from safari hunts. Two huge lion skins lay on the terracotta floor. They must have been magnificent animals, their heads mounted with mouths in a snarling position, eyes fierce amber and protruding red tongues. Dorothy was mesmerized by the beasts and didn't hear their host arrive. He was dressed in long khaki shorts, cotton shirt and leather leggings and boots. His long white wavy hair framed a tanned weathered face. The perfect picture of a 'hands on' man.

"Do you like them?" The very English voice brought her back to reality. "Hello, I'm Ramsey. You must be Butler?" He held his hand out to Charles.

"Yes, how do you do Mr Ramsey. This is my wife, Dorothy."

"Pleasure to meet you my dear." Ramsey took her hand and kissed it. "You have a most attractive wife Butler. Now my dear, Phineas will show you to your quarters." He held Dorothy around the waist for a moment then rang a brass ships bell hanging in the hall near the front door.

The man in white who had answered the door for them appeared from nowhere.

"Phineas, will you take this lady to her quarters and help her with her luggage please. There's a good man. Now Butler will you come with me for a moment." Ramsey had clearly taken charge.

They went into an office the size of a huge drawing room. The walls were panelled with wood and two sides were filled with shelf upon shelf of books. There was a draughtsman's table in the corner, illuminated by a dim light on a metal arm. Ramsey explained to Charles his requirements over the coming months.

Charles said goodnight to Ramsey two hours later and found his was to his quarters, a small one-bedroom cottage some two hundred yards from the main house. It was very comfortable with a sitting room, kitchen and bathroom. Gauze frames fitted in each window with a wooden gauzed frame in the doorway. Dorothy had bathed and was cooking in the kitchen.

"Knock knock," said Charles and walked into the kitchen. "This is cosy, isn't it?"

"Yes, I'm impressed. I found some food in the kitchen and meat in the fridge. How do you fancy curry and rice?"

"Mmmm. Sounds great. Old Ramsey seems to fancy you," said Charles casually.

"Do I sense a little jealousy? I'm honoured," she joked. "Charles darling, come off it, he's old enough to be my grandfather."

"Yes, that's the problem. The older they are, the worse they are." They both knew they were engaged in a fun, nonsensical conversation.

"What's that sound of a motor in the distance? It hasn't stopped all evening." Dorothy was stirring the curry on the little two plate stove.

"It's a generator. Runs on diesel. Pretty effective according to Ramsey and provides electricity to the main house, this cottage and the staff quarters. You probably had a hot bath. He says it heats the geysers."

"Luxurious camping. Glad I came with you! Keep your nose clean Charles and make my life easy." She gave him a quick kiss and got back to the stove.

They enjoyed their meal on a tiny but adequate table in the sitting room. The lights flickered intermittently in unison with the generator as it coughed and spluttered in the darkness way beyond the staff quarters.

Charles had to be up before dawn and they were in bed early. It was a small double bed on a terracotta floor with loose colourful Indian carpets scattered on the floor. An old wooden wardrobe stood in the corner with hanging space and draws, quite adequate for their six-month stay. Dorothy slid under the white starched sheets next to Charles and lay back on the pillows, tired but content. Charles rolled over and lay next to her and tried to kiss her.

"Charles darling. I'm not in the mood. I keep thinking about the girls in boarding school and I feel very guilty."

"They'll be fine and they'll love it. I'm sure they're glad to see the back of us for a while." Charles tried to convince her.

"Another time," she pecked him on the mouth and rolled away from him. "Night night."

Charles had gone when Dorothy woke. The room was bright and the sun was well up. She made herself a pot of tea and got dressed, her shorts and sleeveless shirt adequate for the day. She wanted to explore the surroundings in daylight. The garden was extensive and there was a huge orchard at the back of the house. She saw two gardeners and greeted them in Swahili that they barely understood but they muddled through quite well in broken English. They showed her the orchard with dozens of different fruits from guavas to oranges, to avocado pears, bananas, peaches and the end of the orchard had a long wire fence covered in granadillas. The rich soils, hot summer sun and copious rainfall were any gardener's dream.

On the 'mountain' as the Indian shopkeeper had called it, or rather on the steep hill scattered over a wide area on either side of the driveway, were dozens of avocado pear trees almost growing wild and laden with fruit. They hadn't noticed them in the dusk the night before. Dorothy stood halfway down the slope and looked out over the trees and she saw a vast expanse of bush shimmering in the heat stretching as far as the eye could see.

The girls were having a rough time at school. They all shared one dormitory and there was no electricity at the school. They carried paraffin lamps with them at night and some were placed at intervals in the passages and hallways. Avocado pear trees lined the avenue leading to the convent and the girls often had a diet of avocado spread on slices of bread for breakfast lunch and supper. They'd sometimes be given Blanc mange for pudding, a varying treat for their taste buds. The girls were hungry most of the time.

On Sundays they went up the hill above the convent in crocodile formation along a footpath to the big cathedral for the service and was attended by the local Roman Catholic community. They always walked in the same order, Betty in front then Diana and Barbara at the rear. One Sunday they stopped at a little niche in a rocky outcrop to look at a small statue of the Virgin Mary.

Diana spent a long time looking at it. "I think I want to be a nun and float along in my habit saying my rosary."

"Me too," said Barbara as they collected wild flowers and placed them at the feet of the statue. They thought it a wonderful vision of life.

"You'll never be nuns," said Betty. "You're far too naughty. The nuns would never let you in. Come on, we'll be late."

They ran off giggling and laughing knowing Betty was quite right.

It was mid-term and their excitement increased. Dorothy would be picking them up for the school holidays. They waited at the entrance of the convent and were expecting Dorothy at 3 o'clock. They were still in their uniforms with floppy hats, luggage piled neatly. A pickup drove towards the convent along the avenue lined with the avocado's they had grown to hate so much.

"Is that her?" Barbara sounded excited.

"It's not her car," said Diana and as the pickup neared, "Yes, it is Mummy!"

The girls ran around the battered pickup like excited puppies and ran alongside the driver's door as Dorothy brought it to a stop. In her hurry to get out she took her foot off the clutch too soon and it lurched forward and stalled.

"Hello my darling." She wrapped her arms around them and hugged them tightly. They looked thin, their bare skinny arms and legs dangling out of baggy uniforms. Their backs felt bony as she hugged them. "Oh my darlings, you've lost weight."

"They've been starving us," said Diana.

"We're sick of avocado's and bread," came Barbara's contribution.

"What do you mean?" Dorothy was concerned.

"That's all we get for breakfast lunch and supper," said Barbara.

"Yes and sometimes a pudding at night," said Betty.

They were all trying to speak at once, telling Dorothy their tales of woe.

"They don't teach properly. The nuns hand us cards with the task for the lesson written on them," said Diana.

"And we're not allowed to ask any questions. If we talk the nuns tell us to keep quiet," said a concerned Barbara.

"They can't speak English, they're either German or French or...."

Dorothy cut Betty short. "That's it." Dorothy was on the war-path. "Load up the truck girls. I'll be back in a minute." Dorothy stormed into the convent. She knew where Mother Superior's office was and marched straight to the door. It was closed and she hammered on the door. No reply. She knocked harder and the door opened.

Mother Superior looked at her with her head tilted to one side. "Yes my dear?" She had a German accent but spoke good English.

Dorothy wasn't going to weaken with the sight of a sweet little nun in front of her.

"Mother Superior," started Dorothy. "I'm getting horrendous reports from my girls about the treatment they've received here. They were not being fed properly. It seems they've been on a diet of avocado pears. How can they learn if they're handed a card with notes on them *and* not be allowed to ask questions?" Dorothy was enraged and was blurting out anything as she remembered it. "*And* to top it all, my girls have lost weight. They're skin and bone."

Mother Superior looked sweetly at Dorothy, hands clasped together under her habit and head still tilted.

"Well?" snapped Dorothy, her blood pressure rising. "We're doing the very best we can," came her reply.

Dorothy knew she was wasting her time and wouldn't get satisfactory answers. "Well your best is not good enough for me or the girls. They won't be coming back to the convent next term." She left without waiting for an answer.

The girls were squashed in the cab waiting for Dorothy. She squeezed into the driver's seat. "Right. Let's go home. I've spoken to Mother Superior and told her you're not going back to the convent." Dorothy's eardrums nearly burst with screeches of delight.

"Are we coming with you to Blantyre then?" asked Betty.

"No, that won't work. I don't know what I'm going to do. I'll have to think about it."

Dorothy was to be with the girls for three weeks, during their school holidays. It worried her leaving Charles on his own and as much as she wanted to be with the girls, she was keen to get back to him to keep him on the straight and narrow. She knew it was in the best interests of the girls, which eased her feelings of guilt. It would only be for a few more months.

Limbe was a very small town and they had become friendly with a few families, one in particular was Mr and Mrs Peterkin. Mrs Peterkin was a darling, a motherly woman who always made them feel at home and the girls felt they had always known her. Dorothy kept thinking about them and wondered if the girls could stay with them.

They sat down to supper, the third night out of their prison. Dorothy was feeding them well, filling up their skeletal bodies with plenty of vegetables, roasts, roast potatoes and fresh fruit. Avocados were off the menu.

"Now girls. I will have to go back to Daddy in Blantyre for a few months and I'm wondering what to do with you lot."

"We'll stay here and look after the house," said Betty.

"No you won't. How would you like to stay with Mr and Mrs Peterkin?"

"Ooo, yes please!" said Betty.

"Yippy, we like her. It'll be better than that stupid convent," said Barbara.

"Hmm, OK, but we'd rather be with you." Diana had reservations.

"You know I'd like that but it's not feasible at the moment. Let's go and see them tomorrow."

They all piled into the pickup next morning, all happy to sit in the back. They drove for half an hour on dusty potholed roads, the girls loving the sun beating down on them and the smell of cattle dung and dust. They arrived at the Peterkin's farm with a lovely old rambling granite stone farmhouse, large lawns and exotic plants. They knocked on the door and heard footsteps on the bare wooden floorboards.

"Dorothy my dear," a tall plump woman with rosy cheeks and greying hair stood in the doorway. She was wearing an apron around her waist. "Hello Betty, Diana, Barbara." She remembered their names and they were glad she got the order of priority right. "Come in, come in. It's lovely to see you."

She took them into the sitting room filled with leather couches and chairs. The large low windows and French doors overlooked a swimming pool and lush green lawns. Flamboyant trees with their spreading branches provided a shady backdrop at the bottom of the garden.

"Now make yourselves comfortable and I'll put the kettle on."

"We've got a suggestion to put to you when you come back Jenny!" Dorothy knew she'd oblige.

Mrs Peterkin returned ten minutes later with a tray of tea and buttered scones. "Put me out of my misery!" she joked.

"As you know Charles is working around Blantyre and I've been up there with him. He's been there for three months and has another three to go. We had the girls at the convent in Limbe but it wasn't satisfactory. We're wondering if you'd like to look after the girls for the remaining three months?" She took a cup of tea from Jenny.

"My goodness. We'd love to have your three lovely girls. All to ourselves too! Would you like that girls?" Jenny looked at them.

They all replied together, "Yes Mrs Peterkin."

"Just call me Mrs P. It's much easier. When can they come over?" Jenny was keen to have her guests.

"Well, I only arrived a few days ago. Perhaps in a weeks time, if that suits you?" asked Dorothy.

"Yes, lovely, whenever you're ready Dorothy. We're not going anywhere. What about their schooling?"

"I wanted to ask you about that. I believe there's a private tutor in the area. He uses a motorbike. Do you know him?" asked Dorothy.

"Mr Smallie. He taught my boys and he's first class. I can contact him and ask him to come and see you if you like?" The Peterkins had lived in the area for many years and knew everyone.

"That would be lovely. Thanks Jenny." Charles was earning a good salary and they could easily afford a private tutor. " I'll bring the girls over next Friday and I'll return to Blantyre."

Everything had fallen into place for Dorothy and her brood. The girls got on like a house on fire with Mr Smallie and Dorothy was happy with his credentials and the good reports from Jenny. They were way behind in their education and Mr Smallie was to teach the girls Monday to Friday after they had had another week of holidays. Dorothy took the girls to the Peterkin farm as arranged and when she drove away and waved she felt quite happy that they were in good hands. Mrs P was reluctant to take any board and lodging fees but Dorothy insisted.

The girls had the time of their life on the farm and played ball games on the lawns. There was a netball court, which had been used by the Peterkin boys when they were younger and kept them occupied for hours. Mrs P was a superb cook and they were fed three good meals a day, not to mention the homemade bread and cream scones for tea. They helped her in the kitchen in the evenings with the cooking and washing up. It was an easy life style compared to those hard days in Nairobi. Dorothy made the girls promise they'd never tell anyone about those dark days. It was in their past now and to be forgotten.

Mr Peterkin was a kind quiet spoken man. He was never without his felt bush hat with its wide brim and leopard skin band and Mrs P had to remind him to take it off every time he came in the house. The girls joked about his hat and wondered if he went to bed with it on. He was clean-shaven with a leathery face and a woolly head of black hair greying at the temples.

The girls came in to the house after dark one evening and smelt something delicious. They headed for the kitchen and Mrs P was cooking a leg of lamb.

"Smells good," said Diana. "Can I help you with anything?"

"There's a standpipe in the back garden with mint growing near it. Be a good girl and bring me a handful of leaves."

Diana was always keen to help in the kitchen. "What's this for?" she asked.

"Mint sauce. Haven't you heard of it?" queried Mrs P.

"Nope," answered Diana.

"You have mint sauce with roast lamb. Wash the leaves under the tap then cut the leaves very small and put them in this jug of vinegar," explained Mrs P. "And mind your fingers, you don't want to lose any more!"

"Right, now sprinkle a teaspoon of brown sugar over the mint and leave it to permeate into the vinegar. There, you've learnt something new today."

Betty and Barbara set the dining room table and went to join Diana in the kitchen. Mr P come in and he had his hat on as usual. Mrs P was attending to the vegetables on the stove and had her back to him. "Hat!" she bellowed as a matter of routine, much to the amusement of the girls.

They enjoyed a first class supper of roast lamb, lovely crispy roast potatoes, pumpkin and green beans out of the garden. Pudding consisted of layered sliced pears covered with a sponge, fresh cream poured liberally on each helping.

"Thank you Mrs P," said Barbara. "That was a million times better than avocado sandwiches!"

"Who wants to come with me tomorrow to see the tobacco fields and watch the cattle being dipped?" Mr P knew the answer.

They had a breakfast of scrambled eggs, tomatoes and freshly baked bread then jumped in the back of Mr P's pickup. They drove through miles of tobacco fields and stopped outside the barns. He showed them the bundles of tobacco hanging up to dry from long poles. Big fires were being stoked outside the tobacco barns and kept blowing hot air into the barns to cure the leaves. They were fascinated and loved the strong smoky smells.

They drove on to the cattle pens. Fifty or sixty head of cattle had been herded into a large pen made from sturdy gum poles, and a narrow passage also a gum pole structure, led from the pen to the cattle dip. A gate allowed a few cattle at a time into the passage to prevent chaos and stampeding. Farm labourers whistled and prodded the cattle with sticks, controlling them as they bustled along single file to the dip. They jumped in the deep end one after the other holding their heads high and swam five yards to a sloped shallow end allowing the cattle to walk out of the dip and gather in a holding pen on the other side. The pens were dust bowls from continuous use and the smell of dust and trampled cow dung tunnelled into their nostrils. It was exciting and vibrant.

Charles completed his six month contract in Blantyre and they returned to their house in Limbe with the girls joining them.

They spent another year in Limbe and enjoyed a sociable happy time. Charles miraculously stayed away from his gambling and Dorothy always wondered if he had changed his ways or he never had the opportunity to engage in his horrendous activities from the past. The girls private tutor, Mr Smallie continued to teach them at home and their education progressed in leaps and bounds. He was with them Monday to Friday, mornings and afternoons and at the weekends they'd climb trees, play cricket and generally ran amok like wild animals, anything to let off steam and enjoy themselves.

On Saturdays they'd walk with Dorothy down to the local African market to buy vegetables and eggs. To assure customers the eggs were fresh, the vendors would have an enamel bowl of fresh water on a stand and each egg was tested before handing it over. If they sunk to the bottom of the bowl they were fresh; if they floated they were rejected. The African vendors would cook sweet potatoes in old tins filled with charcoal embers and the girls would eat the deliciously hot potatoes covered in ash but soft and tasty inside.

After church on Sundays they would sometimes accompany Charles up Zomba Mountain. They would drive for miles through the forests and the tea and coffee estates, until they reached the stream where trout fish abounded. He taught the girls to 'tickle' the trout to the surface with his rod and flies. They would proudly take their catches home to Dorothy who knew how to clean them and would roll them in oatmeal and fry them for supper.

They enjoyed the close community life in Limbe for two years and they thought it would last forever. As with all contract work it had to come to an end.

It was time to move on again. They all hated the prospect of going to yet another strange place and starting all over again. Once again the suitcases and trunks came out and the packing started not knowing what lay ahead. Charles had decided they should head for Salisbury in Southern Rhodesia. Mr Ramsey had told Charles it was an up and coming British Colony with good prospects of work. Old Ramsey had his finger on the pulse and Charles was relying on his word.

They boarded the train in Limbe to take them back to Tete on the river and the paddle streamer with the chanting pole-pushers. Charles was talking to the captain and came to tell Dorothy the news.

"The captain tells me this is the steamers last journey carrying train passengers. They're about to open the new Zambezi River Bridge and the railway line will cross the bridge. He's got some bubbly on the foredeck and wants the passengers to have a glass when we go under the bridge!"

"That's interesting," said Dorothy. "History in the making and we're part of it. I'd never have thought we'd be drinking champagne on the Zambezi!"

The huge wooden paddle churned the water as they steamed towards the bridge. It loomed larger as they neared it, a massive suspension bridge spanning the mighty

Zambezi. It looked incongruous with its mass of steel and intricate wiring like a monster deposited in the dusty African bush yet a marvellous feat of engineering in such remoteness. Glasses were filled and the steamer's hooters blared as she sailed under the bridge for the last time carrying her regular train passengers. It was the end of an era. The steamer would probably continue carrying local inhabitants and hauling cargo but it's glory days were over.

CHAPTER 8

Salisbury. Southern Rhodesia 1934. They went from hotels to boarding houses for a few months until Charles secured survey work with an electrical company. They moved into a furnished company house and the girls were able to attend another convent, far superior to the hideous education they had had at the Limbe convent. They felt unsettled in their house, wondering and waiting when the next move would come. It did come and Charles was transferred to Gatooma, a small mining and farming town about a hundred miles south of Salisbury.

Dorothy was distraught with the moves and tired of the girls changing schools. Charles was able to finance their education and to Dorothy's pleasure he was actually saving. She hoped it was towards their future.

Charles became friendly with a couple, Harold and Eve Gordon, owners of a gold mine near Gatooma.

"Remember the Gordon's I spoke about?" Charles asked Dorothy. "They've invited us to tea on Saturday."

"Town talk has it they're very wealthy with a very profitable gold mine. I wonder why they want to invite us," said Dorothy, sometimes and understandably suspicious of Charles' activities.

"Actually, he's offered to show me how to find gold. We might strike gold and be able to retire to a life of luxury." Charles wasn't sure whether to act seriously or not.

"Oh for goodness sake Charles. Not again. You're the eternal optimist. Don't waste your time and money on that."

"Nothing ventured, nothing gained. There's no harm in trying," Charles tried to assure her.

Charles and Harold were engaged in conversation at the far end of the veranda for the entire afternoon. Eve was a quiet woman, happy to show Dorothy and the girls the house and garden, almost on a par with the Peterkin's house in Limbe they thought.

"Those two are doing a lot of talking." Dorothy hoped to glean some information from Eve.

"Oh, I'm used to that," laughed Eve. "There's a lot of gold around here and Harold's always willing to part with his knowledge. Some people have been quite successful."

"Is it a costly exercise?"

"It can be, digging the mine, setting it up and so forth. If one's sure there's gold there, it's worthwhile," said Eve casually.

Dorothy didn't like what she heard. If Charles got a bee in his bonnet, nothing would stop him. She'd been there before with him.

Dorothy's and Charles' conversation that night took her back to Hong Kong and Nairobi, a regurgitating nightmare.

"All we have to do is a bit of prospecting and if there's gold there, we'll dig for it. It's quite easy," said Charles.

"What do you mean 'we'? And what's it going to cost to dig the mine? I think it'll be a disaster Charles. Leave it alone, please." There was a tone of despair in her voice.

Charles won the argument and the following Saturday they went prospecting. Dorothy and the three girls loaded the pickup with hammers, picks, sample bags and the all important picnic basket.

"All aboard," bellowed Charles happily.

The girls still loved the back of the pickup even though they were all young teenagers now. Not only were they tomboys, wild little bush pigs, they were very attractive young girls all with blond hair and blue eyes. Charles had a rough map on a piece of paper drawn by Harold. They drove for about ten miles, partly on strip roads then a rough bush road until they reached a rocky outcrop.

It was September and springtime in southern Africa, the warming sap in the msasa trees inciting the green shoots to fabricate a shady canopy over the bush in the shimmering haze, all nature's announcements that the long awaited rainy season was approaching.

"Harold thinks the area south of this kopje might be a good spot." Charles drove off the bush road and the truck rocked over uneven ground and flattened dry bushes, scraping the underbelly and side of the truck. He headed for a big msasa tree and stopped under the spreading branches.

"Will this do?" he asked Dorothy.

"Yes, there's plenty of shade here," she said.

The girls had already jumped off the truck and were climbing a kopje, up the granite rocks and hanging on the trees growing out of the craggy outcrop.

"I often wonder if they were fathered by an orang-utan."

"Me orang-utan," said Charles in a deep voice, thumping his chest with his fists.

"Go on. Go and find your pot of bloody gold." She slapped him on the shoulder. "I'm going to make a fire in those rocks."

Charles put the hammers and picks in a sack and called the girls. They walked about two hundred yards south of the kopje. He showed them what to look for and they spent the next two hours chipping away at likely quartz.

"Tea time." They heard Dorothy's voice in the distance. They left their prospecting tools in situ and headed back to the camp.

"Reminds me of our hut life," said Barbara as she sipped the smoky flavoured tea.

A slice of homemade cake, another cup of tea and they were back to work.

"Some of this looks good," said Charles. "Put them in the sample bags."

It was late afternoon when they left, Charles excited with their find, Dorothy sceptical. He took the samples to Harold the next day and he arranged to send them for analysis.

Three months passed and Charles was still working in Gatooma and spent every weekend at his gold mine. He had employed a gang of workers to help him sink a shaft in the spot where he had prospected with the girls. It had been a lengthy costly exercise. He obtained a mining licence and concession to mine in that area. The timber, equipment and wages had drained his savings.

"Can I say 'I told you so'?" asked Dorothy wearily. "I may as well talk to a brick wall."

"We just haven't come across the seam yet. Indications are it's there. We just have to find it." Charles sounded convincing.

"You keep putting money in to it and you're getting nothing out of it. My advice is – drop it. Drop it before you get any deeper in debt. You've borrowed on the strength of your concession. If you sell everything to Harold, you'll probably break even and get out unscathed."

Charles sat in a big linen-covered floral chair in the sitting room, his stretched out legs crossed at the ankles, his hands clasped behind his head. He grimaced, deep in thought.

"Are you listening Charles?" She could see him weakening under her pressure and she had to maintain it.

"Hmm, I'm thinking." He didn't move for a few minutes.

"Will you think of the girls for once Charles," she hesitated "and me, for that matter."

Charles sighed deeply, lent forward and put his face in his hands. "Alright, you win."

"It's not a matter of winning, you're just being sensible." She was relieved.

"I'll see Harold at the weekend. I know he'll take the equipment off me."

To Dorothy's delight, Charles came out of the mining venture having only singed the tips of his fingers. That was bad enough but she knew how bad it could have been.

They enjoyed nearly twenty months in Gatooma, made some good friends and had social gatherings at the local sports club. The girls had settled at school and picnics in the bush were a regular weekend activity. All was well until Charles had to drop another bombshell on Dorothy and the girls. He was to be transferred yet again, this time to Bulawayo, a town about two hundred miles south of Gatooma.

"I'm tired of all these moves Charles, but it's good to know you're in demand."

"At least it'll be at the end of the school term. Betty finishes this year; Diana has one or two years to do and Barbara a few years yet. There are some very good schools in Bulawayo."

"I hope it'll be our last move." Dorothy sounded tired. She had no idea what lay ahead.

December 1937. Once again they were on the move. The pickup was packed with suitcases, gardening equipment, kitchen utensils, tins of plant cuttings; everything but the kitchen sink. It was a long journey to Bulawayo on the strip road. The two narrow strips of tarmac mingled with loose stones, dust and occasional potholes. It wound through the bush avoiding rocky outcrops and hills. They would get partly off the strips for oncoming traffic leaving them in clouds of dust. The girls and all their possessions were covered in dust when they arrived in Bulawayo.

Dorothy always felt devastated arriving at furnished company houses. She had her growing family and nothing to show for it. They were never anywhere long enough to put down roots and have their own home. Like their other temporary homes, it was big and rambling. There was electricity but they found a chip geyser at the back of the house that required a fire to heat the water.

They settled well in Bulawayo. It was a big town with a growing population and industrial base. New departmental stores and businesses were springing up in the town centre and it was a hive of activity. Diana and Barbara were in school again. Betty had a flair for art and was gainfully employed as a sign-writer working with window-dressers. It was a friendly town and the girls got to know neighbours and children their own age. Climbing trees became less frequent. They'd bang on an electricity light pole at the junction of the gardens to summons their young neighbours then play cricket or rounders in the gardens.

Dorothy hadn't been well during the year and had paid several visits to the doctor. She had pain in the abdomen and waist and the doctor put it down to her stress and tension over the years and thought it was probably an ulcer. She was a strong woman and put on a brave face and seldom mentioned it to Charles or the girls.

Charles muddled through the year. He was paid well and had accumulated a little nest egg but was concerned it would never be enough for them to retire on. He wanted the very best for his beloved Dorothy. He knew he had to generate more income and put his ideas to Dorothy. He thought the time was right one Saturday afternoon as they both relaxed on their garden swing.

"I've been giving a lot of thought to a suggestion Harold made when I told him we were moving here."

"Oh?" Dorothy wasn't that interested.

"There are some very successful gold mines around Essexvale and…." He knew she'd interrupt.

"I'm convinced you've got a loose screw."

"Will you just hear me out. I heard the other day that the Mining Department are issuing concessions left right and centre for the area and it's obviously a hot spot. The chap who was telling me says there's an existing mine there and apparently the owner, a chap called Sullivan, wants to sell up due to illness. I checked with the Mines Department and they say it's a viable mine but needs more excavating."

"I really wish you wouldn't do this."

"We've been married for about twenty years now and all we have to show for it is a pile of suitcases and cardboard boxes. I want to be successful for you Dorothy."

Dorothy sighed. "I give up with you Charles."

Charles was excited. He knew that was the green light.

They went to Essexvale the next day to see if they could locate the mine and it's owner. It was a good twenty-mile trip. They drove through the Essexvale Hills, a scenic area of rolling hills and rocky outcrops. The rainy season had started and the bush was green and lush. Essexvale was a very small village of farmers and miners and Charles was able to get directions to Sullivan's mine.

They found an old man loading a truck with a gang of workers. Charles approached him. "Are you Mr Sullivan?"

The man was bent and using a walking stick. "Yes," he said with a croaky voice.

"Hello. My name is Butler. I believe you may be selling your mine?"

"That's right. I can't manage it now. You wanna buy it?"

"Well, I'm considering it."

"I'll show you the assay reports if you like." He limped slowly to a grass hut several yards away before Charles could answer.

They made some sense to Charles having learnt a bit from Harold.

"There's gold down there but needs more digging and I can't do it now." The old man's story confirmed what the Mining Department had told Charles.

They haggled over a price taking into account Sullivan's small loan.

"I want to get this behind me. I'll meet you at the Mining Department tomorrow. There'll be change of ownership forms and a lot of other guff to complete," said the old man and shook Charles' hand.

Charles and Dorothy drove back to Bulawayo. "Signed and sealed," said Charles.

"We forgot to ask him about accommodation. Where's the house?" asked a concerned Dorothy.

"He uses those huts. Didn't you hear him?" asked Charles.

"You must be joking! How can we live in those?" Dorothy couldn't believe it.

"It won't be forever darling. Once we have a good income from the mine, we'll either rent or buy a house. Don't worry!"

"You are such an optimist and now you're chasing your pot of gold. If I asked you, you'd probably tell me it's definitely at the end of the rainbow." Dorothy had a pain in her gut and she wasn't going to argue with him.

Charles was nine months into his mining venture. Betty was working in Bulawayo and was living with a friend. Diana and Barbara had to leave school. Charles put all his savings into the mine and school fees were low on the list of priorities. Dorothy's health deteriorated, she lost weight and her pain continued. She seldom visited the doctor and didn't want to worry the family with her problems.

Their accommodation at the mine was a large square hut used as a sitting room cum office, with a lean-to kitchen off that with a wood stove. Next to that were two rondavals, used as bedrooms. The walls were whitewashed mud with thatched roofs. A small narrow enclosed room made with thatching grass served as the shower. A wooden platform at one end held two ten gallon metal containers complete with hoses. Gravity brought hot water through the hoses and the flow was controlled with plugs at the end of each hose. Their toilet was another separate thatched, roofless hut; a long drop like the Nairobi nightmare.

Diana and Barbara helped Dorothy and Charles with the domestic chores and in the mine. They were back to paraffin lamps and their water was carried from a nearby river in drums slung on a pole between two strong workers. Dorothy went along with the routine yet secretly she hated their existence and knew it wouldn't last long. Charles kept digging but the seams weren't improving. He was finding gold, keeping abreast with the expenses but making very little profit. They realised he was putting in a great deal of effort for little in return.

"This isn't going to work." Charles lay on his bed in their hut, almost thinking aloud.

"You were saving more with the survey work," said Dorothy casually, "and not working so hard."

"I'll advertise it tomorrow and let the Mining Department know it's up for sale. They may know someone who wants to take it further."

Dorothy felt a sense of relief. "Very good idea darling," said Dorothy tactfully. "Do you want to go back to survey work?"

"I'll have to. There's a huge railway expansion going on. There's no shortage of work. Your health concerns me." Charles changed the subject. He rolled over on his bed and looked at Dorothy lying on her bed on the other side of the hut. The wick on the paraffin lamp had burnt down and she was barely visible in the dim light. He got off his bed and turned up the wick on the lamp. "That's better. I've been so bogged down with that damn mine, I hadn't noticed how much weight you've lost." Charles walked over to her, held her head in his hands and kissed her briefly on her lips. "Are you all right?"

"Of course I'm all right. I get a pain now and then in the belly but the doc. says it's probably an ulcer. Don't worry about it." She wanted to be positive.

"Why does he say *probably*? It's either an ulcer or it's not. And why have you lost weight?" Charles was getting concerned.

"Will you stop worrying Charles. Running around the mine, carrying wood, helping with the water from the river and heaven knows what else, is enough for anyone to lose weight."

Charles drove to Bulawayo in the morning and placed an advertisement in the local paper and visited the Mining Department. They assured him they would refer interested parties to him at the mine. He had got to know the chief engineer on the railways, Gordon Robinson, through his survey work with the electricity company and decided to visit him. Charles went straight to his office at the railway headquarters and knocked on his door.

"Well I'm damned. Hello Charles. Come in."

"Hello Gordon. Good to see you again," and Charles held out his hand.

"I understood from Garth you had gone gold panning or something," laughed Gordon.

"Well almost. I bought a mine in Essexvale but it hasn't been that profitable. It needs more money into it but I'm not prepared to take it further," said Charles and got to the point. "I'd like to get back to surveying and wondered if there are any positions on the railways?"

"You must be psychic. We've got an advertisement in tomorrow's paper. Let me give you an application form. You can complete it now if you like, it's pretty straightforward. We'll go through all the applications when they come in but I know how you work and I like you Charles." Gordon didn't beat about the bush.

Charles drove back to Dorothy and the girls at the mine feeling much better and confident. A far cry he thought, from the Nairobi days when he walked the streets looking for employment. He shook his head when he recalled those bad days. "Bloody fool," he said to himself. He was about a mile from the mine when he passed an oncoming car on the narrow dust road. It just passed him when the driver hooted repeatedly. Charles stopped and looked back. The car had stopped; the driver got out and ran back to Charles' pickup.

A man in a suit approached him at the window. "Are you Mr Butler?" The man was out of breath.

"Yes. What's wrong?" Charles thought something had happened at the mine.

"My name is Rabinovitch. I was at the Department of Mines this morning and they told me you may be interested in selling your mine?"

"That's correct." Charles was surprised things had moved so fast and let Rabinovitch take the initiative.

"Do you have the time to show me around now?"

"Yeah, sure." Charles drove on to the mine. He greeted Dorothy and she was about to tell him about Rabinovitch's visit when she saw his car.

"You must have met him on the road?" said Dorothy. "He seems interested in the mine," she whispered as Rabinovitch approached them.

Charles showed him the mine, explaining his unwillingness to put more capital into it. Rabinovitch said he had a few gold mines around the country all of which were managed by his staff. He was primarily an investor.

"I'd like to see the assay reports."

Charles showed Rabinovitch to their square hut. It was dusk and Charles lit the paraffin lamps. They talked for nearly an hour and Dorothy wondered if it was a good or bad sign. They eventually emerged from the hut. Both men seemed happy and Charles showed him to his car. They shook hands in the dark and Rabinovitch's car disappeared into the darkness, dust churning up in the taillights.

"He-he", said Charles, cheerfully rubbing his hands. "I asked him to make me an offer and he offered more than we paid for it! Have we got any bubbly to pop?"

"Would you prefer French? Shall we have a look in the cellar?" joked Dorothy sarcastically. "There might be a bottle of South African wine in the kitchen," said Dorothy excitedly.

"This was all so unexpected and happened so quickly. I've got an advertisement in the paper tomorrow so if people come looking, you can tell them it's sold! I'm meeting Rabinovitch in town tomorrow to finalise everything."

A week later Dorothy, Diana and Barbara were packing up again and moving back to Bulawayo. Dorothy thought she must have cherished Charles with untold love and kept asking herself what other woman would have tolerated such upheaval and squalor in their lives. "Love holds no bounds," she said out loud to herself.

"What did you say Mummy?" asked Diana.

"Oh nothing. Just talking to myself."

The pickup rocked slowly along the dusty road. Diana and Barbara sat quietly and patiently in the back with the suitcases and cardboard boxes containing their worldly possessions, as they watched the mine and huts become more indistinct amongst the trees. They had become accustomed to this morbid lifestyle. Morbid with their continual moves and no close friends or place to call 'home.' They drifted like a leaf in a gentle breeze not knowing where it will fall.

Charles secured a position with the railways and he worked closely with Gordon Robinson. They had a Dutch gabled house belonging to the railways in the suburbs of Bulawayo. Betty stayed on in the boarding house with her friend. Barbara went to short hand and typing classes and Diana, who wasn't able to type with her little hand, stayed at home with Dorothy and helped in the house. Dorothy continued to be unwell.

"What's wrong Mummy?" Diana was concerned about Dorothy who had spent most of the day sitting on the veranda. "It's not like you to be so quiet. You're always doing things," said Diana sadly.

"I know. I just don't have any energy and I have a bit of pain."

"Where's the pain?" Diana wanted to help. "Do you want to go to the doctor?"

"I don't think he can do anything."

"I think you should go. I want you to get better." Diana hugged Dorothy for a long time, sniffed hard and ran inside.

Dorothy wiped her eyes. She too wondered what was wrong with herself. She had an uncanny feeling when they left the mine; a feeling that it would be her last move, a feeling that a permanent resting place was waiting for her. A sense of peace had enveloped her, peace mixed with sadness.

She pulled herself together and called Diana to help her in the garden. A storm was nearing and Dorothy wanted to cut some roses before the rain ruined them. "Bring me the scissors out of the kitchen will you darling," she called out to Diana.

Diana was delighted Dorothy felt better, helped her cut the roses and took them into the kitchen. They arranged them in two vases and they looked particularly special. Dorothy's pain returned and she had to sit down. Charles arrived home after work and noticed Dorothy wasn't herself.

"Your skin is yellowish my darling. I'm very worried about you and I want you to see the doctor tomorrow."

Charles drove Dorothy to the doctor. She felt too unwell to argue otherwise.

"Come in, Mrs Butler. What have you been up to since I last saw you, please, sit down." Doctor Scott looked at Dorothy's card. "You were last here a year ago."

"I've been feeling very tired recently with a fair amount of pain around here." Dorothy pointed to her upper abdomen.

"Could you lie on the bed please."

Doctor Scott poked and pushed her abdomen for a long time, tapping here, tapping there. "You're quite yellow. I'm sure you have a gall-bladder problem and we probably need to whip that out. I'm referring you to a surgeon and if he agrees, it will be best to go ahead with the operation." Doctor Scott scribbled a letter and sealed it in an envelope. "Will you make an appointment with the sister to see Mr Corrie. I'd like you to see him today."

"Thank you." Dorothy didn't know what to say. The thought of hospital and an operation horrified her.

Charles had waited for her in the car. "What is it?"

"He says it's a gall-bladder problem and wants me to see a surgeon, a Mr Corrie. He's had a cancellation and can see me in half an hour," said Dorothy quietly.

"Well Mrs Butler. You have gallstones and I think we should remove your gallbladder. You won't feel so ill and the pain you're getting is from the stones. I think the sooner we do it the better. Are you happy with that?"

"I'm not happy about any operation but if it's going to relieve the pain, then yes, we must do it."

Dorothy was admitted to the government hospital in Bulawayo three days later. Charles and the three girls accompanied her, devastated that she had to have an operation.

"Now my darlings," Dorothy spoke to her three beautiful daughters. "I don't want you to worry. Betty, Barbara. I want you to carry on with your work and Diana darling, you find yourself a good job. You're very capable and organised."

"Take care of the girls Charles whilst I'm in here."

"We just want you home Mummy," said Barbara.

"You mustn't stay here long. We love you." Diana sat on Dorothy's bed and held her.

"Come on now you lot!" joked Dorothy. "Get yourselves home now and organise your supper." She tried to be their positive strong mother, their mentor, but she felt tired and weak.

Dorothy had her operation the next day. Only Charles visited her in the evening on the advice of the hospital. She was still asleep and Charles thought she still looked a pale yellow. He held her hand by her bedside for a long time, hoping she'd wake but she didn't.

The following afternoon Charles took the girls to the hospital. They walked down the corridor to her ward, hating the smell of disinfectant and mentholated spirit. Dorothy lay motionless her yellow face stark against the white bed linen. The girls look their turn to hold her hand each hoping their touch would waken her.

"Let's all hold her hand together to give her strength," said Diana. They huddled together and grasped Dorothy's thin pale hand. It felt cold. They could feel tears welling up inside but they wanted to stay strong for their mother.

Dorothy's eyes flickered and opened and she gazed momentarily at the girls. Her eyes were lifeless, glassy, eyes without a soul. They closed and Dorothy's hand moved briefly in theirs. They rubbed her hand desperate for another sign, something to say she was all right. It never came. It was like a broken umbilical cord, the very core of their life being torn away.

Charles stood on the other side of the bed, speechless. Deep down he felt she had to get better. She was his strength, his reason for living.

A sister came into the room jogging them out of their reeling sorrow. "I think you should let Mrs Butler rest now," she said gently. "Come and see her tomorrow."

"Why isn't she awake and talking to us?" asked Diana.

"Why is she so weak?" came Barbara's question.

"She's had an operation and she needs to rest," answered the sister. "Come now." She encouraged them out of the room. They walked silently through the hospital. Charles saw Mr Corrie at the entrance and stopped to speak to him.

"Just wait in the car girls, I'll be with you in a minute," said Charles. He turned to Mr Corrie. "Hello Mr Corrie. We're very concerned about my wife. She looks very weak."

"Yes," concurred the surgeon. "May I have a word with you?" He led Charles into an empty office off the corridor. "I intended removing your wife's gall bladder yesterday as you know. When we opened her we saw she had very advanced cancer."

Charles covered his face with his hands. "Dear God no." His voice was shaking. "No," he said again.

"I'm very sorry Mr Butler. There was nothing we could do."

"How long? Will she come home?" Charles knew he was asking dreadful questions but he wanted to hear something positive.

"I believe she has only days. I'm very sorry. Would you like someone to drive you home?" Mr Corrie seemed concerned.

"No," said Charles. "No. Thank you. I'll be all right." He walked out of the hospital and to the waiting girls, all squashed into the cab of the pickup, no time for fun in the back. Charles broke the news to them as they drove back to the house.

The phone rang at the house at seven o'clock the next morning. Charles' heart sank. It was the hospital and they wanted them to go there right away. They walked silently along the corridor to Dorothy's room and the sister was waiting for them.

She had to tell them the news. "I'm sorry, Mrs Butler died a short while ago."

The girls shrieked and burst into tears. They looked at Charles, his face covered with his hands. They held out their arms to each other and they hugged each other for support. The sister waited a few minutes. "We've prepared her and you might like to see her."

"Oh Mummy," said Betty. They continued to hold onto each other.

"Come my darlings." Charles seemed to draw inner strength and for a fleeting moment he believed it was Dorothy, watching them in the passage. The sister opened the ward door and they filed in, in ritual crocodile formation, the unwritten law of seniority falling into place as it did so many times before on the dusty footpaths in their adored bush. This time Dorothy was well ahead of them, waiting. They stood at the foot of the bed, grasping one another. They found it hard to look at Dorothy. Only her face was visible above the white linen bedcover, her eyes closed. The sisters had put little pink rosebuds around her head.

Barbara spoke first. "Mummy would hate those rosebuds."

"They're just not Mummy," added Diana.

There was an air of frivolity in their statements, mitigating the gravity of the moment and cognizant of veiling the profound reality before them.

Charles kissed Dorothy on the lips and held his head against hers for a moment, tears in his eyes. He beckoned the girls and the line of seniority followed once more. The sister was standing quietly in the corner of the room. "Can I take you for a cup of tea?" They left the room in silence, not looking back as though being guided to go forward now with their lives.

CHAPTER 9

Their lives shifted to another gear after Dorothy died and they couldn't pretend everything was the same. Barbara stayed in Bulawayo whilst Charles, Betty and Diana moved to Salisbury in search of new lives. Romance blossomed soon after for the three girls. Diana married a young police trooper, Barbara also married into the uniformed forces and not to be left out, Betty married her commanding officer and moved to England. Charles moved to South Africa after his girls' married and he married a childless widow. He died a few years later from throat cancer.

Diana and William had three daughters, Margaret and Jill who were born two years apart then they had Beth who was nine years Margaret's junior. Diana often wondered, having been blessed with three girls herself, if her childhood would be mirrored all those years later.

They lived in a police training camp. William was a riding instructor and it was mandatory that all police rookies learnt animal husbandry and how to ride horses and William played a major role in instructing the recruits. It was a huge camp with so many opportunities to play games, have fun and get up to mischief.

Margaret and Jill went to a senior girls school about four miles away in the avenues. They would cycle to and from school each day. Beth was too young to attend school and helped Diana in the house. The girls loved climbing trees and Diana was convinced it was in the genes. With the help of Margaret and Jill, William built a massive tree house in a jacaranda tree in the garden and they'd spend many hours in it with their friends. Beth was many years their junior and was regarded as a pest and a thorn in their side. Many a time she'd be barred from entering the tree house with the others busily engaged in 'meetings' and important activities. Beth would run off to Diana for support and pleading intervention in the impasse.

When Margaret and Jill left school and started working, Beth had the run of the camp with friends of her own age. The stable hands would meticulously pack bales of hay into huge neat stacks but Beth and her entourage would mutilate and completely re-arrange the organised bales in to secret hideouts and they would play there in the sun for days on end.

The rainy season always heralded a new game. Huge heavy canvas marquees were frequently erected on the playing fields for cricket fixtures and the corners of the marquees filled with water after a heavy rainstorm. Beth and her friends would climb the guy ropes to the top of the marquee like a troop of monkeys and jump wildly into the rainwater that had collected in the sagging canvas. When there was no rain the temptation to jump off the top of the marquee into the hollowed canvas below was too great. They'd climb the ropes repeatedly and leap into the hollow below, until one day Beth took her turn and jumped recklessly into the hollow but this time the canvas didn't hold her. It ripped wide open and she tumbled through the gaping hole and came to rest sprawled on the ground fifteen feet below, having cut her lip on a metal table in the marquee.

Beth's antics at times went to extreme. All offices, buildings and messes were strictly out of bounds to all children. Saturday mornings in the camp were sacred and top brass inspected the camp. On one particular Saturday William was part of the inspection party and on entering the billiard room in the Sergeants' Mess they interrupted a game being played between Beth and her friends. A highly embarrassed William bellowed, "Get outa here." He had to back up his total disapproval in front of the top brass by lambasting Beth a number of times across the rump with his instructors' cane. She cried all the way home unable to sit on her bicycle saddle. Beth was delighted when Diana sympathised with her and chastised William for his action.

To Diana and William's horror, Beth's escapades extended to the junior school she attended near the camp. She became very friendly with a schoolmate, Sandra, and the two became partners in crime. They would giggle in assembly and slide down the banisters on the stairs, both activities forbidden and frowned upon by the headmaster and he would summons Diana to the school complaining about her bad behaviour. Once more Diana was reminded of her early days, sliding down the stairs in the London hotel and turning park benches upside down. She loved Beth and tried to keep equilibrium between her misdemeanours and the headmasters' disapproval.

Things turned worse when Beth and Sandra were caught jumping on the beds in the sick bay and once more Diana was summonsed to the school and it was decided detention and extra homework would reform the wild tomboy. It helped for a while until Beth was found, by the headmaster to make matters worse, swinging on the massive velvet curtains in the assembly hall. Sandra had been with her but she had run away and escaped his beady eyes. At the end of his tether he immediately called Diana to the school. It was agreed the headmaster be given authority to cane Beth, should further 'crimes' be committed. Only boys received a caning and Beth made history being the first girl to be eligible for the cane. Perhaps the memory of William's cane across her rump changed her ways as the cane was never used. Despite her misdemeanours she was liked by her teachers and received prizes for hard work.

Diana was very domesticated, spending her time cooking superb meals, making clothes and keeping a lovely garden. It was quite easy for her; she had electricity, running water and everything at her fingertips. Well, four fingers and two thumb-tips. The four stubs on her right hand were never a burden to her and she managed any activity with ease. She could turn on a tap and get hot water now and not worry about carrying it from the river and making a fire to boil the water. Those chores were just a dream for her now.

But one reality from her childhood followed Diana into her marriage. She began to fear the dark and for years had to sleep with a dim light on in her bedroom recalling that old Masai man under her bed and Girlie's threat to have them taken away in a sack by the Masai if they misbehaved.

Most Sundays were spent at 'the lake', a huge expanse of water twenty miles from their home. William was a great sailor and the girls frequently sailed with him.

Beth sometimes pursued her own interests canoeing from the jetty, walking barefoot in the water crushing bilharzia snails underfoot, oblivious to the dangers of the waterborne disease carried by the snails or the crocodiles that lurked in the waters. Diana was quite content organising the food and camp for William and her three tomboys. Their shorts and bare feet were a reminder of her days with her two sisters.

Margaret had a wild passion for flying. Diana and William offered to pay her flying lessons if she did well at school. Needless to say she excelled and began her lessons. Ironically Margaret didn't have a driving licence and relied on the family to drive her to her flying lessons. She loved the old aircraft, the smell of the oil and fuel and she was convinced she was the reincarnation of a World War ll pilot and spent many hours learning in an old Tiger Moth. Diana hated the thought of her flying in the flimsy little machines but she knew her brood had to follow their dreams and she gave them the freedom to dream and live them. Margaret, proud of her ability to fly, wanted to take Diana and William for a flip. They were terrified at the thought but couldn't disappoint her.

Beth pursued William's love of horses and when he visited the house on horseback during his early morning rides, he'd hoist Beth into the saddle for a ride around the garden. As she got older she was given a pensioned police horse, Julian, and would ride for hours through the bush, sometimes accompanying William on his daily rides in the camp and beyond. The smell of the horses, the creaking sound of leather, the suns' rays breaking over the trees and hills were special and the early morning dew on the dry elephant grass had a unique smell only found in Africa.

William would ride his long established friend Chain-shot, a seventeen hand bay gelding. They worked in unison in dressage and jumping, winning many prizes and they were a magnificent pair on mounted escorts with mirror shiny leather, flagged lances and white pith helmets. They were an inseparable team.

Life had lavished copious congenial days on them but they rolled rapidly into months and years then decades, a cursory juncture bestowed on their lives until it was time for William to retire from the police. Diana and William moved to Bulawayo to start a new life and be nearer Barbara where she now had a family. Margaret moved to South Africa and Jill remained working in Salisbury.

Diana felt some nostalgia as they packed up for their move remembering the many, many times she moved with her sisters and parents, but now happy they had actually accumulated their own furniture and many other treasures. One such treasure breathed and had life and her name was Suzi, a huge black standard poodle. Diana, William and Beth moved to a lovely house rented from Barbara and her husband John, situated on the side of a kopje amongst picturesque granite rocks and dotted with shady jacaranda and flamboyant trees.

Beth started school and at 13 was lucky to be attending her second school. William was appointed personnel manager with an international company because of his excellent rapport with people from all walks of life. He was diplomatic, well liked and slotted in perfectly in his new appointment.

Diana the homemaker got to work in the new house and garden. Near their two acre garden was an old disused storeroom and William got to work on it and converted it into two first class stables.

A few months later the last two pieces of their treasures arrived at the railway station, Chain-shot and Julian. Chain-shot was due for retirement and joined William but it was only the former that would be out to graze. Julian was already on early retirement, his unruly behaviour not in keeping with well-disciplined police horses.

Beth soon made friends with other children in the area and once more the 'gene syndrome' came to the fore because anything that resembled a tree had to be climbed. Beth and her close friend Sonnet would climb a big leafy jacaranda tree a distance from the house and smoke cigarettes. They would watch Diana through the leaves as she worked in her sewing room and their ability to spy on Diana added to the excitement of their wicked deed. They'd climb massive granite rocks and sit right on top like monkeys and would suck through a gouged hole in tins of condensed milk. It was all good clean fun. It was also fun at school for Beth.... fun for a while.

She did well at school and took her work seriously but Beth was very independent, like her mother and had a mind of her own.

"You'll be writing your mock 'O' level history in four weeks," announced Mrs Wilkins, their regular history teacher. "Next week Miss Paterson, a student teacher, will be taking over until the end of term."

Beth liked Mrs Wilkins but hated history and made a concerted effort for her. "Why do we have to have a student?" asked Beth who was never shy when the cause was right.

"Miss Paterson must do her teaching practise. She'll only be doing revision with you," explained Mrs Wilkins.

Beth studied day and night, hating every moment. She believed history should remain where it belonged, in the past, and one should look forward not back. She wanted to pass for Mrs Wilkins but Beth didn't like Miss Paterson. She decided she wasn't going to like her even before she met her. She was never impolite to her teachers but was well able to speak her mind, with reason, if the need arose.

The big day arrived and Beth had crammed her head with dates and all the useless information needed for the exam. She wrote the exam, bored with the detail but believed she had her facts right.

Miss Paterson collected the papers. "Right girls. I'll give you the results on Monday."

Beth's heart sank and she wondered if Miss Paterson was to mark the papers. She restrained herself and decided not to ask her and await the results. Beth's weekend was filled with more books, studying for further mock exams in the wings. There was no time for fun and riding horses.

Monday morning came too soon and Beth had an uncanny feeling that things wouldn't go well. The history period was set for late morning. Miss Paterson read out the results and percentages obtained for each pupil. The pass mark was 50%.

"Beth, 48%." The words pounded in Beth's head. She was oblivious to the other results being announced by the young Miss Paterson. Beth didn't believe it. She must be wrong she thought to herself. She had worked hard for the exam. Miss Paterson finished reading the results.

Beth had to speak. She should have raised her hand and waited for Miss Paterson to give her permission to talk.

Beth had very high ideals and she found it difficult to be polite to someone who wasn't worthy of respect.

Beth stood up. "I don't think I've failed Miss Paterson."

"Will you sit down," came Miss Paterson's response.

Beth still stood and remained composed. "Can you tell us who marked the papers?"

"*I* marked the papers," said an indignant Miss Paterson.

"I want Mrs Wilkins to mark my paper. I don't believe I've failed." Beth was not rude but believed she was right to defend herself.

"Will you *sit* down." Miss Paterson was annoyed that a pupil had the audacity to query her ability.

Beth didn't want to let it slip. "I would like my paper re-marked."

"I'll have to report you to the headmistress. Wait outside the classroom."

Beth was pleased there would be higher intervention and walked out of the room.

Minutes later Miss Paterson came out. "Come with me."

Beth followed in silence as she led her towards the headmistress's office.

"Hello Miss De Beer. Can I have a word with you?" asked the young student and they disappeared behind a closed door, Beth left to wait outside.

That's great, thought Beth. I'm not able to defend myself. She waited patiently.

Miss Paterson emerged five minutes later and walked right past Beth.

Miss De Beer stood at her door. "Come in," she said without a smile.

Beth walked gingerly into her office. Girls are *never* caned in girls senior schools, she thought reassuringly to herself. She stood in silence, hands clasped behind her back. Miss De Beer was a tall elegant woman with a wrinkled face and dark grey wavy hair that was never out of place.

"Why did you query your exam result?" she asked quietly.

"I don't think I failed Miss De Beer," said Beth pointedly.

"Your paper was marked and I have no doubt it was done correctly."

"I just wanted Mrs Wilkins to check it," added Beth.

"We can't have staff running around checking papers. There isn't the time. I'm quite satisfied with Miss Paterson's ability. This was a mock exam and I want you to try harder for the main exam at the end of the year," Miss De Beer tried to reassure Beth.

"Yes Miss De Beer." Beth knew better than to argue with the boss.

"Now get along and get back to your lessons." She gave Beth a kind smile.

"Thank you Miss De Beer." Beth left her office. There was something special about that smile and she believed Miss De Beer thought she was right and was on her side. She liked her for her wise judgement.

The following week was the mock 'O' level French exam. The girls waited in the classroom for the invigilator.

Horrors of horrors, snakes alive thought Beth. Miss Paterson walked into the room clutching a folder of papers. She started handing out the papers placing them upside down on the desks.

"This is a two hour paper. When you've finished, you're to remain seated until the two hours is up," said Miss Paterson obviously keen to assert her newfound authority.

The girls glanced at each other. They knew that was never the case. When they finished a paper they were always allowed to leave the classroom. Beth was sure she was meeting out a moral injustice. Beth and injustice were like oil and water. It was an unhealthy combination when Miss Paterson came into the equation.

They started writing and needless to say Beth finished after one and a half hours. She knew she should have remained seated but she couldn't do it. Miss Paterson was grossly unfair with her instruction and Beth would have nothing to do with it. She collected her pens together off the desk, got up, placed her exam paper on the student teacher's desk and walked towards the door. As she did so, she looked through the row of windows separating the classroom and the veranda outside and she saw a tall elegant woman with a wrinkled face and grey hair walk past the classroom. Bad timing thought Beth, but she had made her decision and continued to walk out of the room with Miss Paterson on her tail shouting at her to return. She followed Beth onto the veranda and instructed her to return to the classroom. The grey haired woman heard the commotion, stood still on the veranda and looked impassively at Beth but behind that façade was an air of justice and integrity. Beth accompanied her quietly to her office.

The headmistress asked Beth to explain herself. Miss De Beer knew the rules and regulations regarding mock exams – she probably made them. Once again she gave Beth that knowing smile and Beth knew justice had been done. That was doubly confirmed when she was amongst one of the few pupils to receive the schools' 'deportment badge,' awarded not only for being immaculate and well dressed but for good behaviour. Beth believed it should have been for 'just' behaviour in her case.

Beth wisely summed up the woman with the wrinkled face and grey wavy hair as an extremely astute and wise intuitive old girl. Beth's prudent perception of the headmistresses' character would be verified and reiterated with the decisions and heartfelt integrity she'd encounter later in life.

Diana and William were thrilled with her award. Their wild tomboy wasn't as wild as they believed and the thought of canes was permanently out of the window. Beth passed her 'O' level and started the 'M' level year with her school buddy Kathy, both wanting to be teachers. Beth had reservations and being a believer not only of justice but liberty, her liberty, wondered if she was pursuing the right career. Restricted to a classroom would send shivers down her spine?

Their 'base', their main classroom, was the biology laboratory with Mrs Arthur their class mistress and biology teacher. Beth and Kathy excelled in biology and were clearly teachers pets. Leading off the lab. was a storeroom containing multitudes of laboratory equipment including the girl's favourite piece de resistance, a human skeleton dangling like a medieval corpse on a flimsy metal frame. The girls had named him 'Charlie Bone Shaft.' Kathy always thought it resembled Beth, tall and decidedly bony and Beth was honoured with the same nickname.

"Let's dress him up." Beth had wanted to do it for years.

"We've got a test just now and Mrs Arthur won't be impressed," said a cautious Kathy.

"She won't mind. It might put her in a good mood." Beth knew Mrs Arthur liked them and they wouldn't get into trouble. They had never seen her angry or agitated and she always gained the girls' respect. "Quick, let's do it now."

Beth and Kathy got to work. A white towel was draped over his shoulders. Kathy cut out two circles of paper and drew two perfect eyes and placed them in his eye sockets.

"Perfect," said Kathy.

A floor mop with long tassels of cotton stood in the corner. Beth struggled with the mop and removed its head and popped the mop on Charlie's head. The whole class burst into laughter.

"He looks great!" said Kathy.

"Wait. Wait." Beth had another idea. She rubbed a piece of red chalk on the end of a long white piece, prized open his jaw and his teeth grasped the homemade cigarette.

They placed Charlie near the blackboard as they heard footsteps in the corridor. They rushed to their stools at the laboratory tables and stood as she came in. "Good morning Mrs Arthur," came a collective angelic greeting from the girls.

She placed her basket and folders on her desk and looked at Charlie Bone Shaft. She never showed emotion, only concerned with her professional approach to teaching. A very slight conservative smile emerged.

"Need I ask who did that," was her only response. "Right. We've got a test this morning. Put your books away." She walked around the room handing out the blank paper and question papers.

Heads were down and they started. Beth was aware of the few rouges in the class and she observed a biology book strategically placed in a sink on the lab table in view of one of the rouges. Beth ignored it. If she wants to cheat be it on her own head, she thought. Mrs Arthur walked slowly around the room and passed the offending sink. Beth was sure she'd seen the book. She carried on walking round the tables and back to the same spot, like a Geiger counter zooming in on offensive material. She leaned over the table and slowly removed the book from the sink, closed it and continued her patrol. She never uttered a word; she didn't have to. She was too clever for that.

Test over, she collected the papers and continued with the ongoing biology lesson.

There was a knock on the classroom door and Doreen walked in. She had come to see Mrs Arthur on a personal visit. She was dressed in a uniform with a light grey starched shirt, blue tie and epaulettes and a smart skirt with inverted pleat.

"Hey Kathy," whispered Beth. "I didn't know Dor. had joined the police!"

"Neither did I."

"I know she left school at the end of last year and I lost contact with her. I'm impressed. I like her uniform!" Beth was hooked on that uniform.

William collected Beth from school at lunchtime and they drove home. Beth had to tell her parents about that uniform.

"I think you've fallen in love with the uniform, never mind the job," said Diana. "You've started your 'M' level now and you can't just leave school."

"Why not. If there are vacancies, I want to join." Beth was determined.

"I'll make some enquiries this afternoon." William probably knew every policeman in the country.

Beth ran out to the car when William came home that afternoon. "Pa, what did you find out? Can I join?"

"Just hold your horses," said William. "Let me have a cuppa."

They went inside with Beth champing at the bit for information.

"I phoned the recruiting office and they're recruiting for a women's squad to go into depot in August...."

"Great," shouted Beth not allowing William to finish. "Can I join?

"What about your teaching degree?" asked Diana. She wasn't sure if Beth was taking the right path.

"Ma I don't want to do that now. I just want to join the police," said Beth.

"You're really hooked, aren't you? What happens if you don't like it?"

"I will. I know I will."

Beth passed the interviews with flying colours. They left Bulawayo the day before her attestation day, the car loaded to the gunnels with mounds of cleaning material. William stayed in Bulawayo to look after the animals. Diana accompanied Beth on the 250-mile journey to Salisbury for moral support.

"Good luck my girl. Success. Write and tell us all your news," said William.

"Thanks Pa. I hope I'll complete the training."

"You will. You'll be fine and your Ma and I will come up for your pass out parade."

Twenty miles outside Salisbury they encountered a problem.

"The alternator light's come on."

"What's that um, the battery, no the fan belt I think," Diana thinking of similar problems with Dorothy, Charles' and William's cars over the years. "We'd better stop and have a look."

Beth stopped the car off the road, partly in the bush and lifted the bonnet.

"The fan belt's broken. Look." Diana pulled the broken fan belt from its pulley.

"Oh that's great," said Beth. "That's all we need."

"Dad used to put a stocking on the pulley. It's a temporary measure but it works," recalled Diana.

They dug in their suitcases for a pair of pantyhose and tied a leg around the pulleys.

"Start the engine and let's see if it works," said Diana.

Beth turned the key and revved the engine. "The light's gone out."

"It's done the trick," said Diana with her head under the bonnet and thrilled with her mechanical expertise.

They were up early the next day, Beth having to report to police headquarters at 8 o'clock. She loved her mother dearly and it was the first time they were going to be apart. They hugged each another for a long time.

"I'll miss you. Don't forget to write." Beth was always strong emotionally but felt it hard to hold back the tears.

"Do your very best, that's all you can do and the four months will be over in no time," Diana reassured her. "I'll fly back tonight but the house will be very quiet without you."

The first week into the training Beth and her seven squad mates didn't know if it was day or night, if they were coming or going, Arthur or Martha or their left from their right. They were issued with their kit of blankets, sheets, pillows, mosquito nets, training shoes, track suits and the pièce de résistance was a grey one piece cotton dress like a dust coat but the girls likened it more aptly to prison garb. Beth was horrified because it wasn't like the uniform she had seen on Doreen but she learnt that those were issued when they finished their training. Beth was now back at the training depot where she grew up. She was one up on her squad mates; she knew every nook and cranny in the depot.

Their squad instructor was Inspector 'Squeaky' Morgan a tall, muscular and sun tanned individual. His uniform consisted of a pair of heavily starched khaki shorts, starched khaki tunic full of brass buttons, leather belt with Sam brown and leather boots and leggings. He was always immaculate and everything that had to shine, shone like a mirror. The only thing that wasn't immaculate was his voice. He wasn't nicknamed 'Squeaky' for nothing. When he gave an order he would bellow at the top of his voice and the last word in a sentence ended in a high-pitched squeak.

Their first morning and subsequent mornings thereafter they paraded at 6 o'clock for physical training in spotless tracksuits and white training shoes. A one mile jog to the training ground and woe betide anyone who lagged behind or was out of line. It was unfortunate for the squad if the horses had gone out before them and had deposited their droppings on the quiet depot roads.

They soon learnt. They headed straight for a pile of droppings, fresh and steaming in the middle of the road. The two jogging rows of girls split into two to avoid the mass of land mines deposited in the road, proud they had kept their training shoes clean but that was not what Squeaky had wanted.

"Squaaaaaad *halt!*" he squeaked at the top of his voice. "Squaaaaad about *turn!* Quick *march.*"

They couldn't bear it. They knew what was coming. Surely he wouldn't do it? He did. He marched them straight into the muck splattered on the road.

"Squaaad *halt!*" came another squeak. "Maaaark *time!*"

Left right, left right, left right. Squish squash, squish squash.

"Lesson number one. When I give an order, you obey. Do you understand?" he bellowed, his rage reflected by his red face.

It's All Just Nuts

"Yes sir!" shouted the girls in unison, keen to get out of the mashed horse excrement beneath their feet.

"Squaaad *halt*! About *turn*! Quick *march*! On the *double*!" Four squeaks in quick succession.

They were pleased to be out of the muck but as they jogged the excrement flew off their shoes and onto their immaculately cleaned tracksuits. Then it was exercises for an hour, more jogging and back to their barracks two hours later. They had to change into mufti, have breakfast and be on parade in their much hated prison garb, brass buttons and all by 9 o'clock.

"Fall in!" Inspector Morgan was there is all his glory in his starched uniform and shining leather.

"Bet you he's got a batman to do his uniform," whispered Beth to Ellen.

The girls lined up on the parade ground in two rows with the larger male squads on their left, each squad inspected from head to toe by their respective squad instructors.

"Squad."

Everyone braced.

"Squad *shun*."

The squad leapt to attention. Not a movement in this position. Eyes straight ahead. They were barely allowed to breathe.

Inspector Morgan marched up to the squad, the metal reinforcements under his boots clicking on the tarmac parade ground. He stopped at each recruit ensuring everything was clean and in its place. He stopped in front of Beth.

"What's this." He poked his instructor's cane under her belt. "You were taught how to put on your belt weren't you?" he bellowed.
"Yes sir," shouted Beth.
"That makes you a bloody fool, doesn't it?"
"Yes sir," replied Beth.
"It makes you *what*?" shouted Squeakie in her ear.
"A bloody fool," replied Beth.
"I can't hear you. Say I'm a bloody fool, *sir!*"
"I'm a bloody fool, *sir!*" shouted Beth.
"Can't hear you," shouted Squeakie again.
"I'm a bloody fool, *sir,*" bellowed Beth at the top of her voice.
"That's better. Get that belt on correctly after the parade," shouted a formal Squeakie.
"Sir!" shouted Beth.

That's what it was. Four months of gruelling routine and discipline pumped into them. 6 o'clock physical training, 9 o'clock parade and inspection, 2 o'clock parade and inspection. Saturday mornings were different. Beth knew all about Saturday morning inspections and the vivid memories of that cane across her rump. Every Saturday the top brass inspected their barrack rooms, which meant Friday nights were spent polishing floors and brasses on windows, cleaning doors, walls and windowpanes. Bed sheets had to be ironed perfectly and laid out according to instruction with blankets and mosquito nets. Everything was measured precisely with a ruler. Everything had to be so perfect the squad slept on the floor of their rooms on the Friday night, ensuring everything was shipshape for the next day.

Diana and William knew what was required of rookies and deep down they wondered if Beth would manage the strict discipline. They wrote religiously every week to keep up her spirit and morale. They soon learnt she took to it like a duck to water. Discipline was fine in Beth's mind if it was meted out fairly. Sometimes it wasn't fair but that was part of the training, teaching the rookies to accept abuse and rudeness from the public. It was par for the course and taken as a learning curve.

Between the hours and hours of lectures on law were the exciting bits. The big day arrived, the one they'd so looked forward to; well *some* had looked forward to. They were to attend a post mortem examination at the local mortuary, but not before the 9 o'clock parade. Squeakie's boots clicked towards the squad on the tarmac and one by one they were inspected, his beady eyes peering at them from under his peaked cap.

"Crap on your badges." Squeakie had seen dry polish on Tanya's epaulette badges. "You're an arse hole," screamed Squeakie in her ear. "What are you?"

"I'm an arse hole, *sir!*" shouted Tanya with a tone of amusement.

Ellen was standing next to her and started to giggle. Squeakie clicked his way to the front of the squad in quick time. "This is not a bloody amusement park. I'm not here for your bloody entertainment. You two," he pointed to Ellen and Tanya with his cane, "twice around the parade ground. Move! On the double!"

They fell out from the squad and started jogging.

"I said on the *d-o-u-b-l-e!*" came his ultra high-pitched squeak, reserved for his high blood pressure moments.

The girls broke into a fast run and had to keep up the momentum in fear of further reprimands. Huffing and puffing they got into the Landrover that was to take them to the mortuary with their squad mates.

"I hope there's not too much blood and guts," said a nervous Sue.

"They say there's not a lot of blood when the body's dead," said Ellen.

"Yuck, we'll soon find out." Sue wasn't happy about the visit.

The Landrover pulled up near a small white building at the back of the hospital.

"Ooo, it looks ominous." Sue wasn't at all confident.

The squad huddled together for support outside the door to the gruesome building. A horrendously foul smell hung in the air. Nothing in the world smells worse than a decomposing body. They put their hands over their faces in a vain attempt to rid their nostrils of the smell.

"Heck. That pong is *dreadful*," said Beth.

A man in a long white plastic apron and white Wellington boots came to the door.

"Right ladies. We've got something special for you. I'm Dr Baker the pathologist and I'll be doing the post mortem. If any of you feel faint please leave the room and return when you're feeling better. Follow me."

The squad walked into a large airy room with three stone examination slabs evenly spaced in the centre of the room. A body lay on the far slab and Dr Baker asked them to gather around it.

"We have here an adult male aged about twenty five years. You will note the body is bloated with maggot holes on the skin surface. There is bruising and damaged skin around the neck."

Ellen was notably pale and held her hands over her nose and mouth. She swayed slightly. "Oh boy," she said and walked out of the room.

Dr Baker continued. "The deceased was found hanging from a tree in the bush. We believe he'd been dead for about a week before he was found hence the decomposition of the body."

The stench was beyond comprehension. Dr Baker slit the chest and abdomen with a scalpel and having disturbed the skin hundreds of white maggots wriggled out of the body, some falling on to the stone slab then struggled to find their way back to their rotting host. He cut through the abdomen wall and exposed the gut; the large bowel and guts were packed into the belly like a mass of discarded entrails from a butchery. Beth wasn't going to weaken but the smell was viler than the sight of the body and it's intestines.

Ellen regained her senses and came back into the room as Dr Baker cut through the sternum and ribs to expose the lungs.

"Told you. Not that much blood is there?" said a composed Ellen.

Dr Baker removed each lung and placed them on an adjoining sink and continued his incision through the neck to expose the damaged trachea.

"There you are ladies. You did very well." He herded the squad still holding their noses towards the door and they gladly left the stench-filled stony room and went into the fresh air and sunshine.

"Phew, that was a real smelly one. If we can handle that we can handle anything," said Tanya.

The squad were driven back to camp and their delicate appetites lingered in a fragile state when they were served liver and bacon and red jelly and custard for lunch.

Half way through their training the squad were given four days off over the Easter weekend. Margaret drove up from South Africa for the long weekend and a holiday with the family and Jill, transferred to Bulawayo would join the family. Beth had befriended a fully-fledged police officer Gail, who had had brief dealings with the squad with first aid lectures and she joined Beth on her car journey to Bulawayo. Beth loved being home and with Diana and William. Diana cooked Beth's favourite meal for supper on her first night home; roast chicken, beautiful crispy roast potatoes, scrumptious gravy and fresh veggies. Margaret and Jill were with them and they caught up with news at the supper table. William popped a bottle of wine happy to have his three girls at home again.

"None for me Dad," said Jill.

"Why aren't you having wine?" asked a curious Beth.

"Because," said Jill.

"Because why?" joked Beth.

"Because I'm not allowed," replied Jill.

"How come though?" Beth's quizzing continued.

"I was drinking in Salisbury. They say I'm an *alcoholic!*" Jilly was an eccentric soul, often aloof.

"You had a rough time in Salisbury darling. I'm just pleased you're in Bulawayo now." Diana sliced into the huge bird on the table.

"What's wrong with Chain-shot and Julian?" Beth changed the subject.

"They're just getting old now Cock." William often called Beth 'Cock' as a term of endearment.

"Can't you do something, give them something to perk them up?"

"If I could I would. Their body functions are winding down. They have a little while to go." William, like Beth, wanted them to go on forever.

The four days ended all too soon and Beth drove Gail and Margaret to Salisbury as Margaret was to spend a few days with old school friends. They left Bulawayo mid afternoon and started the five hour drive to Salisbury. It was dark when they were half an hour outside Salisbury. Beth was driving and she and Margaret noticed taillights and head lights a few hundred yards ahead of them. The headlights disappeared for a moment and the red taillights seemed to spin and veer to the right of the road.

"What the hell," said Beth and started to brake.

"There's been an accident. It's just happened now!" said Margaret.

"Pull over," came a voice from the back seat. Gail had been dozing.

Beth stopped on the side of the road and Margaret and Gail got out and ran towards a smashed car in the road whilst Beth manoeuvred her car enabling the headlights to shine on the crushed metal, barely resembling a car. A massive articulated pantechnicon had stopped fifty yards up the road. Margaret and Gail were looking in the car on the road whilst Beth sat in the car too terrified to get out and help. She sat fixed to her seat. It was a dark night with nothing but bush for miles around, only the lights from Beth's car illuminated the horrific macabre scene. It was a good tarmac road and Beth saw something shining on the road and she shuddered and wondered if it was blood or oil on the road. Twisted metal and glass, which vaguely resembled the remains of a car door, lay gruesomely on the road and formed eerie shadows in the car lights. Don't be such a fool, thought Beth, you'll be a qualified police officer in a few months but she couldn't move.

Gail ran up to her window. "Will you get your ass out of there and come and help. You're supposed to be a policewoman."

"I'm not qualified yet," came a nervous answer.

"*Out!* Come on!" shouted Gail. "The woman in the car's dead. She's mangled."

Margaret had found the driver of the car on the far side of the road, groaning and lying in the dust and grass on the verge. He had a gash to the head and was bleeding profusely.

"Where's Pam? How's Pam?" The young lad wanted to know the condition of his passenger. He couldn't move his legs.

Margaret knew she was dead but had to reassure him to prevent further shock. "She's in the car. She's OK," Margaret lied.

There was a car approaching. Beth's car lights were still on the car in the road and she stood in the beam and waved her hands at the oncoming car. Luckily it saw her and slowed down. "Can you find a phone and report this to the police. We'll need an ambulance chop-chop," said Beth more in control of her emotions.

The driver of the pantechnicon approached them and said he didn't know what happened. There were only two cars involved in the accident.

Beth braced herself and walked over to the car in the road. It was a tiny bubble car with the engine at the rear of the vehicle. The driver's door had been torn off and the car had been smashed from the front, so much so that the front of the car and the bumper were now near the back seat. The woman was mangled like mincemeat in the twisted metal, blood smeared over her deathly white skin. Beth could just make out the remains of her head in the shadows of the cars' headlights. A piece of metal had sliced through the right side of her face and bone and skin dangled from her head and blood flowed like a tap from the pulverized meat. She shivered at the sight and thought a dead body on a mortuary slab was a more pleasing sight, even with the smell.

The police and ambulance arrived half an hour later and after giving them their statements and particulars, Beth was pleased to be on the road again.

"That was revolting," said Beth.

"You'd better get used to it," said Gail. "There'll be lots more and you won't be able to run away."

The next two months were more gruelling than the first. Law lectures were endless, as was the first aid, physical training, self-defence, armed combat, helicopter drill. It went on and on but it was exciting. They were measured up by the police tailor for their full dress ready for their pass out parade and their daily working kit.

Two weeks to pass out. The drill and discipline were relentless. Everything had to be perfect. A mock parade was arranged with the male and female squads in full dress. Squeakie Morgan clicked onto the parade ground and bellowed the parade to attention, ready for the camp commanders inspection. The hatchet faced commander appeared in his black cap plastered with gold braid, commonly referred to in the military as 'scrambled egg.' He spoke to Squeakie and marched towards the parade. He walked slowly down the lines of troops meticulously inspecting each one.

Despite the mass of bodies on the parade there was absolute silence except for Squeakies clicking metal reinforcements under his boots. Click, halt and silence. Click, halt and silence. It was very formal, very quiet. Then a fart, an uncontrollable can't hold it in fart ruptured the official mood. Shoulders started shaking, lips grimaced, the atmosphere strained. The entire squad was giggling en mass, desperately trying to control the pestilent wave that had engulfed them. Such highly infectious giggling in such a controlled environment could have got perilously out of hand; the rookies knew it and hatchet face knew it.

"Sort 'em out," croaked the commander and retired to the back of the parade.

Squeakie marched to the front of the parade. "You're a bunch of bloody haemorrhoids." Squeakie bellowed at the top of his voice, emphasizing his disapproval to the commander. "What are you?" he screamed at them.

"Bloody haemorrhoids, *sir!*" the parade echoed back.

"The whole parade is confined to barracks for three nights commencing tonight." Squeakie was red in the face and clicked his way to the rear of the parade to speak to the commander.

"Inspector Morgan," whispered the commander, "I'm intrigued. Why haemorrhoids?"

"A pain in the arse sir," Squeakie replied quietly. "They're well versed with the term sir."

"New one on me. Good. Now will you get this bloody lot onto foot drill."

Three days before the pass out parade, tensions were high; kit was being ironed to perfection and spit and polish was flying in all directions. The squad were ecstatic at the thought of family and friends watching their pass out parade and marquees, stands, benches and tables were appearing around the parade ground.

The squad were attending a lecture when a messenger came in with a note. Beth was to see the camp commander. She walked across the camp to his office and wondered why he wanted to see her. What had she done wrong? Had she failed dismally and they were kicking her off the course? She knew the commander from her younger days in the camp and William had worked with him for many years. He was a strict disciplinarian and had never spoken to Beth on a personal level during her training. She waited outside his office.

"Come in," came his gruff voice.

Beth marched in nervously and saluted him.

The commander was a tall well-built man with a rugged stern face and Beth had always been afraid of him. He was barely a few feet from her now and his face was bigger and more forbidding than she'd ever realised and he was as round as a two hundred pound sack of maize as he sat in his chair. He cleared this throat.

"I've had a telegram from your mother." The commander handed her the telegram. "The clerk will let you make a short call to your mother. That'll be all."

"Sir," said Beth and saluted the commander. She left his office and her eyes immediately scanned the telegram. 'William involved in accident but OK. Only self attending parade. Di.'

Pass out day arrived. Guests gathered in the marquees and the military band was forming on the side of the parade ground. The squads fell in, in all their regalia and inspected by their respective squad instructors. Old hatchet face was to be the parade commander. The squads marched onto the parade ground and were halted. The Commissioner had arrived and was standing on the dais as the band conductor raised his baton; a single drumbeat signalled the massive band to play a regimental march. The squad instructors bellowed to their respective squads.

"By the left, *quick march!*" The parade ground came alive and the military mass marched in precision timing to the band and on towards the guests and dais.

They were a proud lot, marching with heads held high and arms swinging like well timed pendulums. Beth kept her head straight but her eyes searched the crowd like a radar beam, hoping for a glimpse of Diana but to no avail.

The top recruits in each squad were presented with their awards. Beth was pipped at the post and came a close second in her squad.

The recruits passed out and gathered in the marquees where the young police officers met their families and partook in the ritual of 'cucumber sandwiches and tea and tiny cakes.' Beth searched the crowd for Diana and when she saw her rushed through the maze of bodies and attracted Diana's attention. Beth wanted to hug her forever but conscious of the crowds, gave her a quick kiss on the cheek.

"How's Pa?" She couldn't wait to ask her.

"He's still in hospital and very badly bruised but nothing broken. We were devastated that he couldn't come. He is so proud of you and wanted to be here so much darling."

"What happened anyway?" asked Beth.

"A stupid woman lost control of her car on a left hand bend and drove straight into his car. She went right over on to the wrong side of the road."

Beth was posted to Bulawayo and the following day she and Diana started their journey back home and to a new life.

CHAPTER 10

Beth continued to live with Diana and William in their beautiful home in Bulawayo, which they eventually bought from Barbara. At long last, at the age of 49, Diana had roots and was able to work in a garden she could call her own. The acre of bush garden in front of the house fell away down a steep kopje with multitudes of large and small granite rocks. Diana worked tirelessly with the gardener planning and building quaint granite pathways up and down the kopje, linked with narrow rustic steps into secret and serene areas. Granite stonewalls were built as retaining walls for numerous flowerbeds, scattered between the meandering paths and steps. It was a magical transformation blending huge natural rocks and indigenous trees with the granite walled beds of succulents and cacti.

The garden around the house was even more serene with green well-maintained lawns with more granite walled flowerbeds painstakingly made from the granite rock on the property. Massive jacaranda and flamboyant shade trees dotted the surrounds of the upper garden. The front of the house led out onto a massive slate patio with rustic wooden roofing lovingly made by William and the gardener that provided welcoming shade from the relentless sun that beat down most days of the year and a few yards from that, the bluest of blue swimming pools. A metal framework behind the pool housed Diana's cherished hanging baskets containing a variety of Fuchsias. It was the perfect home, not overlooked by a living soul except birds, squirrels and lizards.

Beth revelled in her police work and took it very seriously and it all blended in perfectly with her parents and a home and garden many would die for. She loved her parents and was always honest with them in every aspect of her life, except her love life. Perhaps she was shy or embarrassed to show her emotions but that's the way she was.
"Ma, I'm going to play squash," Beth told Diana one afternoon when she'd returned from work.
"Who are you playing with?" asked Diana.
"No one in particular. I'll go down to the courts and see who wants a game." Beth patted Suzi and walked out to her car. Suzi loved the car and had to be told to 'wait' if she wasn't going for a ride. She was a highly intelligent pooch, well trained and she understood every word. "Find Mum. Go on. Find!" Suzi turned around, tail wagging and ran to the patio where Diana was standing. She waved as Beth drove off down the long driveway. Diana was always there. She always gave a goodbye wave to William, Beth or friends.
Beth drove five miles to the local sports club and walked upstairs to the spectator's gallery in the squash courts. They were busy. The sounds of the squash balls slamming against the walls, shoes squeaking on the wooden sprung floors and shouts from the players made the atmosphere vibrant and alive. It was a warm evening and Beth wore a pair of white shorts, white T-shirt and

white lightweight canvas shoes. She had a perpetual suntan. A tracksuit top was slung over her shoulders. She had light brown short-cropped hair neatly combed and Diana's blue eyes. The perfect epitome of a tomboy.

A tall well-built man sat next to her, also dressed in white squash kit. She watched the game below wondering if she would be able to play a game with someone.

"Hi." The man next to Beth looked at her.

"Hi," said Beth. Beth wasn't particularly interested in the male species but was game if he wanted a game of squash with her. "Are you playing with anyone?"

"The chap I was teaming up with tonight couldn't make it but I decided to come down. Anyway, I'm Eric Bond."

"Hi. I'm Beth. You're not James. James Bond." Beth was often dry. "Do you want to have a game with me?"

"Yes, sure. I'll check the schedule downstairs," said Eric.

Eric came back and they sat together for a few minutes. "Where do you work?" asked Eric.

"I'm in the police," said Beth.

"I thought so."

"What do you mean?" asked Beth, not really concerned with his questioning.

"You look like a policewoman," joked Eric and gave her a big grin.

"Huh, thanks," replied Beth blandly.

They continued to watch the match in silence for a few minutes.

"And you?" asked Beth.

"I'm the manager of an insurance company."

"Oh." Beth wanted to get on with a game.

They managed to sweat out several games. "Thanks Eric. That was great."

"Can we play again?" asked Eric.

"Yes, but I don't know when." Beth hated being tied down.

"Here's my phone number. I'm here two or three times a week," said Eric.

Beth drove home and was greeted as usual by a receptive Suzi.

"Hi Ma." Beth greeted Diana in the kitchen.

"Have a game?"

"Ya. Was OK." Beth poured herself a cup of tea. "Played with a bloke called Eric. He wants to play again but I'll see."

Eric went right out of her mind. Beth was very busy at work and enjoyed the garden, swimming pool and her parents company after work. Jill was living with a workmate Nora, and they enjoyed Jill's visits although they were usually brief and over a weekend. Jill held down a responsible position in the bank and had had a chronic drinking problem. If she had just a few drinks, she would be as she called it 'as drunk as a skunk,' and she'd find it hard to stop. She was an alcoholic. Diana and William wanted to help her but she chose to go it alone, declined any family involvement or help and relied heavily on Nora. For years Beth called Jill a 'rodent,' as a term of endearment and was meant and accepted in a fun, friendly spirit. Over the years it changed to 'Roe-Roe' and there it stuck.

Weeks passed and Beth needed to vent her energy on another game of squash. She didn't phone Eric but went on the off chance he might be there. If he wasn't there, too bad, she'd find someone else for a game. Diana stood on the patio and waved as usual to Beth, all routine and taken for granted.

Eric was at the squash courts, sitting in the spectator's gallery.

"Hi." Beth sat next to Eric.

"Hello." Eric sounded pleased and smiled at Beth. "Long time no see."

"I've been busy. I only play occasionally anyway. How are you?" asked Beth.

"Oh fine. I've been quite busy as well but I've been coming down most nights hoping to see you." Eric was casual but to the point.

"Well tonight's your lucky night," joked Beth.

They played a good game and Eric tried to nail down Beth.

"Can I take you to dinner sometime?" Eric smiled at Beth. He had a nice friendly smile but she hated his hair. It was thinning on top and he grew it long on one side and combed it over his balding pate and it flew all over the place when they played squash.

"I never know what I'm doing," said Beth. She was quite happy with her own company and routine at home. "I'll try and give you a ring in the coming week."

"Promise?" asked Eric, still smiling.

"I'll try," said Beth, not keen on Eric's persistence.

Beth enjoyed her drive home, heading for a lovely garden and caring parents, not forgetting an intelligent Poodle. She was content with her life. Diana and William were watching TV in the sitting room.

"Hi." Beth put her squash racquet on the couch.

"Hello darling. There's a pot of tea in the kitchen," said Diana.

"Hi Cock," said William.

Beth had a few cups of tea and a bath and they sat down to supper.

"We're having a dinner party on Saturday." Diana and William loved entertaining and were renowned for their excellent parties.

"Oh good. Eric's asked me to dinner sometime, so I'll go on Saturday and leave you guys to enjoy yourselves. Is that all right?"

"Now who's this Eric. Tell us about him. Where does he work?" asked Diana as she served their food at the table.

"Uh, nothing exciting. He manages an insurance company. I can't be bothered really but I'll go out for a change."

Diana and William never saw Beth in a relationship and were curious where this friendship would lead knowing she was a free spirit and quite content to do her own thing. Beth was apprehensive about them meeting Eric. She waited on the patio for him and when she saw the car lights went into the garden to greet him. Diana and William heard the car and went onto the patio. Beth wanted the introduction very informal, like the relationship. Eric and Beth stood in the security light beam in the garden.

"This is Eric," she said casually. "Eric, my folks."

"Hello," said everyone.

"OK, we won't be late. Enjoy your party." Beth hated the thought of being in any form of relationship. In a lot of ways she felt committed to her parents and felt comfortable with that. Eric liked Beth and enjoyed her company and wanted to see her again. She promised to see him again at the squash courts.

Chain-shot and Julian were getting very old and slow and their health was deteriorating in unison with their old age. They had been lovingly looked after but the time for them to move on was getting painfully near. William believed it was overdue and kept putting off the moment. He had terminated the life of many police horses with a single gun shot, painless and quick but there were other more humane methods and William wanted to take that route. There was a lot of bush near the house and on top of a nearby kopje was a small quarry, the remains of a feeble attempt to excavate granite rock. Diana, William and Beth had skimmed over the subject of putting them down, nobody keen to say anything or even believe it would ever happen. William was conscious of the family's feelings and in his true tactful way purchased the necessary equipment and stored it in the tack room. He had to wait for the right time, the moment his inner self could manage the task.

"Where's Pa?" Beth asked Diana one Saturday morning.

"He's gone on the kopje with the horses." Diana couldn't say more and Beth knew what she meant.

Beth felt terrible and knew she had to give William moral support but it would be hard. She walked through the bush and up the small kopje and before reaching the top saw William holding a bottle of liquid in the air with one hand and reassuring Chain-shot with the other. A plastic tube led from the bottle to the neck of the beautiful animal. Beth had a lump in her throat. The pitiful sight of William putting down his precious friend, his friend for so many years on their early morning rides, their team work in dressage and jumping competitions and their mounted escorts in full regalia was too much for Beth and she wanted to turn and run away but she had to give William support. The final few yards to the top of the kopje were dreadful but she pressed on and stood near William. He always appeared a strong man emotionally and even now he controlled his emotions but he had few words to say.

"Everything's going fine." William's words were controlled

"Good," said Beth. Like her father she seldom showed her emotions and kept them bottled up and camouflaged.

Beth glanced towards the quarry and caught a glimpse of Julian's belly. He was lying in the quarry and William had already attended to her poor friend. She didn't want to look further.

"Did you have a problem with Julian?" asked Beth.

"As they lose consciousness they fall in. Quite painless." William kept his words short.

"Do you need any help?" Beth would have helped but wanted desperately to leave.

"No Cock."

"See you back at the house." As Beth left Chain-shot started to sway.

William and Beth knew they needed time to themselves.

Beth's police work was varied and exciting, driving Landrovers, investigating crimes first hand and preparing cases for court. Beth was the senior officer on duty at a small sub-station one particularly busy Sunday night. She and her staff had attended cases of assault, road accidents, reports of theft and all the paper work had to be completed for each case.

They had had an hours reprieve from relentless phone calls from the public late on that Sunday night. She sat at her desk in the charge office, folders and papers chronologically placed to one side as she hammered furiously on an antiquated but serviceable Remington typewriter. It was a hot summers night and insects and hard-backed rain beetles enjoyed easy access to the charge office through open windows, flying in and out with impunity. Beth knew Africa, its weather patterns and the significance of the different types of insects. There was an air of excitement amongst the staff at the little station and although engrossed in her work Beth felt the excitement as well.

The rains were coming. Winter had been dry and not a drop of moisture had fallen on the ground for eight months. Dust was everywhere and the bush grass was crisp and brown. The air was still and humid. A rumble in the distance stirred further excitement. Moments later there was another rumble but louder and nearer and the station lights flickered momentarily. The station was abuzz with chatter. Beth bashed away at the typewriter with two fingers, keen to finish her reports whilst the lights were working. Electrical storms were known for tripping the mains switches in the electricity sub-stations and although the equipment was of high quality the first storms of the season were often ferocious, the dry air pushing cumulonimbus clouds towering into the sky causing severe lightning strikes.

There was another rumble, then two in quick succession. The sound of thunder was a beautiful sound, a sound so complex and with such meaning it could never be reproduced on a musical score by any of the worlds greatest composers. The rumbles were particularly deep and everyone knew it meant the clouds were heavy and full, full of life-giving moisture. A few big drops of rain fell on the corrugated iron roof of the police station, then a few more. Beth could smell those few drops that had fallen on the dry grass and powdery dust, an indescribable smell, a heaven-sent aroma only experienced with the first rains of the season and only a soul conversant with Africa could fully comprehend the magical significance of it.

Beth couldn't contain herself. It was pelting down now and she joined the boisterous staff standing on the veranda watching the thick silver threads bombarding the ground as they passed through the security-light beams. There was so much noise they could hardly hear the charge office phone ringing.

"Someone's reported a snake in his house," said the officer who took the call.

"Oh heavens, that's not our department," said Beth but she knew good public relations were important. "Come on, let's go." She leapt into the Landrover with one staff member and drove down the quiet streets, the wipers struggling to keep up with the pounding rain. They found the house and approached the open front door to find a tall muscular specimen of a male standing nervously near the door.

"Good evening," said Beth. "I believe you have a snake in the house?"

The strapping rugged man smiled sheepishly at Beth. "Uh, um, yes. It's in the dining room. Can I show you?" He was clearly embarrassed having to ask a young female police officer to see to his slippery visitor but was obviously too afraid to attend to it himself.

"Yes please," said Beth politely. She walked in the house and saw a woman and two young children huddled together at the far side of the kitchen beyond the dining room. The poor woman thought Beth. That epitome of masculinity can't sort out a snake in the family home. The tough man remained in the hallway whilst Beth went on the hunt.

"Have you got something I can control it with?" asked Beth.

"I'd rather you killed it," said the man and he went outside to find a weapon and returned with a garden spade.

"Well, if I can but it'll make a mess on your carpet," said Beth.

"Don't worry about that," came the woman's voice from the kitchen. "Please kill it for us." She sounded desperate.

Beth had looked all over the dining room and couldn't find the uninvited guest and thought it must be under a heavy sideboard. She called her fellow police officer standing nervously at the doorway, hoping not to get involved. They pulled the furniture from the wall and Beth saw the snake, at least five feet long. She had mounds of work to do back at the station and wanted to get the ordeal over with. She dragged the spade along the skirting and the snake slithered towards her and with one swift movement jabbed the edge of the spade behind the offending creatures head. It wriggled madly and Beth started a sawing movement behind its head. Blood oozed onto the carpet. She kept up the sawing motion and its head separated from its writhing body. She scooped the head onto the spade, picked up the body by the tail and put the decapitated specimen onto the lawn.

"Sorry about the mess," said Beth.

"That's quite alright, thank you," said the big tough man.

Beth drove back to the police station chuckling to herself. She felt in control of her life and she certainly knew she didn't need a member of the male species in her life. She double de-clutched through the gears on the heavy Landrover, confident.

On Jill's visit to the house the following weekend, Beth related the story to her and to Diana and William. The three sat on the patio, shaded from the midday sun whilst Beth lay on a sun bed next to the pool. She wore a tiny bikini and her long brown arms and legs lay motionless in the scorching sun.

"You had better watch that sun my girl." Diana was always reminding Beth and she always ignored her sound advice.

"What a jerk hey Jill? Why did the guy call the police for such a stupid thing? Did he think we had nothing better to do! Typical male," said Beth.

"They're not capable of doing anything, so what's new," said Jill.

William got up and went inside. He never liked Jill and Beth running down men, which they did quite frequently. Diana always took an open-minded non-committal view.

"I must go," said Jill.

"You've only just got here," said Beth.

"I've got things to do. Bye Mom." Jill stood up and kissed Diana.

"Bye-bye darling. Come again soon." Diana went inside to attend to the lunch.

"Come," whispered Jill to Beth. "I've got something to tell you." Jill had a fun jovial nature at times and it always amused Beth. She liked it and she enjoyed her big sisters' company and was sorry she didn't see more of her.

They walked out to Jill's car. "Nora and I went to Salisbury last weekend to a bank seminar and I met a great bird." Jill was whispering and was being quite humorous. "She's butch and gorgeous."

"You're impossible," laughed Beth. "You and your birds!"

"We've invited them to Bulawayo and they'll phone us when they can come down."

"Who's *they?*" quizzed Beth.

"Her name's Emily and she's in an affair with Jenny. You'd like Jenny." Jill was smiling.

"What do you mean *I'd* like her? You have some strange ideas," said Beth, not really taking the conversation seriously. She was used to Jill's weird comments that came forth occasionally.

"Come on. You're gay," said Jill.

"Bloody hell, what makes you think that?" asked Beth.

It's All Just Nuts

"Of course you are," said Jill as she started the engine.

"Balls," came Beth's reply.

Beth often wondered if Jill was gay. She lived with Nora and they were both pretty tough, rather butch, never any men around. Diana and William never said anything and it was just assumed something might be going on.

Jill reversed slowly. "We'll bring them round here when they come down." Jill was still grinning, a naughty, fun grin.

Jill's nuts thought Beth as she went back to the poolside. She might be a bit anti-male but she wasn't a flipping queer. She shrugged it off and lay down in the scorching sun. It was serene, tranquil, not a cloud in the sky only the sound of the pool pump humming in the distance and the water gurgling from the filter system. Poor old Suzi was lying on the grass next to Beth and cooking under the blazing sun with her woolly black coat but she was Beth's shadow when Diana wasn't nearby.

"Come Suzi! Come and lie in the shade." Beth walked onto the patio and encouraged Suzi to follow her. Suzi was an obedient hound, a lovely animal and she followed Beth. "Good dog," Beth patted her, "that's much cooler you nit."

"Coke my girl," William handed her a glass of coke. Diana and William enjoyed a lunchtime beer at the weekends but Beth seldom touched the stuff and was content with non-alcoholic drinks.

"Thanks." Beth lay on the sun bed again. Diana and William sat on the patio and nattered over a beer, Beth oblivious to their conversation. Diana was cooking a weekend roast and the whiffs of roast beef drifted through the air. Life was good.

The following week Beth received a parcel at work, hand delivered by a messenger from Eric's office. She was too busy to open it and placed it in a filing cabinet in her office. When she finished work she opened the parcel in the car at work.

"Bloody hell. He's mad," Beth said out loud and laughed. It was a blue nylon short nightie. "Just as well I didn't open it in the office."

Beth showed the nightie to Diana. "Look at what that mad character's given me."

"Hmm, he fancies you and obviously wants you to wear it for him!" laughed Diana knowing Eric was wasting his time. She knew as well as Beth that it was *not* her. Tomboy Beth wouldn't be seen dead in a frilly sexy nightie.

"The guy must be mad. I'm not wearing that. You can have it Ma."

A few days passed and Beth hadn't acknowledged the parcel as she was too engrossed in her work and didn't regard the present as significant. She was at her desk recording a statement from a witness when her phone rang.

"Hello," came Eric's voice.

"Oh hi," said Beth. "Thanks for the parcel but I couldn't wear anything like that," she laughed.

"Perhaps I can persuade you." Eric sounded sincere. He actually had quite a deep sexy voice she thought.

"Never. It's not me." Beth didn't pull her punches with him.

"Would you like to go to the Oasis on Saturday?" asked Eric.

Beth had a witness with her and didn't want to talk small talk on the phone. "Yeah, OK. Seven thirty at my folks place?"

"Great." Eric sounded pleased.

"Must fly." Beth put the phone down and got back to her witness.

Beth told Diana about the invitation. "I'm not crazy about going, but it'll be something different."

"If you don't like him, tell him you don't want to see him," said Diana. "He fancies you and he won't let up."

"Ugh, I'll go along with it for now. I can pull out any time." Beth was secretly fascinated by Eric's persistence. She'd never been pursued with such vigour. The odd flutter when she was at senior school but this was different.

She was in the kitchen with Diana, drinking her favourite beverage. "Hmm, curiosity killed the cat," joked Beth as she sipped her tea.

"Yes, and you know the rest don't you!" said Diana.

"What?" said Beth.

"Promiscuity made her fat!"

"Ha-ha," replied Beth dryly. "Not my scene, thank you." It was a thing with Beth. She couldn't show or discuss her feelings of a romantic nature with Diana yet she had a very close relationship with her mother. It bugged Beth sometimes then she'd shrug it off, telling herself she wasn't concerned with that nonsense. Romance and all the complications that went with it was, in her mind, a waste of time and energy.

Eric arrived bang on the nose at 7.30 on Saturday. She thought she'd better let Diana and William get a better look at him and she invited him into the sitting room. He was wearing a jacket and tie and had that dreadful hair plastered over his balding pate. Old Eric was pleasant and polite and had a sincere friendly smile.

"OK, I'll see you later. I won't be late," said Beth. She was wearing a smart pair of black trousers and a colourful shirt. Beth never wore dresses if she could help it and the few she did have were invariably reserved for weddings and funerals.

Eric had reserved a table at the Oasis. It was an upmarket nightclub, with an à la carte menu, candlelit tables and live cabaret.

"You look very nice tonight." Eric sat opposite Beth. He always smiled when he spoke to her and he'd look deeply into her eyes, or at least try to.

"Oh nothing fancy really." The waiter gave them the menus. "Thank you," said Beth.

"Hmm, I'm hungry," she said.

"For what?" Eric leaned over the table and grinned at her.

"Oh piss off."

The band started up and played a series of quiet instrumental melodies. Beth enjoyed quiet romantic music, that 'nightclub shuffle' stuff. A strumming guitar, the gentle thud of the drums, the tapping of cymbals, a whispering piano all sent her hormones on the route march. But one thing was sure; she'd never tell anyone. A woman appeared near the band holding a microphone.

"Hi everyone. Good evening." A whisky-hoarse voice came through the speakers. "We hope you'll enjoy yourselves tonight. If you have any special requests, we'll try and oblige. Thank you. Let's go boys." The female vocalist turned to face the band and the drums and cymbals rolled into life. She started singing a country and western song which wasn't Beth's scene.

"Like to dance?" asked Eric.

"Maybe later. Let's eat first." Beth wasn't crazy about dancing.

They went through a bottle of wine and they were ticking nicely after dinner. Beth was actually responding to Eric's overtures, soft language flowing back and forth across the table. Beth wondered if it was the sensual rhythm of the music and Eric's sexy voice that made her responsive, or perhaps it was the Irish coffees.

"Shall we?" Eric nudged his head towards the dance floor.

Beth got up without answering. The floor was packed and they shuffled close to each other. Eric was tall, about six foot four and Beth put her head on his chest. She was a real romantic when it suited her and as they danced she knew her feelings were more platonic than physical. They seemed to dance forever and the pace got slower.

"Coffee at my place?" suggested Eric.

"OK. Don't get any ideas," said Beth, spoiling his fun.

They walked up the stairs to the first floor and to Eric's flat. It was a large flat on the edge of the city.

"Do you like it?" asked Eric as he walked into the kitchen.

"Yes, it's fine." Beth sat on the couch. "Been here long?"

"About two years. It's convenient for work and the sports club up the road," said Eric.

They drank their coffee. Eric smiled at Beth and held her chin. "You're special." He kissed her passionately and she responded. They kissed for a long time. "Grrrrr," Eric growled and in a second picked her up and carried her to the bedroom and lay her on the double bed. She was still feeling nicely pickled from the wine and Irish coffees.

"Huh, you'd never have got me here voluntarily," she joked.

He lay next to her resting on his elbows and looked into her eyes. "Shall I take you back to the sitting room?" His voice was deep and soft.

Beth pulled his head towards her and kissed him.

Beth had been transferred to the traffic branch. She had attended many accidents since that fateful night when she was still training and nothing was too gory or difficult for her now.

The traffic branch buildings were in a perfect setting amongst leafy trees, lawns and flowerbeds. The offices were immaculate and the floors, as William would aptly say, 'shone like shit on a barn door.' Beth would have to attend accidents in police patrol cars and to drive those she had to pass the advanced driving course. She passed a rigorous three-week course, driving to a particular system, learning to handle a vehicle at speed in awkward situations and controlling a vehicle on a skid pad. The patrol cars were the flagship of the force and they had to be immaculate.

Beth had her own office and the large window looked out onto the lawns. She was highly disciplined and had the respect of senior and junior staff. Because of the efficient way she handled cases she was given all fatal and serious accidents to investigate either for inquests or prosecution.

It was late morning. Beth lay on an inflatable mattress in the pool. The sun was beating down from a blue sky.

"Life's hard, isn't it," joked Diana as she stood on the patio watching Beth.

"Yup, it's hell." Beth scooped water onto her grilled legs and belly to cool off.

"We'll have lunch in an hour. Mind that sun."

"Thanks Ma." Beth knew Diana spoilt her. She didn't have much on her mind. She was on night shift and had to leave for work at 2.30. She was the senior traffic officer on night shift that week ready to attend any accidents. She heard the phone ring.

"It's Eric," said Diana.

"Blast. Please tell him I'm not here," said Beth.

"I'm not making your excuses for you," said Diana firmly.

"I've managed to fob him off for a few months, but he won't take a hint."

"If you don't want to see him any more, *tell* him and don't string him along." Diana always gave wise advice but Beth seldom listened.

"Yeah I know. He's a pain." Beth intended being brief with Eric but to her surprise he told her he was being transferred to Cape Town. He wanted to see Beth before he left but she knew it would be a futile exercise.

Beth put on her uniform, a smart skirt, starched shirt, tie, lanyard and epaulettes with badges of rank and perfectly ironed white cotton traffic sleeves. Diana did all her ironing and she knew she was thoroughly spoilt but she was very appreciative of all Diana's work. They stood on the patio saying their goodbyes.

"Suzi's very quiet these days. I wonder what's wrong with her." Suzi stood next to Diana and Beth patted her. "That's a very subdued wag my girl. She's not smiling today."

"It's probably the heat. Come on, you'll be late. Bye-bye darling." Diana was always the same, always sincere and always there. She was an honest, just woman who always kept her word. She was slim and wiry with a permanent suntan; her fair hair always shortly cropped with a perm and Beth loved her.

"Bye Ma. Hope I'm not late. I'll phone you." Beth walked to her car and Diana waved from the patio as she always did.

Beth had a mound of work to attend to; current ongoing investigations and she had three new cases in her 'in' tray. She needed a brief statement from a witness and hadn't the time to see him personally. She recorded it over the phone then typed it out. She'd get him to sign it when she had time. She couldn't make appointments when she was on night shift and on call for accidents.

What could she clear she thought. She sat at her desk and paged through various dockets. "Ah, I need a post mortem report from Dr Rankin." Beth spoke out loud to herself. "Then that's ready for court." She called the junior officer who accompanied her on patrols.

"I want to go to the hospital and see Dr Rankin. Are you ready?" Beth asked him.

"Yes ma'am," replied her assistant.

Beth passed the traffic administration office on her way outside.

"Hi June. How're you? Busy?" Beth liked June. She was part of the furniture and knew the ropes at traffic department. She was a tall, well-built woman much older than Beth and a keen sportswoman.

"Oh well, you know," laughed June, "bit of this and that." She always had a naughty look in her eye. "When are you coming to play softball? We're really looking for new players."

"Yes I'd like to. I'll chat to you when I come back," said Beth.

Beth got in the patrol car with her assistant. She automatically went through the system. Ignition on; check indicators, gauges on dashboard, horn, mirrors, seat belts, adjust seat and start engine. The vehicle was clean. Good she thought. She didn't want a bollocking from the boss.

Her assistant turned on the VHF radio. "Control room, this is traffic one, over."

"Go ahead traffic one," the voice came through clearly on the radio.

"We're on patrol," said the assistant.

"Roger, traffic one."

Beth drove straight to the hospital and parked at the back. Dr Rankin's office was right next to the mortuary. What a place to have an office thought Beth; the dead centre of town, she chuckled to herself. She popped her head in his office. There was no one there. She walked along the corridor to a set of swinging doors and put her head through the door. She saw Dr Rankin's back.

"Knock, knock," said Beth.

He turned around. "Hello Miss Maynard, come in. I've been meaning to phone you." Dr Rankin was conducting a post mortem. "You're here for the report on that pedestrian in the hit and run?" He carried on working.

Beth had come in at the wrong time; he was sawing off the top of a skull with a hacksaw.

"Yes, that's right." Beth had seen many post mortems but hated the sawing of bone, be it sternum or skull. It left her cold.

"He must have been paralytic. His reading was 120/100. Well pickled, wouldn't you say?" said Dr Rankin. "We also found a few pieces of paint flakes in his hair. I've got everything in my office."

"That's great. The driver gave himself up the next day as you know and intends pleading guilty but it's good to have forensic backup in case we need it. The point of impact was well into the road and the deceased's sobriety, or otherwise, shouldn't have a bearing on the driver's negligence but that's up to the magistrate." Beth was trying to weigh up the pros and cons of the case.

"I'll just be a minute." Dr Rankin pushed his fingers into the eye sockets of the body on the slab and the brain popped out of the hole in the top of the skull. "Bob's your uncle," he said and put the slimy white organ on a table. He went over to the basin and turned on the tap lever with his elbow and put his bloody rubber gloves under the running tap, removed them, untied his white plastic apron and hung it near the door.

"I'm dying for a cuppa, come and join me," he wasn't taking no for an answer.

"Thanks Dr Rankin. I can't stay long."

Beth drove back to the traffic department, pleased with her documents from the pathologist. She wanted to talk to June about softball and as she was about to park the patrol car the VHF radio burst into life.

"Traffic one, control room," came the voice.

Beth's assistant grabbed the microphone. "Control room, traffic one. Go ahead."

"Roger, we've had a report of a code 5 on Luke's Road near Park Avenue. Can you attend, over."

"Control room, traffic one. Wilco," said Beth's assistant.

"Damn it," said Beth as they drove back onto the main road. A code 5 was a serious accident and they were to advise if an ambulance was required. She flicked two switches on the dashboard. The piercing sound of the siren came to life and the blue light on the roof of the car spun into action. Beth manoeuvred the patrol car at speed through the city centre, cautiously through red robots and controlled intersections. They reached the accident in less than five minutes.

"Not much sign of an accident," Beth told her assistant as they got out of the patrol car. There was a five-ton truck parked partially off the main road, it's offside wheels on the road. A small crowd had gathered at the back of the truck and Beth went to see what all the fuss was about. A racing bicycle lay under the back of the truck and a young male lay on the road also at the back of the truck in a pool of blood. He had a massive compressed wound to the top of his head, parts of the skull exposed with upright splinters protruding around the blood filled hole.

There was no need for Beth to render any first aid or check the carotid artery.

"Did anyone witness the accident?" asked Beth.

A man in the crowd came forward. "Yes. I saw the whole thing." His voice was shaking.

"Could you hold on a moment." Beth went to the patrol car and pulled the mike out of the window on its spiral cord. "Control room, traffic one." There was no response. "Control room, traffic one," she called again.

"Go ahead traffic one."

"Roger, this is a code 11 on Luke's Road. We have one deceased cyclist and request a body box over," said Beth.

"Roger traffic one. Do you need assistance, over," asked control room.

"Uh, roger, negative. We'll manage. Seems pretty straight forward, over," was Beth's reply.

"Roger traffic one. We'll get a body box to you, over."

"Roger, thanks. Out." Beth got her clipboard from the car and went back to the witness.

The only witness was driving his car about a hundred yards behind the deceased who was cycling at speed on his racing bicycle with his head right down, as they normally do during races or training. The truck was parked partially on the road ahead of the cyclist and he saw the cyclist ride straight into the back of the truck. The front of the bicycle went under the overhang of the truck and the full force of the impact was the deceased's head on the tailgate of the truck. The road was on a slight decline and the witness believed the deceased was travelling at about 40mph at the time of impact.

It was nearly 6 o'clock when Beth got back to traffic department. Everyone had gone home and Beth and her assistant were left in charge for the rest of the night. She sat down at her desk to sort out her paperwork and thought about June. She had wanted to talk to her about softball. It was common knowledge that the gay community dominated the softball crowd and Beth knew June was gay and she lived with her partner in the suburbs. Beth wasn't fazed or particularly interested. Curious perhaps but not interested. Plenty more opportunities to talk to June she thought. She had a pile of work to get through.

Beth finished her week of night shift and looked forward to the weekend off. She wanted to bath Suzi on Saturday morning but Beth noted she was very subdued again.

"Look Ma, her belly is swollen. I wonder what it is."

"Yes it is," said Diana. "I hadn't noticed it before. I think you and Dad had better take her to the vet."

Beth went to find William pottering in his workshop. "Pa, come and look at Suzi. Her belly is swollen." William knew a lot about animal husbandry.

"Come my girl," William called Suzi. She had her head down and gave a feeble wag. He felt the area around the belly. "It is distended but soft. I don't know what it is. We'd better have her checked out."

Suzi loved the car but this time they had to assist her onto the back seat and William and Beth drove her to the vet.

The news wasn't good and they drove home with little conversation.

"What's the diagnosis?" Diana was in her 'workshop', the kitchen.

"He says it's lung oedema." William had to explain. "Bigger dogs can get it when they get older apparently. It's fluid in the lungs and there's very little they can do. He suggests we monitor her and if it gets any worse we'll have to put her down."

"Oh heavens, no William." Diana was devastated.

Suzi was lying in the dining room and Diana knelt down next to her. "Hey my girl, what's wrong?" She held her head in her hands. She was such a clever well-behaved dog. She'd be told to 'ask' for her food or a biscuit and she knew to sit down quietly and bark.

Suppertimes were special. She knew she'd be asked to lie down, so she did so in anticipation of the order but lay with her head up. Diana taught her to take it a step further and she'd sometimes tell Suzi to lie down *real* and she knew she would have to lie flat with her head on the ground. She was a wonderful watchdog when Diana was on her own. She never barked for the sake of barking. If she barked, Diana knew someone was there and the tone of the bark told her if it was friend or stranger. And now her dear friend had a sad look in her brown eyes and Diana felt helpless.

"Where's Beth?" asked Diana.

"Not sure. Probably sunbathing. She hasn't said much but she's obviously upset," said William.

Beth resembled a lizard, basking again in the midday sun. She tried not to think about Suzi. She was part of the family and the thought of her not being there was unbearable. She heard a car door slam and minutes later Jill appeared on the patio.

"Hi Roe-Roe." Beth was always glad to see her big sister. Jill was secretive in a lot of ways and kept her relationship with Nora to herself and never asked the family to their home.

"Hi. I've got some news for you," Jill spoke softly and had her mischievous look on her face. "I'll tell you later."

Jill sat on the patio and talked to her parents and always had their undivided attention. Diana especially would stay and talk with Jill whilst William would drift off to do his chores. Beth heard her tell Diana she'd been promoted at work and would be in charge of her department.

Beth spoke from her sunspot near the pool. "Will you be transferred away from Bulawayo?"

"No. I wouldn't move anyway," said Jill.

"That's good," replied Beth.

Diana said cheerio to Jill and left Beth to see Jill to her car. She knew they liked to chat together and was happy to give them their space.

Jill was like a big kid when she was alone with Beth; big sister coming down to little sister's level. Beth thought she was fun and amusing. "Listen, Emily and Jenny are coming to Bulawayo in a few weeks. They're spending the weekend with us." Jill spoke in her low secretive tone.

"So?" said Beth. "Why the big secret? Why don't you tell Ma and Pa?"

"I told you they're gay and I really like Emily. I want you to meet them," said Jill, still with a fun air about her.

"Hey Roe-Roe, you're nuts," joked Beth. "Yeah alright but you'd better phone first in case we're not here."

Beth walked back to the house, bemused. She didn't like to keep things from Diana and William but Jill had spoken to her in confidence and she had to respect that. But it was sensitive stuff for Beth anyway. Relationships were hard for Beth to talk about and now gay relationships were mind boggling for her, a very grey area. She put the conversation out of her mind. She preferred swimming, sunbathing, pottering in the garden with her parents and cleaning her new car.

The following evening the three of them were in the sitting room. Suzi had been lying on the grass under a tree for most of the day and had turned her nose up at her supper. They were worried about her and it was late evening when they realised they hadn't seen her for a while.

"Where's Suzi," said Beth as she walked towards the open French doors to the patio. "Bloody hell. Pa, come and look at Suzi." She was lying on the patio and Beth could see a white liquid on the ground around her head. "I don't want to look."

Diana and William looked at Suzi. William got down on his knees and examined her. "Poor girl. She's gone," said William quietly. He would know, he was a boffin with animals.

"Oh William, no," said Diana. What's that white stuff? It's in her mouth as well."

"It's from her lungs, it's the oedema. The poor girl; she suffocated," said William. "I'm quite sure she didn't suffer; if she'd been distressed or uncomfortable she would have walked around the patio discharging the liquid. There's no sign of that. She probably lay down feeling unwell and just died."

They buried Suzi in the garden the next day.

They vowed they'd never have another dog. Beth felt the same but at the same time knew that Suzi had been great company for Diana who was on her own all day at the house. Beth kept an eye in the newspaper for a new dog. It would have to be a pup they could train themselves but what breed? Standard poodles, like Suzi, were like hens teeth. Her woolly coat had been a nightmare to maintain; grass would stick to her coat and Beth often had badly blistered fingers from the scissors when she gave her a hairdo. No, thought Beth, we need a smallish smooth haired pooch but small dogs were yappers and they had no time for yapping dogs. She thought she was looking for the impossible.

Ten days after Suzi died, Beth scanned the Pets for Sale column in the newspaper. Bassett Hound puppies; six weeks old. Diana was a great fan of the cartoon, Fred Bassett. That's it, thought Beth, perfect. She left the office before her official lunch break and headed for the address in the paper.

There were four puppies to choose from, two bitches and two dogs. Definitely a bitch thought Beth. They were all gorgeous but Beth took a particular liking to a little bitch sleeping under a hedge in the garden. The others were very playful but when Beth lifted the little one from under the hedge, she wobbled on her legs and looked sleepily at Beth. She was tri-coloured and by far had better colourings than her brothers and sister. Maybe she's the dunce of the litter thought Beth.

"I'll take this one please," Beth told the owner and put the wobbly pup in a box on the back seat of her car. She drove home and the hound made far too much noise for her size. Beth began to wonder if she'd done the right thing. They didn't like noisy dogs. Well, we'll just train her she thought, but Diana would probably reject her outright anyway. Beth knew she should have asked Diana first but if she had, Diana would have put her foot down; both feet actually. Diana was a Taurus and could be quite stubborn when she wanted to be.

The moment of truth had arrived. Beth drove up the long driveway and parked on the lawn under a shady jacaranda tree. She left the yapping creature in the car and ran to the front of the house. Diana had heard her and came outside.

"Hi Ma. I've got something to show you. Come," said Beth and ran back to the car.

Diana heard the din. "No thank you. We don't want another dog. You can take it straight back."

Beth knew Diana too well. When she spoke like that, she meant business. But Beth was an Aquarian and also stubborn. She knew she had to *try* and convince Diana in the nicest possible way.

"Just wait! You haven't even seen it," said Beth desperately.

"I don't *want* to see it. I don't want another dog Beth." Diana was being very firm and it made Beth nervous.

"Wait Ma," Beth persisted and took the yelping bitch out of the box and put her on the lawn. The body of the noisy creature was all of six inches long, in lovely shades and shapes of black, brown and white. It's springy brown tail, the size of a little finger, fluttered precariously in the air with a white tip at the end, the famous Basset periscope.

"You can take it back from where it came Beth." Diana was adamant.

The small beast wobbled on its feet and sniffed the grass. Great folds of skin hung on its little body, its ears so long and floppy they dragged on the grass. Beth picked her up and held her with ease in one hand.

"Look!" laughed Beth and she lifted the folds of skin on its body. It had mounds of it. It was just a ball of fur, skin and ears. Beth held the puppy directly at Diana. Its little forehead was a mass of wrinkles with outsized ears hanging on either side if its face. It stared at Diana for a moment and nudged its nose towards her and gave a short yelp, almost a bark.

"Look at the size of her feet!" exclaimed Diana. "They're *huge*! Everything's out of proportion; too much skin, feet too big, ears too big!"

Whoopee, thought Beth. She's hooked!

"I hope she is a she?" asked Diana.

"Yes. She was the quietest of all the pups but her colourings were much better than the others. Isn't she beautiful?"

"Oh Beth darling, I don't know. We said we wouldn't get another dog after Suzi."

"Yes I know Ma, but she'll be company for you and hopefully a good watch dog. Can we keep her?" Beth knew she'd say yes.

"Let's ask your father when he comes home." Diana didn't want to give in.

"She's not housetrained, so we'd better put her on the back veranda for now. She won't get through the wrought iron gate."

"I'll take her. You'd better get back to work," and Diana took the tiny mite from Beth. "Look, she fits in my hand!"

"Bye Ma, we'll have to think of a name. I thought Sally might be good, but you can decide." Beth drove off, late for work.

Sally was soon housetrained. William stopped her nightly yapping and she would settle down in a tiny cardboard box in the kitchen at bedtime. Various names had been thrown around, even Freda, in partnership with the cartoon strip Fred. Diana and William had a friend called Freda so that would've been an unwise move. Sally somehow seemed to flow; it was a warm and friendly name.

Three weeks later Beth was cleaning her car on the lawn in her customary shorts and that day she wore a particularly moth eaten, torn and miss-shaped T-shirt. She knew that the older and thinner it was and the more holes it had, the cooler it would be on a hot day. They were her favourite shirts and she had many of them. It was a tragic day when heart-rending decisions had to be made to re-classify them as a holey cleaning cloth.

She heard Jill's car on the long driveway and stop under the jacaranda tree. There was a big succulent elephant bush between her and the car park and Beth heard three or four car doors slamming. She knew Jill had brought her friends.

Beth had her car bonnet open and was cleaning the engine with a cloth, with equal amounts of grease on the cloth and her hands. She was unaware of a greasy mark on her chin. Sally was helping her, frolicking in and out of her legs and lying under the car in the shade when the scorching sun burnt her young folds of skin.

"Hi Roe-Roe." Beth wasn't shy using Jill's nickname and she knew Jill wouldn't mind.

"Hello," said Jill slowly and distinctly with a big grin on her face.

"Hi Beth." Came another greeting, this time from Nora.

Beth noticed their two Salisbury friends were with them and decided to greet everyone en mass. "Hi everyone." Beth carried on fiddling with her cloth under the bonnet.

Diana heard the car and was standing on the patio ready to greet her visitors. She was very proud of her home and a great hostess. "Hello darling," she said to Jill. "Hello Nora."

They sat on the patio and Beth heard William had joined them. Beth had little time for natter and small talk but thought she'd better be polite and join them. She was also curious to meet this butch Emily that Jill fancied. It was a new ballgame for Beth.

"Come puppy," Beth called Sally from under the car and the little horror bounced out and into Beth's hands. "Let's go and meet these funny people."

Beth joined them on the patio, clutching Sally for support.

Jill did the necessary introductions. "Beth this is Emily and Jenny," indicating who was who. "Emily, Jenny. Beth."

'Hello's' flew in all directions. William had served drinks of various sizes and colours to everyone.

"Coke my girl?" he asked Beth.

"Not just now. Maybe later."

Jill had met Sally a couple of times but the others saw her for the first time and they fell in love with her. Beth put her on the ground and she scampered around to everyone, sniffing and wagging and greeting each person in turn.

"She hasn't grown into her skin and ears yet but she's getting there," joked Diana. "We're very attached to her and she's got a lovely nature."

Beth virtually lived in sunglasses and she was particularly grateful she could insulate her eyes as she scrutinized Jill's friends behind the safety of the darkened lenses.

Jill was chattier than usual and Nora chipped in now and again. Beth found Emily and Jenny normal and wouldn't have suspected them as being gay. She always assumed a gay woman would look very butch or masculine. She wondered what Jill saw in Emily and thought there was no accounting for taste.

It was getting on towards lunchtime and Diana was relieved when Jill said they had to go. She was a whiz in the kitchen but she hadn't mastered the miracle of feeding the five thousand. She had a small chicken in the oven for the three of them and it would have been difficult to stretch it seven ways at such short notice.

Beth worked night shift again the following week. She was in her office typing a case for court when the phone rang. It was a Saturday afternoon and she'd had a surprisingly quiet few hours. It was Nora. She never phoned Beth.

"Sorry to worry you Beth. Jill has been drinking and she's absolutely paralytic. I can't talk any sense into her and I was wondering if you could help." Nora sounded calm but desperate. Big Nora was a Samaritan and could handle most situations.

"Yes, sure Nora. I don't know how I can help but I'll pop around. It seems crazy but the folks and I don't know where you live. Jill's very secretive, as you know. Can I have your address?"

Beth didn't waste time getting there. They lived in a house in a bushy area on the outskirts of the city with a big garden that was fenced and gated. Nora was at the gate to meet her and Beth saw Jill lying on the grass near a bushy, rocky part of the garden.

Beth knelt down next to her. There was a strong smell of beer. "Jill, what the hell have you been up to?" There was no response from Jill and Beth shook her shoulder. "Hey Roe-Roe," joked Beth.

Jill grunted and opened her eyes. She gave a slurred 'hello.'

"Jill, where are you hiding the beer?" asked Nora. Nora didn't allow any liquor in the house. She knew it was like poison to Jill and if Jill brought any home she knew she would have to hide it.

Jill sat up. "I haven't got any bloody booze." Her speech was slurred and she was aggressive. "Just bugger off Nora." Jill tried to stand up and Beth and Nora helped her.

"That's it. Get your blood circulating and get that rubbish out of your system," said Beth. They hung onto Jill as she staggered across the lawn.

"Let's take her to the barn," said Nora.

"The barn?" Beth sounded surprised.

"She lives in that little stone cottage." Nora indicated a building about fifty yards from the main house.

"Piss off Nora." Jill slurred her words again.

"That's very nice. I'm just trying to help."

They put Jill on the bed in the barn. "I'll go and make some coffee," Nora went outside.

"Fuck off," said Jill. She sat on the edge of the bed and swayed slightly and looked at Beth. "I like Emily. Want her to live here." She had a dazed look in her eyes.

"Well what's this boozing got to do with it?" asked a confused Beth.

Jill sat on the bed with her shoulders forward and head down and she shook her head. She started to cry. Her thin scraggly hair surrounded her small face. Beth felt sorry for her.

"Come on you big nit. Where's my fun Roe-Roe? The boozing won't help, you know you can't take the stuff," said Beth and Nora came in the barn with a tray of mugs.

"I'll be with you in a minute," said Beth. She went out to the patrol car parked at the gate. "Everything quiet?" she asked her assistance.

"Yes ma'am. No reports."

"I won't be much longer," Beth told him and she went over to the bushes where Jill had been lying. She lifted some of the branches lying close to the ground and saw three bottles of beer in the leaves. "The little rat," said Beth and left them on a table in the hall of the main house and returned to Jill's barn.

She stood in the room and gulped down her coffee. "I must go. Can I come and visit now I know where you live?" she asked.

"Of course you can," said Nora.

"OK Roe-Roe. I'll see you. Just stay off the you know what." Beth rubbed Jill's shoulder.

Nora accompanied Beth to the gate. "I found three bottles of beer under that bush," she told Nora. "I put them in the house."

"She can be fine for months on end then she goes off the rails," said Nora. "Thanks for coming."

Beth told Diana and William about the incident. They weren't surprised as Jill had been on and off the bottle for a number of years. Beth however didn't tell them about Jill's apparent attraction to Emily. Jill could tell them if she wanted to and anyway, it was Beth's proverbial grey area.

Diana and William were happily settled in Bulawayo, made many friends and attended and held private dinner parties. They joined a private club where members cooked exotic Eastern dishes with the venues at members' homes. Only those who had connections with the East and Far East were eligible to join. Not only did Diana's birthplace make her a perfect candidate, she was a culinary expert in producing delicious Chinese food. Even William excelled in the kitchen and he was always looking for new exciting recipes.

Barbara's son and his new wife lived nearby, as did Barbara and John and the families frequently got together enjoying bar-b-q's in their expansive beautiful gardens. They would enjoy month upon month of fine weather and blue skies. Life was being very kind to Diana and Barbara after the upheaval and turmoil of their youth. Diana seldom spoke to Beth about her childhood but she knew Diana had lived a difficult life from the little she told her. She spoke of her mother on occasions and told Beth how she had died, that she was buried in the local cemetery but she never went to visit the grave. It was never discussed but a visit would have upset Diana and she felt she had to go forward with her life.

Beth had spoken to June about softball and joined June's club, which meant rigorous training a few times a week after work and matches at the weekends. Beth was friendly with June at work and she also coached Beth's team and consequently they saw much of each other.

It was a new ball game for Beth as she was thrown from her private secluded lifestyle into a rowdy but very friendly crowd of softball players. There was an openly gay bunch of women amongst the players, June one of the oldest and most well known. Beth was intrigued and fascinated by it all and as Beth soon learnt, some of the women were fascinated by Beth and scratched their heads in wonder at this new kid on the block with thick shortly cropped hair and her trousers or shorts a permanent feature.

June knew Beth well enough to be straight with her. When Beth had the time she'd join the team in the clubhouse for an after training drink and chat.

"Hi Beth." June sat next to her on an empty bar stool. She always had a naughty twinkle in her eyes and a dry sense of humour. "There's a lot of interest in you amongst the gang," she said in her serious yet fun way. "Is she or isn't she, you know!" June gave a deep secretive giggle.

"Bloody hell June!" laughed Beth. "Perhaps I should say I'm honoured but actually I'm intrigued. I don't know who's who in the zoo myself."

"What do you mean?" June sipped her beer.

"Who's the butch one, who's the fem. Gets confusing!" said Beth.

June put her head back and gave a deep belly laugh. "Half of them don't know themselves." She carried on laughing. "Oh my goodness, I like it! Actually they think you're gorgeously butch."

"Oh, come on June!" June had Beth laughing now.

"I'm telling you," said June in her jovial tone.

"Well it's just a figment of their imagination my darling," laughed Beth.

Beth felt a hand on her shoulder. She turned around. It was Olive. Olive was a coach and umpire and although getting a bit long in the tooth, she still played occasionally. To Beth's inexperienced eye Olive was butch, very butch. She was fairly short and dumpy but looked like a rugby scrumhalf.

"Hi Ju. Hi Beth." Olive was a fun individual and had a voice like a foghorn. "Ju, we're a couple of players short for the inter provincials in Salisbury in a fortnight. We thought about Beth coming along as reserve. What do you think?"

Beth butted in. "*Inter provincials*! I haven't played long enough for those."

"Beth's doing well. She runs like a rabbit in the outfield." June gave a belly laugh again. "Can you make it? Smiler should give you a few days leave." Smiler was the boss of traffic department, a rather wretched individual and was known inaptly by his nickname.

"You must be pretty desperate but yes, why not." Beth wasn't over the moon but didn't want to let the side down.

Jill visited the family that Saturday. It was her first visit since her affair with her beer bottles a few months earlier.

"Hello darling." Diana greeted her with a kiss. "Where have you been?"

"Hi Mom. I suppose Beth told you about the fun and games." Jill sat on the patio and Sally started chewing her handbag next to her chair. "Gee, she's growing. Hello puppy." Jill put the squirming hound on her lap.

"Yes you silly girl. I thought you were over all that," said Diana.

"No harm in a fling now and again," replied Jill. "I'm big enough and ugly enough to look after myself. Where's Beth?"

"She's gone down to the garage. She'll be back in a minute." As Diana spoke they heard Beth's car come up the driveway.

"Dad's gone to town to do some chores."

"Hi Roe-Roe. A real rodent eh!" joked Beth.

"Pull the other one," snapped Jill.

Beth went into the kitchen to make tea and left them to talk together. She went out the back door, around to her car and drove it onto the lawn. She wanted to clean it before her trip to Salisbury the following weekend. Beth kicked off her leather sandals and hosed down the car. It was a hot sunny day again, the fine weather taken for granted. She wet the chamois and started drying the windows and paintwork. Sally heard her and bounded over to the car and tried to attack and maul the hosepipe lying on the lawn.

"Hey stop it! Don't you put those needle teeth through the hosepipe madam." Beth picked her up and patted her gently on the rump. "No," she said sternly.

It's All Just Nuts

Beth heard Jill saying her good byes to Diana. Her half hour visit was over thought Beth and Jill came over to her at the car.

"Ma said you're going to Salisbury on Friday. Is there any room?" asked Jill. "I've been wanting to go up for weeks. Emily's been phoning me and apparently she and Jenny are having major problems and their affair is virtually over."

"June from the club was going to come with me but she's taking her own car now. She's got all the kit to take and my car's not big enough," said Beth. "So yes, looks like there's room."

"I want to come. Old Nora will want to tag along," said Jill. "Where are you staying?"

"I thought about Molly, but I don't know yet."

"Emily and Jenny have a huge flat apparently. We can all stay together with them. I'll phone them and double check. So is it on? Friday afternoon after work?" Jill sounded her usual self again, full of nonsense.

"I think Nora must come so she can keep you in check." Beth was serious.

Beth, Jill and Nora arrived at Emily and Jenny's flat at 9 o'clock on Friday night. Jill had arranged everything and they were happy to have their three visitors for the weekend.

They went to the door of the flat and they heard voices inside.

"Oh great," said Beth. "There's a row going on."

The shouting increased and they heard what sounded like a chair or piece of furniture being thrown.

"What shall we do?" asked Beth.

"The longer we wait, the worse it'll get." Nora didn't hesitate and rang the doorbell.

A few more shouts were exchanged then there was silence. The key turned in the door and Emily opened the door.

"Hello everyone." She was notably agitated. "Sorry about that. Come in."

"We hope our stay will be alright," said Nora. "Are you sure it's convenient?"

"We're always having these arguments. It's nothing new," said Emily.

"What do you mean *we*," said Jenny with a face like thunder. "*You* start them."

"*You're* the trouble maker Jenny," said Emily, not letting up.

"Hey guys. Can we have a cup of tea? We're parched." Beth tried to defuse the argument.

Jenny went into the kitchen and Beth followed. "Can I help at all?" asked Beth.

"I'll just put the kettle on. We haven't cooked anything. All we've been doing is arguing," said Jenny.

"Don't worry. My Mom made us some egg and bacon sandwiches and we had them on the road."

Jenny lowered her voice. "Emily is such a trouble maker. I've had enough and I'm moving out next week." Jenny had a nice smile when she wasn't growling like a wildcat, thought Beth.

"Where will you stay?" asked Beth.

"I'm going to stay with my brother in Salisbury then I'm moving to Holland in a few months."

"Holland? That should be exciting." Beth didn't know what to say.

Jenny gave Beth a friendly big smile. "Yes, they're more liberal there." She made a big pot of tea and they went into the sitting room.

Jill and Nora were sitting with Emily. She had been crying and she blew her nose with the tissue in her hands.

"Stop your acting Emily." Jenny became a feline again.

Emily ignored her. "Can I pour you some tea?" Emily asked her guests.

"Have you got anything planned for the weekend?" Jill asked their hosts.

"Not really," said Emily.

"We can watch some softball if you like," suggested Jill.

"Yes, check out those butch birds." Jenny gave a hearty laugh and smiled again at Beth.

Jill grinned at Beth. "There you are. You'll have some spectators."

"Ha ha," said Beth. She was feeling very embarrassed.

Beth went to the sports club on her own in the morning, the others promising to follow later. June and Olive were there before her and they'd started warming up with the team. Beth joined in, the team throwing and catching balls with their leather mitts, loosening up their arm muscles.

"Come on girls," shouted Olive, once the game was underway. "We're gonna win today! Let's flatten 'em!" It was the usual softball rhetoric to build up team spirit and confidence. Their team was winning and they had three loaded bases. Pam went up to bat; she knew she had to bring the girls on the bases home. "Bring 'em home, bring 'em home!" The crowd was ecstatic, the team shouting and egging on Pam. The pitch threw the ball like a missile at Pam and she ignored it. "Good eye, good eye!" bellowed the catch behind Pam, the ball slamming into her leather mitt. She threw it back to the pitch. The ball came again at Pam at the perfect angle and not at lightning speed. This is the one she thought and braced herself. She flexed her muscles and threw all her weight at it, the bat and ball cracking together in perfect unison. The ball flew beyond the outfielders. Eardrums vibrated as the crowd bellowed and screamed at the loaded bases to come home. Third and second bases stamped their feet victoriously on home plate. The ball had been retrieved in the outfield and was flying through the air back to the catch. She threw off her wire mesh face protector for a better view of the ball. She was braced, one foot on home plate, the crowd screaming. First base was on the home run yards away from the plate. The ball was hurtling towards the catch. It was touch and go. First base slid onto home plate in a cloud of dust and somersaulted towards the wire mesh protective screen, covered in dust. The umpire was happy. She was home safely.

Amongst the turmoil and excitement, Beth hadn't noticed Jill and her friends walking towards her on the stands. The other spectators had to move along on the stand to allow them to sit down. Jenny sat next to Beth.

"Hello," said Jenny and gave Beth her friendly smile. "How are you?" she asked.

"Fine thanks. Hi everyone." Beth greeted the others.

"Aren't you playing?" asked Jenny.

"I'm their reserve for the tournament." Beth was feeling a little uncomfortable with Jenny sitting a bit too close to her.

"I want to congratulate the girls. See you in a minute." Beth was pleased to be away and ran down the stands to the team bunker.

"Is she gay?" Jenny asked Jill openly.

"She says she isn't but she is," laughed Jill assumingly.

"Hmm, she's nice," said Jenny.

"Leave her alone," said Emily. "You've ruined my life, don't ruin another one."

"Don't talk rubbish. You're a lunatic," replied Jenny bitterly.

"Who's for an ice cream?" Nora defused a potential confrontation.

Everyone gathered in the clubhouse after the match. Beth, Jill and Nora had cool drinks, Jill for obvious reasons and Beth and Nora seldom touched alcohol. Emily had a glass of wine whilst Jenny had at least three beers in the short time they were there.

"Jenny's knocking them back," Beth told Jill. "Hope she's not driving."

"Oh take off your police hat for once," barked Jill. "She fancies you."

"For Pete's sake Jill. It's not my scene." Beth was fed up with Jill's persistence.

They got back to Bulawayo late on Sunday night. Jill had kept talking about Emily and they had decided Emily would ask for a transfer to Bulawayo and would live with

Jill and Nora. Jill had known Emily for many years when she lived in Salisbury and she was excited at the prospect.

Beth thought Jenny was friendly but she also saw the other side of Jenny with her arguments and frayed temper with Emily. Beth shrugged off the latter and concentrated on her friendly smile that, in Beth's mind, exuded a sense of genuineness. Beth dealt with a lot of people from all walks of life and she thought she had a firm grip on assessing personalities. She didn't realise how wrong she was.

Weeks passed by and Jenny phoned Beth at work on a regular basis. She had moved in with her brother and Emily was preparing to move to Bulawayo. Jenny talked about life in England, Europe and especially Holland. She said she had lived in England and enjoyed the open approach to the gay community there and she'd be moving to Holland in the coming weeks. She wanted Beth to visit her there.

For a long time Beth had wanted to travel to Europe for a holiday. She had taken very little leave over the years, happy with her lot at work and her home environment. She spoke to Diana about the prospects of a holiday and Diana was keen she should go.

Jenny continued to keep in touch with Beth and wrote to her soon after arriving in Amsterdam, giving Beth her new home and work addresses and her phone numbers. Beth hated the thought of imposing on anyone but having supplied her addresses, Beth was sure her offer was genuine. She took the bull by the horns and applied for leave albeit with some reservations.

Beth felt torn between her friendships and her commitment to her home and Diana and William. They gave her the very best and she was reluctant, through her own choice, and Beth did have the choice being the free spirit she was, to become involved in relationships. The loyalty and sincerity between the three of them formed the strongest bond imaginable. Beth didn't tell Diana and William she was going on holiday to meet Jenny, torn miserably between her total honesty with them and not wanting them to know of the friendship. She hated herself for it but knew it was only a temporary situation.

Beth arrived at Schipol airport in Amsterdam late in the afternoon. Jenny was in a new job and it was agreed Beth would find her own way to Jenny's house. Beth hired a car at Schipol and she was completely bemused that all she had to do was show her international driving licence to the car hire company in return for the keys to the car. She couldn't speak a word of Dutch and couldn't read the road signs and had never driven on the right of the road yet they handed her the keys. Oh well she thought, if they're happy, she was happy.

She drove round and round Amsterdam for hours, stopping at garages asking for directions to Jenny's suburb. Night had fallen and she was highly amused with the sights of Amsterdam. She had her own sight seeing tour and found herself, as she learnt later, in the red light district. Ladies of the night sat with suspender-clad legs straddling chairs strategically placed in sleazy, dimly lit windows. Beth laughed, enjoying the new experience, a far cry from sleepy Bulawayo in the bowels of Africa.

It was nearly 9 o'clock when she drove into Jenny's road, a secluded cul-de-sac. She found the house and rang the bell. She saw a figure behind the amber frosted glass in the door and the door opened.

"Hello Jenny." Beth smiled at Jenny. All of a sudden she felt she was imposing on Jenny. She had felt fine until that door opened.

"Hello," came Jenny's response, reciprocating her smile. There was something different but Beth couldn't put her finger on it.

"Are you sure it's alright if I visit you?" Beth wanted to get things right.

"Yes, fine. Where's your suitcase?" asked Jenny.

"Um, in the car. I'll get it." Beth wished she wasn't going into that house and a gut feeling was telling her to drive away.

Jenny had curry and rice for supper and they talked about the trip, Jenny's new job and life in Holland. Beth knew she didn't have to be psychic to realise Jenny had changed, a change she wasn't comfortable with.

Jenny had left for work by the time Beth got up the next day. After the fiasco the night before with her excursion through the red light district, she took a bus into the city. Beth spent the afternoon walking the streets of Amsterdam, fascinated by the architecture, the cobblestoned street and the shops and canals. It was an inspiring experience and she took it in like a kid at a funfair for the first time.

She found her way back to the house with difficulty, having taken the wrong tram on one occasion. It was 7 o'clock when she unlocked the door with the spare key from Jenny.

"Hello," said Beth. The lights were on but there was no response. She heard pans clattering in the kitchen. "Hello," Beth said again.

Jenny looked at her blankly. "Hello." Her usual smile had gone. "What do you want to eat?"

"I'm not fussy. Whatever's going. Can I help?" Beth knew she'd be treading on eggshells for the evening.

Jenny didn't answer and made a deliberate din with a frying pan and saucepan.

"I found my way into Amsterdam, thanks to your directions." Beth hoped Jenny's attitude would change.

Jenny had a face like thunder and ignored Beth.

"I'll be in the sitting room if you need any help." Beth sat on the edge of a chair, paging aimlessly through a magazine wondering what was wrong with Jenny.

Jenny didn't speak to Beth and slammed her bedroom door after supper. Beth wondered if she had come home too late and decided to be at the house when Jenny got home the next evening.

She was making a cup of tea when Jenny came home after 10 o'clock. The front door slammed.

Jenny stood at the kitchen door. "Couldn't you have made supper?"

"If you can tell me what to cook, I'll do it with pleasure."

Jenny sauntered over to Beth with a bitter expression. "You're bloody useless."

Beth couldn't believe the change in Jenny. She was more than capable of looking after herself but knew if she said anything it would only fuel Jenny's anger. She stood against the kitchen cupboard and Jenny pushed her.

"You're fucking useless." Jenny didn't let up.

"What's wrong with you?" Beth had to respond.

"Can't you do anything?" Jenny shouted at Beth, grabbed her collar with both hands and knocked her head repeatedly against the kitchen cupboard.

"Stop it Jenny. Control yourself." It was probably the worst thing Beth could have said.

Jenny lashed out and tried to punch Beth but she broke the attack with her arms and Jenny again pushed Beth's head against the cupboard. Beth wouldn't lower herself by returning the blows. She was astounded at Jenny's actions convinced she had a mental problem.

Beth knew she had to get out of the house. She went straight up to her bedroom, packed her suitcase in a matter of minutes and walked to the front door.

"I'm sorry this has happened," said Beth as she opened the door.

Jenny screamed at her to get out of the house and she felt very relieved to close the door behind her.

"My dog," Beth said to herself. She was shaking from anger and astonishment and told herself not to be so stupid. She had no idea where she was going and drove aimlessly, grateful to be out of that house. She shivered at the reality of the bad feelings she had when she first arrived at Jenny's house. Beth remembered seeing a board advertising rooms to let near a canal but there were dozens of canals and they all looked the same to her.

Beth inadvertently found herself on a main road and had no idea where she was or where the road was leading. She slowed right down looking for an exit and saw a blue flashing light in her rear view mirror. The car drew level with her. It was a police car and they were signalling her to pull over. She got out of the car and greeted the police officer, wondering why she had been stopped.

He started speaking in Dutch and Beth had to tell him she was English.

"Have you been drinking?" asked the policeman.

"Heavens no!" said Beth.

"We noticed you were driving very slowly," and as he spoke he opened a small container. "We need to breathalyse you." The policeman was polite and asked Beth to blow hard into a little tube. She was amused at the prospect of being on the wrong side of the law for a change but the test was well within the legal limit. Beth told them where she was from and they talked about life in Africa.

She drove randomly for an hour then saw an advert on a gate 'rooms to let'. It wasn't the one she had seen before, but it was a start. It was after 11 o'clock when she rang the doorbell. She heard footsteps on a hollow wooden floor and an elderly man opened the door.

"Good evening," said Beth. "Do you have a room?"

"Yes. Daily rates 15 Guilder a night. Bed only." His English was quite good and he knew the pertinent details.

"Can I have a look please?"

The old man took Beth up a very steep narrow staircase to the second floor. There were three doors on the landing and he opened one with a bunch of keys. Beth looked inside. It was a very small room with a bed and table and a basin.

"Can I stay here tonight?" asked Beth.

"Ja, ja," said the man. "You must pay now."

Jenny's change of character was beyond Beth's comprehension. She had never encountered such an extraordinary individual and her investigative mind wanted to confirm that her mood swings were quite abnormal. She knew she wouldn't get very far but she was sure she'd find similar symptoms in print.

Beth returned her hire car assured that trams and buses were more convenient in the city. She was surprised yet relieved that many Dutch folk had an adequate understanding of English and she was able to muddle through quite well. She found her way to a public library in Amsterdam and asked the librarian for directions to the medical section. Beth's plastic anorak made a dreadful rustling noise in the quiet library so she removed it, rolled it up quietly and stuffed it under her arm. As she had anticipated, a lot of the medical books were in English and she went through the different headings on the shelves. Gynaecology, pathology, psychiatry. "Aha," said Beth. She'd found what she was looking for and went through the titles. Psychiatry, Part I and II. That should be enough she thought. She didn't want to study the subject; she just wanted confirmation that Jenny probably had a mental problem.

Beth took the books to a table, sat on her noisy anorak and paged through her selection of books. There was a mound of stuff. She looked at the index; Manic Depressive Disorders. Perhaps she was a schizophrenic. The word popped out of the page. Beth skimmed her eyes over the page, picking up words. 'Believe they are a particular figure' and 'they hear voices in their head telling them to carry out various acts.' She read on. 'They are disorganised and can become agitated, swearing and shouting for no apparent reason.' That makes sense she thought but thought a schizo. had a split personality. She searched for psychopath. 'A persistent disorder of mind resulting in abnormally aggressive or seriously irresponsible conduct.'

It looked like a complex illness but as Beth read on, aggression seemed one of the prime symptoms. *Irresponsible and aggressive behaviour* popped up on the pages. 'Lack of conscience, lack of empathy,' it went on.

She's probably a psychopath thought Beth as she returned the books to the shelves. She thought of Alfred Hitchcock's film 'Psycho' and grinned to herself. She really made the right decision not to hang around and thought about being chopped into little pieces and put in a refuse bag in the canal at the bottom of her garden.

Beth knew her holiday money wouldn't last a month and she found part time work in a motel a few miles from her room. The long hours worked for two weeks provided sufficient funds to tour around Holland.

Beth had been thinking about Jenny and foolishly, wondered how she was. She was reluctant to leave their friendship in limbo and merely wanted to part company on a friendly note although she knew it was more an acquaintance than a friendship. She plucked up the courage to phone Jenny.

"Hello Jenny. It's Beth. I just wanted to find out how you are," said Beth, wondering what sort of response she'd get.

"I'm fine." Jenny's tone sounded fairly normal.

"I'll be touring the country in a few days and then going home and I was wondering if we could meet up tomorrow just to say hi and bye," said Beth.

There was no response from Jenny.

"Hello?" Beth thought she'd put the phone down.

"I'm here. I'm thinking," said Jenny. "I'll meet you at the Galaxy Club at about 6 o'clock tomorrow."

Good thought Beth. "Can you give me directions?"

"It's in downtown Amsterdam. It's very well known and anyone will give you directions."

Beth took a tram into the centre of Amsterdam and arrived at the Galaxy well before the appointed time. As Jenny had rightly said, everyone knew the club and she found it with ease. It was fairly crowded but she sat at an empty table near the door. Beth only realised after a while that it looked like a gay club. Her suspicions were confirmed when a tough looking butch woman sat down at Beth's table. Lord, there's a rugby forward for you thought Beth. She wasn't shy. She started speaking in Dutch and Beth put her hands in the air and said "I'm English."

"Oh that's fine. I speak a little English," said the butch woman. "How are you darling? Can I get you a drink?"

"No thanks. I'm waiting for someone," and as she spoke she saw Jenny come in the door.

Jenny and the mysterious butch woman greeted each other like long lost friends. Jenny ignored Beth and sat at the bar with the rugby forward. Beth was a bit taken aback. Now what, she thought. The whole situation was absurd and she wondered how the hell she got herself into this position in the first place. She knew she should have left it but she wanted to part company on friendly terms, but she wondered if that would be possible. Beth continued to sit on her own, wondering if Jenny would come over but she didn't.

Beth took the bull by the horn and sat next to Jenny at the bar. "Hello," said Beth in a more formal than friendly way.

The tough woman looked at Jenny. "Do you know each other?" she asked.

Jenny laughed almost scornfully, with a tone of resentment. "Sort of," she said.

Beth wanted to leave, hating every moment but said, "Does anyone want a drink?" She knew her ordeal was transient and she could handle the dastardly situation.

Beth ordered two pints for the two women and a half pint for herself. She was ignored for the two hours they were there whilst Jenny talked to various individuals at the club, joking and laughing and showing off.

Jenny eventually approached Beth. "Let's go," she said and walked towards the door and Beth followed like a fool. Jenny got in her car and opened the passenger door from the inside. Beth got in. Jenny didn't speak.

Beth tried to ease the tension but felt inclined not to be too friendly. "Have a good day?" she asked.

Jenny didn't answer. Beth knew she was stupid to have got in her car. Where were they going she thought. Beth's rented room was near a huge concrete tower on the outskirts of Amsterdam and it was an excellent landmark for helping her find her bearings.

Jenny drove onto a motorway and they were heading away from the tower. Beth decided to speak up.

"I live in the other direction, near that concrete tower," said Beth blandly, not wanting to rock the boat. "Where are we going?"

Jenny braked sharply, pulled roughly on the handbrake and got out of the car barely before it had stopped. She slammed the driver's door and seconds later opened Beth's door.

"Get out." Jenny shouted violently at Beth.

"Jenny, please," said Beth, "be reasonable." There was a fair amount of traffic on the motorway and Jenny was oblivious to it.

"Get out," she bellowed again, talking between her teeth emphasizing her anger. She pulled Beth out of the car with both hands on her collar and started punching and kicking her. Beth was more than capable of defending herself, in fact she could have had Jenny flat on the road in seconds but she didn't retaliate, believing such a move below her dignity and they'd only look like a couple of wildcats in the street. During Jenny's continual punching and kicking Beth lost her balance and fell onto the road. She continued kicking her on the ground when two men appeared and pulled Jenny away. She wrestled with them until they let her go and she marched to her car and drove away.

One of the strange men spoke in Dutch then reverted to English. "Are you alright?"

"Yes, thank you," said Beth and they helped her up.

"Can we take you somewhere?" he asked her.

It was like sweet music to her ears. She had no idea where she was and she was a pedestrian on a motorway, not one of the best situations to be in. She pointed out the concrete tower to them, gave them the name of the road where she was staying and got in the back of their car.

"What happened?" asked one of them.

"Oh I don't know. The woman's a lunatic," said Beth flummoxed at her ordeal and the hideous situation she had found herself in.

The next day Beth bought a bunch of flowers from a street vendor and found Jenny's office address, situated in a pretty leafy cul-de-sac. She couldn't bring herself to deliver them and stood twenty yards from the entrance. She stopped a young boy on the pavement. He was happy to deliver the flowers, with a note tucked in the stems: "Good luck. If you ever need any help you can contact me in Bulawayo. Love Beth."

CHAPTER 11

The years slipped by all too quickly, yet life was much the same for Beth and her parents. To Diana's delight she had stayed in her own home for nearly twenty years now and she and William made their garden into the perfect haven. There was a special aura about the garden and the house and visitor upon visitor would comment on the peace and exceptional charismatic charm the property exuded.

The shady jacaranda trees for all their beauty were a gardener's nightmare. They were thirsty trees and their massive root structures with minute tentacles would wind their way into anything in search of water. The flowerbeds were prime targets but Diana overcame the problem with a multitude of metal drums painted dark green and placed strategically in the natural rocky outcrops around the garden. They were filled with an array of plants suited to particular areas of the garden. Huge delicious monsters with their massive slatted leaves gave a tropical air to the slate pool surrounds, whilst other areas of the garden would lend themselves to miniature bougainvilleas of rusts, pinks and crimsons. Natural granite rocks protruded from an area in the extensive lawns not far from the house where they had paved the area with rustic brick and that was home to several drums of roses.

It was late September and summer for the southern hemisphere was around the corner. The last rain that fell on the garden was in February – seven months ago. Diana and Beth were cutting the second bloom of roses of the season. It was late afternoon and it was humid, the air still and close. There had been month upon month of blue skies and now clouds had appeared below that expansive blue dome that had enveloped them for all those months. Everyone longed for this time of year. Clouds would build up and would tease and tantalize then melt and disappear in the sweltering dry heat. This time it was different and Diana and Beth knew it. This time the clouds were building and swirling into bulbous mountains expanding and growing into cumulus nimbus clouds. They were pink, reflecting the setting sun and turned a deeper pink in minutes in response to the sun sinking lower into the western sky.

"We're in for a storm tonight. The garden's crying out for rain," said Diana picking up the cut roses she'd placed neatly on the lawn. "Come on Sally Basset, supper time darling. Are you going to eat tonight?"

Sally was eight years old now and according to the veterinary surgeon it was a good age for a pedigree basset, but her life wouldn't be extended much longer. Sally had cancer of the gums and had managed well with the disease until a week ago when it seemed to be draining her strength.

Diana prepared Sally's supper but she wasn't lying and waiting in the kitchen as she usually did. She was curled up in the dining room not interested in what used to be the best time of day for her.

"Come on my baby," said Beth. "*Do you want it?*" Sally always knew what that meant. It meant a four-letter word beginning with 'F' but tonight she didn't want any part of it. She just wasn't hungry.

"She won't be with us for much longer Beth." Diana knew, and she had to be realistic. Sally Basset had learnt all Suzi's tricks and would lie down promptly when told to, even lie down *real* by lying flat with her head on the ground. She had been a wonderful watchdog, barking with different tones for different situations and visitors, becoming an extended eye for Diana when she was alone and a great friend and comfort to the family.

Sally Bass. didn't eat for three consecutive days. The cancerous growths on her gums had spread and the vet. assured the family her time to depart this life had arrived. Once again poor William was delegated the responsibility of dealing with another family pet. He took her to the veterinary surgeon for her injection to take her to a higher level and the girl was placed in the garden with her friend Suzi.

It was the mid 1980's and Rhodesia had become Zimbabwe and the country was well into her independence although with some movement in the population as people came and went. Zimbabwe was a beautiful country with beautiful people and Diana, William and Beth were very much a part of it and ready to go forward with everyone for the betterment of the new nation.

Barbara's John had a health problem requiring him to live at sea level and they very reluctantly moved to South Africa and to be together, her son and his family followed some time later. Their departure left a void in their lives but to the delight of Diana and William, Jill had become a greater part of their lives with lunch invites between both households a regular occurrence.

Jill was still living with Nora and Emily. They would holiday together and were great outdoor types enjoying camping trips to game parks and natural resorts. They were the inseparable three-some. Beth always believed two's company and three was a crowd. Jill confided in Beth and told her that her friendship with her two female friends was purely platonic and even if that was the case, one wondered how the three managed to maintain a relationship. Nora as a Samaritan was a level-headed sort of individual, Jill's mentor and would easily tolerate Jill's mood swings and tempers. Jill on the other hand was the household 'handyman' turning her hand to car and machinery repairs, plumbing and general repairs and maintenance of the house and gadgets. She was comical and fun when she wasn't having her mood swings, somehow creating a yin-yang balance with her relationship with Nora. Emily was enjoying a peaceful existence and flowed between the two. The three strangely seemed to compliment each other.

Jill and Nora started a safari company nearly twenty years earlier but it wasn't successful and they suffered financially. Finances were always a grey area in their household and caused some dissension between them and Beth and her parents. Jill worked very hard as an accountant yet always told Beth, Diana and William that she never had any money. She was an illusive sort of character and they often wondered how truthful she was. Jill was very complex and difficult at times.

Jill hadn't been away on a trip with Beth or her parents since her school days and agreed to join them for a long weekend trip to the second largest lake in the country to watch a national regatta. William hadn't sailed for years but enjoyed helping out at various sailing events.

It was a four-hour drive through the dusty lowveld to the massive expansive lake set in granite hills. Jill and Beth shared a comfortable stone and thatched huts with en suite facilities and Diana and William shared one next door. It was a well laid out camping site on the shores of the lake with the round huts of various shapes and sizes scattered around the camp and facilities for caravaners and campers with tents. The regatta was well attended and the camp was alive with activity.

The next morning, as Diana met up with old friends and William became involved with the sailing, Jill and Beth had the whole day together. They enjoyed each others company and when they were on their own Jill would take charge yet act like a kid with her little sister, seven years her junior.

"Come, let's walk to the wall." said fun loving Jill.

They started off on their hike after 9 o'clock and, able to see one end of the wall jutting out behind a hill in the distance, mistakenly thought it would take two or three hours to get there and back. They set off wearing their usual gear of shorts, T-shirts and sandals avoiding hats in the belief they were reserved for sissies. They walked through the bush taking a direct route towards the wall. Their feet were brown with dust in no time as they fought their way through the tinder dry elephant grass, hard barked bushes and young trees that had seeded themselves freely in the bush. They couldn't walk in a straight line because of the terrain of granite rocks and outcrops and found themselves climbing a big hill unable to follow the shoreline that was impassable with massive rocks jutting into the lake at the water's edge.

Jill was leading the way and was ten yards ahead when Beth walked off on her own hoping to find an easier route. Jill heard a blood-curdling scream from Beth.

"What's wrong?" shouted Jill as she heard her little sister calling her.

"*Jiiiillll! Shit, shit, shit.*" Beth was shrieking and in a frenzied state. She ran towards Jill with her hands all over the place, fluffing her short-cropped hair and frantically brushing her head, chest and back with her hands.

Jill guessed what had happened and didn't waste time getting over to Beth, running wildly over rocks and through sharp twigged bushes with no regard for her own safety.

Beth had walked into a massive spiders web strongly woven between the trees. There were three or four spiders in the web, yellow and black bodied creatures three to four inches in diameter. She had had her head down watching the rocks and uneven ground and had walked right into the web.

"Bloody hell Jill. Just check my back. Can you see anything?" Beth was panting frantically still brushing her head and trunk wildly and involuntarily with her hands.

"Shame Beth," said Jill seriously. "I can see the bastards from here".

"Where, where!" shrieked Beth thinking Jill had seen spiders on her.

"Over there, between the trees," said Jill. "Turn around, let me see." she told Beth. "No there's nothing on you!"

Jill was terrified of snakes and Beth terrified of spiders and they respected each others phobias.

"Phew, that was lousy. You lead the way and I'll follow," said Beth still brushing herself sporadically with her hands. "Thanks Roe-Roe!"

"That's alright," replied Jill sincerely.

They battled their way through the bush and arrived at the wall nearly two hours later. It was massive, far bigger than they had ever imagined. A two lane tarred road ran across the entire width of the wall. The lake was miles from any urban towns and the road was little used and there were no cars or any signs of life.

It was nearly midday and ironically they were thirsty despite the huge wall holding back such an expanse of water. It never occurred to them to take a bottle of water when they left the camp. They walked to the centre of the wall and looked down at the mighty flow of water gushing out of two open floodgates. They could hardly hear each other talking as copious volumes of water thundered into the gorge below swirling and bubbling below like a witches cauldron.

Jill indicated to Beth they should walk to the far side of the wall and down to the river. Colossal granite rocks loomed forebodingly out of the water on both sides of the gorge. Jill walked down the steep narrow cement steps built against the imposing wall with Beth following and they were now below the towering wall near the turbulent pounding water. The sound was deafening and the two sisters grinned at each other. Jill beckoned Beth again and they walked along the expansive rocks following the flow of the river through the gorge. The rock faces were steep in places and they removed their sandals so they could grip the rock like monkeys. They left the thundering sound behind them and sat on the rocks to watch the river, still swirling violently between the enormous rock formations. It was desolate yet beautiful, the gorge imposing and unyielding and fraudulently engulfing them. Hawks circled high above the gorge, squawking, as though signalling the sight of death below them. A troop of baboons sat lifelessly under trees, growing precariously from cracks in the craggy rocks on the other side of the river, shading them from the relentless African sun.

Jill nudged Beth. "Watch," she said. She stood up and cupped her hands around her mouth and gave out several barking sounds that echoed through the gorge.

The baboons came to life and leapt into their shade trees, staring at Jill and Beth.

Jill made barking sounds again and the tree branches shook vigorously, the baboons excited and agitated. They returned Jill's bark. Beth joined in the chorus and the baboons ran around the rocks anxious and barking ferociously, showing no embarrassment exposing their large pink posteriors. A huge male came right down to the edge of the river and jumped up and down, exposing his long yellow canines as he barked and snarled at Jill and Beth, his black beady eyes peering over his huge square snout.

"Come, let's go," said Beth. "I hope that bugger can't swim!"

Jill and Beth continued along the river mesmerised by the swirling water. The vicious sun was burning hot and they were thirsty. The water looked clean but they knew the bilharzia parasite was prevalent in the waters and they couldn't drink it.

They were tired and hot, now looking for a safe place to cross the river to avoid a long walk back through the gorge in the sweltering heat. Black rocks were exposed in the river but nothing that resembled stepping-stones that would provide a safe crossing. They kept on walking hypnotized by the water, still looking for a place to cross. They heard a gushing sound and saw rapids ahead; the turbulent white water swirling and rushing violently down a descent in the river course.

"Now we're buggered," said Beth. "We could go on and on looking for somewhere to cross. Those rapids could go on for ever." Her mouth and throat were dry, her lips cracked.

"Let's go back a bit," said Jill, "where the river was about five yards across."

They retraced their steps for about fifty yards. "Shall we try here?" asked Jill.

"The rocks look OK on the other side, as long as we can get out safely," said Beth, weighing the pros and cons. "What do you think?"

"The water looks calm although it is flowing," said Jill. "I don't think we'll find a better spot. I'll go first."

"I thought we'd go together, then we can die together," joked Beth.

"No, I'll go first and test the water." Jill enjoyed being big sister. "Here goes." Jill got down on her haunches on the rock sloping into the river and pushed herself into the water. Jill was a strong swimmer and proud owner of a bronze lifesaving medal but neither she nor Beth realised the strength of the current. As soon as she entered the water she was swept downstream, unable to make any headway in crossing the river. The river had taken control of her as she bobbed uncontrollably towards the rapids.

"Shit Jill," shouted Beth as she kept up with Jill on the craggy rocks. "Can you try and swim towards the edge?"

The current was getting stronger and Jill found it difficult to manoeuvre herself towards Beth. The massive rocks sloped steeply into the water and Jill wouldn't have managed to get out on her own and Beth had to keep up with her.

"Swim towards the edge!" shouted Beth again.

Jill made a concerted effort and she came a bit nearer the edge.

"A bit more." Beth tried to hold out her hand to Jill but she was still too far away yet the rapids were in view now, thundering over jagged rocks. "Come on Jill!"

Jill seemed to have more control now and swam crawl one arm over the other, and came nearer the edge. Beth held out her hand again and this time Jill grabbed it. The start of the rapids was barely twenty yards away. Beth had to brace herself and bend her knees to keep hold of Jill but the river fought back wanting to engulf and swallow her in its deceiving grip. Beth pulled and Jill came to the edge of the river but the rocks into the water were too steep and Jill couldn't get out. They grasped each other's arms in a fireman's grip and Jill managed to put her feet on the submerged rock and pull herself out of the water.

They both sat on the rock, panting.

"That was close eh!" laughed Jill, still out of breath. "Phew!" she said.

"Yeah, we'd better abandon that idea. That current's stronger than it looks," said Beth gazing at the water.

"There's a strong undercurrent and it wanted to take me under. I was damn lucky."

They had no alternative but to walk back to the wall the way they came. It was mid afternoon already and it would take at least an hour to return to the wall and two hours through the bush back to camp. Their mouths and throats were bone dry and their lips were cracking, not only from lack of water now but from the sun beating down on them, uncompromising and merciless. They walked in silence conserving energy and concentrating on the rough terrain underfoot.

Beth broke the silence. "Our pink bummed friends have disappeared," she said as they walked past the spot where they had teased the baboons.

"Hmm." Jill's throat was too dry to talk.

They went around a bend in the river and saw the wall looming large ahead, beckoning them. It was in sight now, their goal in reach.

"Hey. I'm so thirsty, I could die," said Beth and stopped walking. "I'd *love* a sip of that water." Beth looked at the volumes of water flowing quickly next to them. The surface rippled and shone like silver in the sunshine. It looked deliciously tempting.

"*Don't*," said Jill emphatically. "It's filthy *and* full of bilharzia."

They carried on walking in silence. The wall was about fifteen minutes away now but it looked like a hundred miles away. They were both strong and fit but they were dragging their feet now, delirious and weary, delirious from dehydration, their bodies crying out for life giving moisture.

"I can't take it," said Beth as she approached the water's edge. She crouched down at the river and cupped her hands and threw the precious liquid over the back of her head. It ran down the side of her face and past her mouth. The temptation was so great but she knew she had to resist and she wiped her mouth on her shoulder. She did it again, this time she threw the water on the back of her neck and it trickled down her back. It must have looked cool and refreshing because Jill joined her and they both splashed water on themselves. Beth finished off with a handful of water over her face. It was cool on her burning skin and she made a rude sound with her lips and wiped her mouth with her shirt.

"I'd give my right arm for a drink," said Jill as she led Beth up the steep gorge to the top of the wall. They didn't know where the road would lead so they walk through the bush as they did on their outward journey. "I'll go ahead and you follow."

"That's an excellent idea. Keep your eyes peeled for spider webs please," said Beth seriously.

The sun was getting lower in the sky but they were sure they'd be back before sunset. The dust from dry elephant grass caught the back of their throats, only increasing their thirst. Their arms and legs and faces were ruddy brown from the sun that had bore down on them all day, with no compassion or regard for their well-being.

"Look," said Jill, pointing ahead of them. "There's the camp."

"Thank heavens," said Beth as they looked down from the hill onto the clearing below with trees, huts, tents and caravans neatly organised. As they neared the camp the sun was just slipping behind the hills in the distance, leaving a massive shadow over the lake and landscape.

"Hi Ma," said Beth as they walked in to Diana's hut.

Diana looked notably worried. "Where in heavens name have you been?"

Beth and Jill walked passed her. They had seen a jug of water and two glasses in the room and they emptied it without a word.

"We told you we were going to the wall," said Beth.

"You went out this morning. We didn't think you'd be away for so long," said Diana.

They looked at her, brown and dusty, their bare arms and legs exposing scuff marks, scratches and dried blood from the hard dry twigs and thorn bushes.

Diana softened and saw herself and her two sisters standing in front of her and recalled the fun and excitement they experienced climbing trees in the bush. "I've just put a big stew on the fire and it should be ready in a couple of hours." She knew her smoky flavoured bush stew would go down well. "Who wants a cup of tea?"

The VHF radio crackled under the dashboard of the patrol car. "Traffic one, control room."

Beth grabbed the mike jammed between the leather bucket seats. "Control room, traffic one. Go."

"Traffic one, report of a code 12 on Barrington Road South, at the canal. Can you attend, over?"

"Control room traffic one. Roger. Proceeding. Out." Beth still had the mike in her hand as she flicked the switches on the dashboard, bringing the siren and blue flashing light to life. She wriggled higher in her seat and held the steering wheel at the ten to two position with her leather and string driving gloves, ready to drive at speed across the city to the reported road accident.

"Just our luck," she said to her assistant. They had had a quiet evening with two minor accidents to attend to. It was now 10.30 and they were due to go off duty in half and hour and be on call for any serious accidents until 7 o'clock the next morning.

Beth was a good driver and knew how to handle a car at speed, double-declutching, turning the wheel without arms crossing over, reading the road and correctly reducing speed at controlled intersections. She had attended accidents in the past where ambulance drivers thought they owned the road with their sirens blaring and lights flashing, only to end up the victims themselves. As they approached the canal they saw a shattered windscreen, broken glass and metal work lying in the road but no sign of a vehicle. She parked the patrol car on the verge near the canal and kept the blue light flashing on the roof.

Onlookers had gathered on the road and were looking down into the canal. Beth looked over the rail. A vehicle was lying on its roof and she saw someone lying in the wide cement canal. The canal was used as a storm water drain and for industrial waste but was dry most of the time.

Beth spoke to the crowd as she slid awkwardly down the embankment into the canal. "Did anyone witness the accident?" she asked loudly.

Beth heard a voice above her. "Yes. We did."

"Can you hang on a moment and I'll see you in a minute." Beth wanted to assess the condition of the person lying in the canal whilst her assistant went over to the car on its roof. A young male lay still on his front, his right leg contorted and twisted and clearly fractured. Beth tried to find his carotid artery and fiddled around for a moment. She felt a pulse and checked he was breathing, then marked his position with a waterproof crayon.

She ran over to the vehicle on its roof and heard a siren on the road above. The ambulance had arrived. Beth shone her torch into the mangled wreckage. A young male hung upside down in the driver's seat, the seatbelt still holding him in position. His head was lying at an awkward angle against the interior of the flattened roof.

A medic appeared next to Beth. "I'm not sure if this chap is alive. He may have a broken neck. Can you check him out? We're going to need the Jaws of Life." Beth asked her assistant to radio for the fire brigade. The other medic was attending to the man with the broken leg and Beth had a moment to talk to the witnesses up on the bridge. She marked the position of the car with her crayon and ran up the embankment.

"Who said they'd seen the accident?" Beth spoke into the crowd.

A man and woman approached Beth and the man started speaking. "We were travelling behind the car. It was speeding and wasn't able to negotiate the bend before the bridge. It skidded and the driver must have overcorrected the vehicle because it flipped and literally bounced over the rail and into the canal."

"It was dreadful, especially the sound when it rolled," said the woman. "It seemed to skid and brake and there was smoke coming from the tyres. It rolled when he tried to correct the skid I think. It all happened in seconds." The woman was notably shaken by the ordeal.

Beth wrote down their statements and noted their names and addresses. "Thank you. We'll be in touch for a full statement." They heard a siren and Beth saw the fire tender approaching. "It's all go," said Beth to herself as she saw four people carrying a stretcher up the embankment.

"I'm taking this chap to hospital and I'll come back for the guy in the car," said the medic. "Won't be long."

Beth got the name of the medic. She knew the importance of the chain of evidence, in case the accident was a fatal. She requested her assistant to give the vehicle registration number to the control room so they could establish the registered owner and notify next of kin.

The fire tender parked on the bridge, the nearest point to the car on its roof in the canal. The hydraulic Jaws of Life operated perfectly on the end of an extended cable from the tender, prizing open the window after sawing through part of the door. They freed the man from his seatbelt, carefully immobilising his neck. The man was unconscious but alive.

They measured and marked the skid marks on the road and marked the position of the windscreen and bits and pieces from the mangled vehicle.

Beth had crossed the t's and dotted the i's and was ready to leave the scene. She had checked in the wreckage for a lead to the identity of the two injured parties but found nothing. They waited and watched the breakdown removal team winch the vehicle safely out of the canal then returned to the patrol car. There were just a few stragglers now peering curiously over the bridge.

Beth got into the patrol car and pressed the button on the mike. "Control room, traffic one, over."

"Traffic one, go," came the abbreviated response.

"Roger, we're proceeding to the hospital to check on the casualties over." Beth hung onto the mike as she drove away from the scene.

"Rrrrogerrr," joked the voice on the radio. "You're late tonight, over."

Beth spoke into the mike again, not following correct radio procedure. "Tell me about it."

She parked outside the casualty department and went through the swinging doors into a brightly lit corridor, clutching her clipboard. The smell of disinfectant hit her. Beth hated hospitals. She walked into the duty room office and spoke to a nurse at the desk.

"You had two RTA casualties in this evening." Beth didn't have to finish.

"They're both in x-ray," said the nurse without looking up from her desk. "One is serious and may have a broken neck and the other seems to have a broken leg. Nothing too serious."

"Are they conscious?" asked Beth.

"Only the one with the broken leg but we've given him morphine and you won't get any sense out of him now," said the nurse leaning back in her chair.

"Control room are checking for the next of kin," said Beth.

"Good. There was no identification on them."

They drove back to traffic department and Beth threw her clipboard and papers onto her desk and sat down. She wound an investigation sheet into a recently serviced Olivetti typewriter, giving off the smell of a well-oiled firearm. She lined up the paper and looked at her watch. It was 1.30am. She'd be another half hour she thought and started bashing on the machine with two fingers.

It's All Just Nuts

Diana and William were in bed and Beth often lay on Diana's bed and talked to her at bedtime.

"So shall I do it?" asked Beth casually.

"Do what?" asked Diana.

They had discussed over dinner earlier that night, the prospect of Beth leaving the police. She had served for seventeen years and thought she needed a change.

"What we discussed tonight," Beth reminded her, "leave the police."

"Oh I don't know. What will you do?"

"Dunno. I'll find something no doubt. I can't stay in forever," said Beth.

"Well, we'll think about it in the morning. Come on. Bed time."

"Oke doke. Night night."

"Night darling," said Diana.

William already had his head down and seldom engrossed himself in their discussions. "Night Cock. Whatever decision you make, it'll be the right one."

Beth went to her room and did a lot of thinking. She felt the time was right, or was it? It had become a way of life, it *was* her life but at the back of her mind she knew it couldn't last forever. She turned off the light and lay in bed for over an hour, wide awake. She knew she had to take the plunge and wondered what sort of life would lie ahead. Beth heard a noise and wondered what it was. She listened carefully for another sound but it was quiet. Squirrels nested in the roof; perhaps it was a squirrel. She lay still, listening intently. No she thought, not squirrels. She tried to recall the sound in her mind but it was weird, hard to recall.

Beth wasn't happy. She decided to investigate and walked into the passage leaving the lights off. If it was an intruder she wanted to catch him red handed. She unlocked the inter-leading door between the bedrooms and the rest of the house, turned the key quietly and opened the door. It was pitch black. She would have liked a torch there and then but knew that wasn't the answer; she'd be a sitting target behind a torch beam. She was in the sitting room now and had to put a light on. Beth headed in the direction of a table lamp, holding out her hands in the blackness feeling for familiar bits of furniture.

There wasn't a sound in the house and for a moment thought she was stupid and had over reacted but that sound still worried her. She found the lamp and fiddled for the switch under the shade. She turned it on and her eyes scanned the room. Nothing. Not a sausage. One end of the sitting room, the bridge, had four huge glass windows overlooking the patio, swimming pool and garden and the heavy curtains were drawn at night. William nicknamed it the 'bridge,' the massive windows reminding him of the bridge of a ship. Beth approached one set of curtains and braced herself, ready to bring her self defence into action. She drew them back. Nothing. This is ridiculous she thought. She went to the next set and pulled them back more casually.

"Bloody hell," shouted Beth involuntarily. A man was standing rigidly on the wide windowsill behind the curtain and there was an enormous hole in the wide windowpane with shattered glass on the windowsill. As Beth took it all in over a matter of seconds, the intruder moved like lightning and made an ungainly dive through the hole in the glass. Beth flew down the corridor to alert William, returned to the sitting room and dashed out the front door turning on the security lights in the process. The garden around the house lit into daylight but she knew she was wasting her time now. There were too many dark nooks and crannies in the garden where the intruder could hide himself.

Beth returned to the house and William was standing guard at the open door.

"Just be careful my girl. I think you'd better come inside," he said, being cautious.

"He took off like a long dog. We won't get him now."

Beth and William looked at the mess left behind. There were spots of blood on the stone patio and a granite rock lay abandoned under the window, shattered glass around it.

"I'll sleep in the sitting room in case he comes back," said William.

"OK Pa. I think we should keep the lights on too." Beth locked the front door and went to tell Diana what had happened. She was still dozing in bed, blissfully unaware an intruder had nearly cleaned out her house.

They wasted no time the next morning and had the entire house alarmed, switches here, switches there and sensors in strategic places. Diana was very happy with the system and everything worked perfectly.

Beth in the meantime took the bull by the horns and submitted her resignation from the police. The furore of the alarm company staff running around the house installing wires and sensors and the time they spent mastering the system conveniently lessened the wretchedness of Beth's decision.

The two months notice went nowhere, Beth anxious about her future.

She sat with Diana on the bridge one afternoon talking, debating, and deciding what to do.

"I think you should go on a long holiday then come back and look for something to do," said Diana wisely. "You haven't had a decent holiday for years."

"Neither have you. You need a holiday too," said Beth

"We've been to see Barbara and Margaret," she reminded Beth of their visits to South Africa.

"Yeah, but you haven't been overseas."

"I'm quite happy here. I don't want to go gallivanting all over the place thank you." Diana was a strong woman and knew what she wanted. "You go and have a nice holiday and enjoy yourself. You deserve it."

"I don't deserve anything," balked Beth, always wanting her parents to have the best and more concerned about their welfare than her own. "Wouldn't mind going to some way out place like Thule in Greenland. Some call it Ultima Thule don't they? Translated as the end of the earth?"

"It feels very strange, unemployed and from tomorrow no fixed abode either," joked Beth. They were all sitting at a big table at the restaurant at Bulawayo airport, Diana and William and Jill and her two mates.

"Beth, tell us again where you're going," said Emily.

"All I have is a ticket to Halifax in Canada and stopovers in Salzburg and Nice on my way back. I've made no bookings anywhere and I'm going to bum around with my backpack." Beth was excited yet unconcerned that she'd made no firm plans or bookings.

"Why Halifax?" asked Emily.

"Well it's the nearest airport on the east coast of Canada and I'll be flying there from London. I'm hoping to get to Greenland from Nova Scotia but I'll send you a post card and let you know where I end up!"

An indistinct announcement came over the public address system, calling for passengers to board the flight to Johannesburg. Bulawayo airport was small and it was the only flight going out that afternoon and despite that, the airport was surprisingly busy.

"Come on darling, you'd better go," said Diana anxiously.

"Let the crowds go first and I'll tag along at the end." Beth was in no hurry. She was going to be away for a month and wanted to spend as much time with the family as she could.

Another announcement came though the PA calling the remaining passengers and they saw passengers boarding the aircraft. They made their way downstairs to customs and immigration and stood at the end of the remaining small queue.

"This is it," said Beth and gave Jill and her friends a hug, leaving her favourites for last.

"Bye Pa." Beth hugged William.

"Good trip my girl. Just enjoy yourself," said William. He never ever said goodbye.

"Bye Ma." Beth left the best 'til last. She was very close to Diana and she was closer to her than William but she loved them both in different ways.

"Bye darling. Have a lovely time and *write*! We have your return flight details and we'll be here to meet you in a month." Diana hugged Beth.

Beth's only luggage was a backpack and she put that through the scanner and gave a final wave to the family and went out of sight for the security check. She flung it on her back and walked out to the Boeing 737 on the apron. She looked back at the airport building and the big open veranda. Diana, William, Jill and the girls had gone upstairs again to see her off.

"Bye Beth!" shouted big sister from the balcony.

"Bye Roe-Roe!" shouted Beth, not embarrassed at the thought of all and sundry hearing Jill's odd nickname.

She stood at the top of the steps of the aircraft and turned around for the last time and waved as though she'd never be seeing them again. The airport was on a plateau and cold winds would blow from the southern African continent in winter, sometimes bearing icy winds from the Antarctic. Winter was around the corner for Bulawayo and the wind had a cold bite but Beth was heading to the northern hemisphere and to summer.

The engines revved and the aircraft moved off slowly and started a sharp U turn to take it to the end of the runway for takeoff. Beth saw the crowd on the balcony cover their ears as the jet engines blasted their ear-piercing whine at them as the Boeing turned around. It seemed to taxi forever to the end of the runway then turned and stopped momentarily. There were no other aircraft in the vicinity; Bulawayo was a sleepy hollow, but a beautiful sleepy hollow. The pilot opened the throttle and the engines spun into life and the aircraft vibrated. She gained speed quickly and lifted off almost level with the airport building and Beth saw the family waving. She felt a sense of guilt leaving them behind.

The Boeing banked south and flew over Bulawayo, a well laid out city stretching about fifteen miles across with the residential suburbs sprawling in all directions around the city centre. She felt at ease knowing she'd be returning to her beloved family and city.

Beth found a comfortable bed and breakfast with a family near Birch Cove, in Nova Scotia. Most houses in Canada were wooden structures but as robust as a brick house. The B&B had five big bedrooms, some with en suite facilities. It was cosy and serene and overlooked the bay in Halifax.

For a very nominal fee the owners of the B&B took their guests on a sight seeing tour of the area. The scenery was breathtaking for Beth having come from a relatively arid region in Africa. The emphasis was on green; it was stunning with fir and pine trees in abundance on the rolling hills and countless lakes of varying shapes and sizes dotted amongst the pine forests.

They went as far as Peggy's Cove just south east of Halifax on the Atlantic coastline. A brilliant white lighthouse that looked as though it had recently been given three or four good coats of paint stood majestically on an expansive rock formation that sloped gently into the sea. There was a peaceful air at Peggy's Cove and the ocean was being particularly kind, the waves gently lapping the rocks incongruously with such a massive unimpeded ocean beyond, but the B&B man assured them that ferocious storms and mammoth waves pounded the area.

Perhaps it was the wrong time of day for fishing because a pile of beautiful wicker lobster traps were placed neatly next to the brightly painted fishing boats tied up at the jetty. It was a picture-postcard scene, tranquil and crisp.

The travel agents in Halifax assumed Beth was mad, asking for information about flights to Thule in Greenland. She spent days trying to get a flight but no one could help her. She needed to travel off the beaten track and a travel agent was able to book a flight to Frobisher Bay on Baffin Island but there was no information about the area or what accommodation was available. Beth was unconcerned and was game for any adventure that lay ahead.

The overnight train travelled to Quebec City on the St Lawrence River. The sun was rising at 6am when it arrived on the southern shores of the river. It was still like glass and Quebec City towered high and stately above the river on the northern shores, the morning sun imparting a dignified glow on the lifeless mass of buildings.

The ferry took commuters across the river and Beth felt dwarfed as she climbed the steep long winding steps from the river to the city, her backpack feeling heavier with each step as she neared the city high in the sky. Top class hotels overlooked the St Lawrence and boats and yachts looked like toys on the mighty river below.

The city was notably French speaking and as she sat at the table of a pavement café enjoying a cup of coffee she smiled as she recalled her encounter with Miss De Beer on that fateful day when she walked out of her French exam. She really was a wise old duck and Beth wondered why Miss De Beers sound judgement still haunted her.

The Boeing 737 left Quebec City for Frobisher Bay with one stop at Fort Chimo. Beth asked the airhostess if she could take a photograph of the plane on the apron and she was given the green light, albeit with the airhostess keeping a beady eye on her. There was movement of cargo and passengers at the sleepy airport then they were off again, heading north over Quebec Province and beyond the tree line.

The tundra and desolation seemed to go on forever until they reached Hudson Bay and the sights of snow and icebergs had her leaping from one side of the plane to the other, fascinated by the strange new sights, the airhostess convinced Beth had escaped from a lunatic asylum.

The aircraft taxied to the Frobisher airport terminal that consisted of a small wooden building where the handful of passengers collected their luggage but there was no sign of Beth's backpack. She waited and waited, certain it would appear but the few passengers and their greeting parties soon disappeared and she was left in the small deserted building like a stray animal. She enquired with a member of staff and after further checks in the plane, a phone call was made.

"I'm sorry but your luggage was removed at Fort Chimo," said the airport official and before Beth had time to reply, "but they've assured us it will be on the next flight tomorrow morning."

"I have no hand luggage. Everything's in my backpack," said Beth, not particularly upset, "even my toothbrush!"

The man made another call and spoke to Beth. "Someone will be coming to see you shortly and she may be able to help you. If you could wait here," he pointed to a wooden bench in the small terminal.

A short fair-haired woman appeared minutes later. "Hello, my name is Emma. Are you the passenger with no luggage?"

Beth stood up. "That's right. I'm Beth," and she held out her hand to the dumpy woman. "I believe it was inadvertently removed at Fort Chimo and will only be here tomorrow. I don't even have a toothbrush." Beth seemed more concerned about that than where she would sleep that night.

"Where are you staying?" asked Emma.

"I don't know. I hope there's a motel or bed and breakfast here," said Beth innocently.

Emma giggled. "There's nothing like that here. Frobisher is primarily a government run settlement and doesn't cater for tourism, but we are trying to get a tourism industry established here."

"Oh I didn't know," said Beth wondering if she would be comfortable on the wooden bench in the terminal building.

"You're most welcome to stay with me and my husband during your stay. How long will you be here?" asked Emma.

"Just a few days. I'm hoping to go into the Arctic Circle. Are there any buses or tours up there?" Beth was unknowingly naïve.

"No, no!" laughed Emma. "Let's get you a toothbrush, then we'll stroll over to my place."

A policeman from the Royal Canadian Mounted Police stood outside the terminal building in his riding jodhpurs, red tunic and wide-brimmed hat, an impressible sight and they talked 'police talk' for several minutes.

"Sorry Emma," said Beth as she followed her along a muddy roadway. "I was in the police in Africa and I tend to zoom in on uniforms."

"Africa!" exclaimed Emma. "You're a long way from home."

"Yes. I wanted to travel somewhere off the beaten track, you know, away from the crowds. We get nearly 365 days of sunshine at home so cold weather and snow is a change for me," Beth explained.

Emma and Beth headed towards a row of wooden buildings on stilts. They entered a very small room and a door led off that into another small room and then into a living room area. Emma had to answer all Beth's questions, curious and interested in the unusual living conditions.

"The temperature can be 40 below in winter and the two rooms at the entrance help to keep the cold out," Emma explained to Beth.

The mid-winter icy colours in the house with white carpets, white walls and white curtains were uninviting with not a hint of warming autumn shades, the curtains a heavy white plastic, injudiciously driving out the welcoming transitory midnight sun in the summer months.

The settlement, inhabited by local Inuits, was a dreary labyrinth of wooden buildings dotted with a multitude of gum poles supporting a wholesale web of wires, the permafrost impelling the water and sewerage piping throughout the settlement to lie incongruously above ground.

Beyond the buildings of the settlement lay endless miles of tundra resembling a barren and desolate atomic aftermath, ground mosses and the enormous mat of tiny colourful flowers the lone survivors, trees and bushes wiped from the landscape.

"I'm very grateful to you both for taking me in. I had no idea what I was letting myself in for up here." Beth had joined Emma and Mike for supper in their winter wonderland home.

"We're pleased we could help," said Emma. "I've been giving thought to the Circle. There's a weekly flight that goes to Pond Inlet leaving tomorrow, taking supplies and passengers to the settlements, *but* it's costly."

Beth was on very limited funds and the news didn't sound good. "Do you know how much it would be?"

"I think it's into the hundreds of Canadian dollars. It's not a very long flight up there but fuel is shipped here which is a costly exercise on its own," explained Emma.

"That'll be out of the question for me. That's all I have for my entire holiday!" Beth tried to sound light hearted. "So near and yet so far."

"The owner of the aircraft lives in Montreal but he's in Frobisher for a few days. I know him quite well and I'll have a word with him." Emma sounded confident and Beth was at a loss as to what she had in mind. Emma was in a hurry to finish her supper then got up from the table. "Excuse me a moment." Emma went into the sitting room and closed the door behind her.

Mike helped Beth to pudding and describing their winters. "You probably noticed luminous poles placed intermittently on the road sides," said Mike.

"Yes," said Beth. "I'm curious."

"The blizzards get so bad sometimes that visibility can be reduced to a few meters and the poles are vital and keep one on the road."

"I can't imagine a temperature of minus 40," said Beth. "One would be frozen at minus 20 anyway," she joked.

"Believe me it feels colder!" said Mike. "The wind chill factor can make it feel like minus 60 sometimes and that is *biting*!"

Emma came in to the room. "Well," she said with a smile, "I've spoken to the owner and explained your circumstances and he's more than happy to give you a free ride to Pond and back to Frobisher." Emma was pleased with her negotiating skills.

"That's fantastic!" Beth was over the moon. "Thanks *very* much. That's really great."

"They're leaving at 5 o'clock tomorrow afternoon and he suggests you be at the Frobisher terminal by 4.30. Is that alright?" asked Emma and carried on without Beth's answer. "I'll lend you my parka. It can get very cold up there."

"Parka?" asked Beth.

"It's a fur lined coat with a hood. Very warm."

She was well in time at the airport with only a handful of people in the terminal. Beth gauged the situation and approached the man who seemed to be in charge.

"Excuse me." Beth got the man's attention. "Are you the owner of the aircraft going to Pond Inlet?"

"You must be Beth. Emma's friend?" the man beamed at Beth.

Beth was relieved. "Yes that's right. I want to thank you for your generous offer. I really wanted to get into the Circle and I wouldn't have managed it without you."

"It's my pleasure. Pleased I could help. I understand you're from Africa eh?"

"That's right. I'm restricted with the amount of foreign currency I can take on holiday. To compensate you, I'd like to send you an elephant skin briefcase when I get home," said Beth.

"Now *you're* being generous. Thank you!"

"If you could let me have your postal address, consider it done."

Beth boarded the twin-engine turbo prop Hawker Siddeley 7. It seemed smaller than a Dakota, with barely half a dozen passengers but loaded with supplies for the three settlements they were to visit. The owner had drawn a rough map for Beth and she examined it as the aircraft shuddered at the end of the runway. They'd fly north east over Cumberland Sound from Frobisher and land at Pangnirtung on the south east coast of Baffin Island. Then to another settlement called Clyde River further north, and finally Pond Inlet on the northern reaches of the island.

It wasn't a long flight to Pangnirtung and they landed on a runway that resembled a dust road in Africa. It ran parallel to the waters edge making no room for error by the pilot, the runway dusty with loose stones but quite adequate for its purpose. They weren't there long when they were in the air again heading up the east coast of Baffin Island to Clyde River over stunning scenery.

Although it was past mid summer, huge glaciers lay motionless on the black rugged mountains, with the occasional iceberg raising its head above the icy waters in the craggy inlets along the coastline. Glaciers on high jagged mountain peaks had only partially melted, like cream trickling from the top of monstrous Christmas puddings, inappropriate in their remoteness. There was mile upon mile of them of varying shapes and sizes, lying lifeless yet majestically in grand eerie silence.

The sky had been beautifully clear but they started to fly through thin cloud as they continued their journey north. The cloud started to thicken, the pilot reduced altitude and the aircraft slowed as though coming in to land. Thick white cloud now enveloped the small plane with visibility down to zero. The engines slowed to a frightening drone, the sound reverberating in the suffocating cloud surrounding them. The drone persisted and when it seemed the engine revs couldn't reduce further, the deep drone slowed even more. Beth peered into the opaque confusion desperate for the sight of ground to get her bearings, having no idea if they were flying straight or circling yet dreading the sight of a rugged mountainside within yards of the window. Beth was nervous, certain the pilot was flying blind. If he was flying by instruments she was sure they'd have landed by now.

The engine revs increased, the deathly drone faded and wisps of broken cloud flew past the windows. Beth sighed with relief as the plane gained altitude and she looked back at the pall lying over the Clyde River valley, black mountain peaks rising out of the cloud like massive coffin nails.

Beth saw a small settlement out of the port window. The plane banked to the left and another African bush road loomed up ahead of them and they landed at Pond Inlet. Passengers disembarked and Beth strolled around the settlement, not venturing too far from the turbo prop plane that looked small against the vast landscape. She was grateful for Emma's parka, the temperature was 5°C at 11.30pm, a month past mid summer. With the sun low in the sky the local Inuit's gathered around the plane the nearby Bylot Island silhouetted majestically before a cold watery sky, their only permanent witness.

Beth stood still, thinking, taking in the moment. She was almost on top of the world, 72° 41′ North. She felt rootless, alone, a million miles from her beloved family and home deep in the bowels of Africa but she knew she'd be back there and with them again and she lightened up.

New passengers were boarding the plane for their flight to Frobisher and Beth strolled back to the plane. They were on the move again, the last leg of the trip back to Frobisher. She had her window seat again and at the stroke of midnight the sun had settled motionless and visible above the desolate arctic horizon.

Beth befriended a fellow police officer at Salzburg airport who found her comfortable inexpensive accommodation in the city. Although years later, the residents of Salzburg were still proud that the film hit 'The Sound of Music' was filmed in their beautiful city and the hospitable policeman took Beth to see the famous places depicted in the film. Beth lost count of the number of times she saw the film and adored being in the Marable Gardens and seeing the Von Trap house at close range. He took her to a traditional farm on the outskirts of the city where they sampled the local fiery schnapps and had an indescribably scrumptious meal cooked by the friendly farmer's wife.

Fortuitously Beth had inexpensive accommodation because she became addicted to the delicious piping hot brown frankfurters in soft bread rolls, served by the numerous street vendors in the cobbled streets of Salzburg.

They were delectably addictive and she went back time and time again for more.

By the time Nice on the côte d'azur was in her sights funds were at rock bottom. She searched addresses at the information bureau at the airport for her usual cheap accommodation, looking at prices as opposed to addresses in the right area and scribbled down an address and called a taxi. It took her along the main road surrounding the bay, dotted with tropical palm trees and expensive looking hotels on her left. The driver turned up a narrow street and stopped just behind the main shops and hotels on the main boulevard and pointed out a huge impressive pink building, assuring her it was the address she had given him.

An address in that area would be beyond her reach but she had nothing to lose by looking inside the pink building. She walked through a grand entrance and stood shocked in amazement at the massive foyer with marble walls and floors, a chandelier hanging from a Gothic ceiling and two curved staircases on either side of the foyer. Its aesthetic appearance was short lived because the address probably *was* correct. It was dilapidated, antiquated and dimly lit without a soul in sight.

"Bloody hell." Beth spoke out loud to herself her voice echoing in the stony tomb as she wondered around the poorly lit foyer. "What a dump." There were two swinging doors slightly ajar on the left of the foyer. Beth pushed one side and it opened. She put her head through the door and the sight was no more impressive than the ruin in the foyer. She was confronted by a long narrow passage poorly lit by a single light bulb dangling from a long flex barely visible through a maze of clothes and sheets hanging on four or five lengths of rope along the passage. "Shit," Beth muttered to herself again.

Her curiosity got the better of her. "Hello, anybody home?" she called loudly.

She heard some movement down the passage and she saw a pair of legs approaching beneath the washing. A woman pushed the clothing and sheets aside and looked at Beth. She babbled in French way beyond Beth's comprehension.

"Speak English?" asked Beth.

"Oui, oui, yes. You want room?" she asked vivaciously.

"Yes, maybe." Beth shrugged her shoulders not wanting to commit herself. "Can I see?" Beth pointed to her eyes but the woman fully understood.

"Oui, come, come," and she led Beth down the passage through her laundry and opened a door off the passage.

The room was tiny with a bed and small wooden chair. Beth opened the wooden shutters on the window and looked out onto a surprisingly well kept garden and a handful of palm trees. The woman confirmed the price as advertised at the airport. It wasn't Beth's cup of tea but it was a bed, a cheap one, and that suited her.

It was nearly 7 o'clock in the evening but the sun was still high in the sky. Beth gratefully removed her backpack and went off briskly and unimpeded for a walk along the boulevard and the pebbled beach and threw flat stones skimming across the still Mediterranean. She looked at the hotels, palm trees, flowers and lawns and chuckled to herself. She would tell everyone she stayed on the French Riviera but she wouldn't tell them she stayed in a ramshackled dump; well she might she thought, just for a giggle. The café prices along the boulevard sent Beth scuttling off to the back streets and she found a clean restaurant with seating on the cobbled pavement. She looked through the menu and ordered a plate of spaghetti bolognaise for a quarter of the price of a meal in the tourist traps.

"You speak good English," Beth told the woman who took her order.

"I'm a French Canadian and spent most of my life in Vancouver so yes," she laughed, "my English is pretty good!"

"Tell me," Beth's investigative mind working overtime, "what do you know about that massive old pink building near the boulevard?"

"That's an old palace. The authorities have condemned it and it's due for demolition shortly. Why do you ask?"

"I'm staying there for a few nights and I was curious about it's history," said Beth.

The woman laughed. "That old woman refuses to leave. She is the only person left in the building and they're having a problem removing her. She's the talk of the town! They say there's a ghost in the palace. It's hownted. How do you say it?"

"You mean haunted?" Beth corrected her.

"Oui, haunted! You know, ghosts."

Beth walked back to her impoverished abode dispelling the theory of ghosts. She went through the main doors and the foyer was in darkness. She looked across the foyer in the direction of the swinging doors where the old woman's washing hung and saw light struggling through the gap in the doors. Good she thought and walked across the foyer, keen to push the door open. The laundry still hung in the passage and Beth was grateful for the feeble yellow light still hanging on its cord. A light was on in the kitchen at the end of the passage and Beth went to see if the old woman was there. She knocked on the open door. "Hello," said Beth.

"Oui!" said the woman cheerfully. She was sitting at a small table in the kitchen sorting out a pile of papers that resembled old invoices. "Café?"

"Thank you," said Beth.

The old woman got up and turned on the kettle. Beth was able to observe her more closely and thought that she was probably the ghost in the old building. She was barely five feet tall and very round. Her unkempt hair was touching her shoulders and was obviously dyed pitch black as tell-tale signs of grey were showing in the parting in the middle of her head. Her lips seemed permanently dyed with red lipstick that extended beyond her natural lip line and her eyebrows were unevenly painted with heavy black mascara. She had a hard battered face but seemed a cheerful old soul.

"Where you go tomorrow?" she asked.

"I'm not sure. I don't know the area," confessed Beth.

"You can take a bus to Monte Carlo. There it's very pretty. I make you some sandwiches and you go eh?"

"Yes, that sounds good. Thank you."

Beth didn't mention the ghost theory to the woman, not wanting to get into a lengthy conversation with the old woman and went off to her room after her coffee. She closed her bedroom door and only then discovered there was no lock on the door.

"That's great," said Beth to herself. She managed to jam the small wooden chair under the round doorknob, content that if anyone tried to enter it would make sufficient noise to waken her. She lay awake for a long time grateful for the glow of the streetlights coming through the shutters.

Beth heard an almighty din as she walked along the laundry-clad passage the next morning.

"Non non pee pee," came the screeches of the old woman in the kitchen followed by clash, bang, clatter. "Non non pee pee," bang bang, crash.

Beth went to investigate and saw the old woman leaning out of the kitchen window balancing on the window sill, her large backside taking up the width of the window as she furiously banged two saucepans together. Beth wondered what in heavens name she was doing.

The old girl turned around gibbering in deep French, her face red with fury.

"Bon jour," said Beth hoping to calm the woman.

She broke into English shaking her head. "Those boys, ugh! They do pee pee in the road. Every day chase, chase, chase." She broke into French again talking to herself and threw the saucepans on the counter in a rage. She sat down at the little kitchen table and put her head in her hands and sighed.

Moments later she looked up beaming from ear to ear, her pitch black hair falling wildly around her weathered face. She slapped the palms of her hands on the table. "Sandwiches!" She opened the fridge and produced a neatly bundled packet. "Inside I put egg, tomato and ham sandwiches. Good?" she asked.

"Oui, oui. Merci madame!" Beth was feeling uncomfortable with her feeble French.

The scenery between Nice and Monaco was exquisite, the rugged cliffs with sheer faces, handsome and lifeless plunging silently into the blue Mediterranean. Beth walked through Monte Carlo, the streets notably void of litter. It was sparkling, clean and pretty. Beth felt out of place in her denim jeans and jacket as she strolled around the pristine shops.

Beth heard a voice behind her. "Oui, monsieur?"

She looked around to find a shop assistant had come to her aid and didn't have time to reply before the assistant came forth with a notable apology. "Oh, pardonnez moi mademoiselle!"

"Don't worry, I'm used to it. I should wear pink ribbons in my hair," said Beth as she combed her fingers through her tomboyish hairstyle.

A creamy coloured building with beautiful architecture and accumulating wealth beyond Beth's wildest dreams stood at the foot of a massive island of lawns, flowers and palm trees. She couldn't believe she was looking at the famous Monte Carlo Casino and her grandfather came to mind. Diana had told her of her grandfather's gambling habits and he would've been in his element had he visited the world-renowned gambling den.

Beth ate her sandwiches in sunshine on the small sandy beach arced around the Monte Carlo bay, gleaning from the locals that it was man made, the fine clean sand imported and placed over the hard pebbles that characterised many of the beaches on the côte d'azur. The sun was warm, like the winter sun in Africa and Beth lay on the beach thinking about Diana and William and wished they were with her but she knew they were content in Africa and especially Bulawayo. She was looking forward to seeing them in a few days.

The flight home took her via Kinshasa in the Congo and Johannesburg. Passengers weren't allowed to disembark at Kinshasa but Beth stood at the top of the steps of the aircraft; the smell of Africa was prominent and she loved it. The flight continued to Johannesburg and there was a few hours wait for her connection to Bulawayo.

It was mid afternoon and Beth had a port window seat. She could feel the sun on her arm and it was warm and inviting. The countryside became less inhabited as they flew over the Northern Transvaal and across the mighty brown Limpopo River lying lifeless in the barren bush. It was late August, the arid countryside having experienced a long dry winter. The craggy Matobo Hills famous for their spectacular granite kopjes and massive rock formations of immense beauty millions of years old lay sprawled out below as far as the eye could see. The beginning of the Matobo Hills was 20 miles from Bulawayo by road and Beth knew they'd be landing soon.

The tone of the engines changed and the plane started to lose altitude and flew low over the city, banking sharply to starboard to line up with the runway in the clearing in the bush. The South African Airways Boeing touched down perfectly, speeding momentarily on the runway until reverse thrust threw both engines into an ear piercing blast. It taxied up the runway and back to the terminal. The grass was brown and dry, a huge contrast from the greenery Beth had experienced over the last month. She peered through the window looking for Diana and William on the balcony. They always stood at one end, stand out from the crowd.

Beth saw William in their usual spot but she couldn't see Diana. She must be there somewhere thought Beth.

She went through immigration and customs and through a short corridor to the waiting families and friends. She scoured the crowd and saw William standing alone and Beth was worried now. They hugged each other and Beth wasted no time.

"Where's Ma?" She sounded concerned and knew something must be wrong.

"Your Ma had a thrombosis and was in hospital for a week but she came home today with strict instructions to rest."

"Oh hell. Is she all right? What caused it?" Beth was full of questions.

"These things happen Cock, but the swelling is down and she's fine," William assured her.

Beth run into the house from the car and found Diana in a chair on the bridge with her leg elevated. "Hi Ma!" They hugged each other for a long time. "What have you been up to!"

"Sorry I couldn't meet you darling. This was so unexpected. My leg swelled up last week and I thought nothing of it but your Dad wasn't happy and took me down to the doc. The next thing I was in hospital." Diana looked well and cheerful.

"Why did you have to go to hospital?" asked Beth.

"They thinned my blood and they wanted to keep an eye on me, but I'm fine darling! Nothing will keep me down. Now let's hear about your holiday."

CHAPTER 12

Over five years passed and Beth was well ensconced in her own business. Zimbabwe was a tropical paradise and tourists were flocking to the country to take advantage of the perfect sunny weather, visit natural game reserves like Hwange and the famous majestic Victoria Falls. It was the fastest growing industry in the country and Beth jumped on the ladder and was successfully manufacturing, marketing and distributing ethnic jewellery to tourist outlets throughout the country.

Everything at home was as good as it always was except for one thing. Beth's attitude to William had changed drastically and she had become argumentative and bitter towards him. It was her own doing and she knew it, as her father continued to be genteel, polite and diplomatic in all situations, even during Beth's vulgar behaviour towards him. Beth couldn't explain her rudeness and put it down to pressure of work. She worked from home for some years and despite that became one of the biggest suppliers in the country and focusing so much on the business probably caused stress and she used her father as a release valve. These were her thoughts on her stance towards her father and she never discussed them with her parents. They seemed to muddle through with Beth's up and down moods.

Christmas was around the corner and Beth went overboard as she did every year showering her parents with presents. Christmas was celebrated in the traditional family way and for a few years now it had been reduced to Diana, William, Beth and Jill, with Barbara and her family having moved to South Africa.

Deep down Beth loved her father but never expressed it. She always had a deeper love for her mother. She feared their passing; her parents were now in their seventies and each Christmas when she wrote out their Christmas gift tags she always hoped it wouldn't be the last.

Christmas Day arrived and Diana had the turkey in the oven at the crack of dawn and William had removed the leg sinews the night before with a pair of pliers. The bird was in and countdown had begun. Diana and Beth set the table on the bridge and were waiting for Jill to arrive before opening the mound of presents under the tree.

"Yoo-hoo!" Jill's voice rang out in the sitting room.

"Yoo-hoo!" replied Diana.

Beth and Jill did their kissing ritual and made kissing noises with a left right, left right motion and greetings flew around.

Jill was wearing her shorts and a T-shirt and Beth noticed she was holding something under her shirt.

"What's that?" asked Beth and poked the small bump. "It feels like a tomato!"

Jill looked at Beth then at Diana. "Shall I show her?" Jill asked Diana.

"Yes go on. Put her out of her misery!"

Jill lifted up her T-shirt still clutching the small bump and the tiniest black kitten popped its head out nervously.

Beth shrieked with delight. "Oh the darling! Let me hold it!" Beth took the little mite from Jill that was small enough to sit in her hand. "Is it a he or a she?"

"She's a she," said Jill, smiling.

"Ma, you asked me what I wanted for Christmas months ago and with tongue in cheek I said a black kitten but I never thought you'd do it." Beth was thrilled with her new friend. "You two must have been in cahoots!"

"I got her from the SPCA yesterday. Her mother and three kittens were found in the bush and someone took them to the SPCA," said Jill.

"Thank you, thank you!" Beth hugged Diana and Jill.

William came in the kitchen and greetings flew between him and Jill.

"Look Pa!" Beth held the kitten in front of William. "Isn't it cute?"

"It looks very young. Must be about six weeks," said William accurately.

"The SPCA said they were probably born in early November, so you're about right Pa," confirmed Jill.

"We'll have to think of a name. How about Choo-Choo? She's as black as a Choo-Choo train!" Diana was bang on and she was christened Choo-Choo.

Choo-Choo tried to venture outside seeking independence but a small leaf danced across the patio but she turned tail, terrified, and scuttled inside wobbling on her young short legs. A small Christmas cracker box padded with pieces of soft material became a cosy den and she slept for hours after an exhausting morning.

William had retired but found plenty to do, doing his own chores and running errands and assisting with the company. They were in effect living under one roof albeit a big one with a huge garden, but it got to Beth. There was no justification in Beth's anti stance towards her father but since he retired, deep down she felt he was infringing on her space and her relationship with Diana. Poor William handled it well like a true gentleman and kept out of Beth's way. She worked virtually seven days a week, fifteen hours a day sometimes and was under pressure. Diana was piggy in the middle and had to balance her time between the two.

"Why doesn't he get a job?" Beth asked Diana early one evening. Beth was sitting on a stool in the kitchen watching Diana at her workbench.

"Your father's in his 70's and he can't find a job now. He wants to work with you. You know he's as happy as a boy in a sandpit when he's helping you and I wish you'd allow him to do more." Diana usually kept her patience with Beth.

"He's a pain in the arse and he gets on my bloody nerves." Beth would get agitated about her father and couldn't stop.

"Will you stop talking about your father like that," said Diana openly annoyed with Beth.

"He gets up everyone's nose and he's a bloody nuisance," said Beth, not letting up.

"He doesn't get up my nose. If you can't talk properly in here, go and find something else to do," said Diana.

Beth felt Diana was siding with William and that annoyed her. "He can piss off," said Beth leaving the kitchen. She was in the sitting room and talking to her self and continued her ridiculing. "He's a pain in the arse."

Beth was working in a room in the house, conveniently converted to an office when Diana called her for supper. The atmosphere around the supper table would vary depending on Beth's mood. She felt guilty that evening when she looked at her father at the end of the table. He *never* argued with her or took offence at her rudeness. He was a gentleman in the true sense of the word. Every evening without fail he would wear a collar and tie after his bath, even on the balmiest of nights. She thought he was wonderful for that but she would still unleash her wild tongue on him.

They now had a factory in an industrial park but Beth still worked at home late into the night, sometimes with cardboard boxes scattered around as they got out late orders. Choo-Choo adored the boxes and would climb in each one to ensure nothing unsavoury lurked inside and without exception would climb onto the highest stack. She'd scramble up the side like a squirrel and lie contentedly on top for hours like a Sphinx and watch Beth through slit eyes as she worked tirelessly into the night.

Choo-Choo understandably was spoilt beyond comprehension. She had turned into a fairly small shorthaired domestic cat with exquisite yellow eyes, her doctor once commenting how pretty she was. Diana wasn't particularly partial to cats but she liked Choo-Choo. She was well trained like all the previous animals in the household. She was allocated one chair in the sitting room, the cushion kept covered with a towel and she knew that was her space. Sharpening claws on furniture was forbidden and she learnt that at a very early age and never attempted the abhorrent exercise. Beds were out of bounds. She was spoilt with a huge garden to herself with an array of trees to climb, gnarled tree roots to sharpen her claws and dozens of bushes and different shady spots to lie under. Choo-Choo would lie in wait in the evenings for tiny shrews to scuttle from under the bushes and she'd pounce on them likening herself to a marauding lioness. She'd toss and tease the shrews on the front lawn under the gaze of the floodlights, delighted with her catch, her belly already full of the finest mince. Young geckos were a gastronomic delight and tickled her taste buds, so much so that once one was caught it would be devoured instantly.

Beth did the marketing for the company visiting prime tourist resorts in the country. She was getting ready for a five-hour journey by road to Victoria Falls that she always undertook alone. A variety of other things had to be done before hand; appointments had to be made with customers and that was a mission in itself. She liked to do that herself and kept an excellent rapport between customers and the company. The company produced a first class product and was reliable with deliveries, back up and after sales attention and Beth ensured that was maintained.

    She sat on her usual stool in the kitchen chatting to Diana the night before her departure. It was early evening and the sun had set and Choo-Choo's routine clock told her it was suppertime. She came into the kitchen and sat quietly and patiently. Diana had already prepared her plate of mince and Beth started the nightly ritual of feeding the family cat who seemed convinced it was of the canine variety.

    "Do you want it?" Beth held the plate above Choo-Choo.

She knew what that meant and gave a quiet 'meow.'

"Lie down for your supper," said Beth.

Choo-Choo ignored her and rubbed up against Beth's legs.

"Lie down." Beth was more firm.

Again Choo-Choo ignored her and rubbed against the kitchen cupboard, purring loudly.

"Just give it to her," said Diana. "She doesn't want to lie down."

"She knows what to do," Beth persisted. "Choo-Choo, *lie down* for your supper!"

She put her head on the floor and rolled onto her side, her paws kneading the air furiously as she purred and looked innocently at Beth.

"You're a good dog!" Beth patted her on her side. "Come on!"

Choo-Choo leapt to her feet and got her head down to her plate.

"She really thinks she's a dog," laughed Beth.

Beth was on the road early the next morning. She had made the trip many times and enjoyed her space away from home and if the truth was known, Diana and William probably enjoyed it when she was away.

It was over 200 miles to Victoria Falls on a good tarred road but through mile upon mile of bush with the odd African village in the distance consisting of grass huts and cattle kraals made from tree branches sunk closely together in the ground. Halfway between Bulawayo and Victoria Falls was Hwange Game Reserve, a famous natural reserve with a huge concentration of wild game including the 'Big Five' consisting of elephant, rhino, buffalo, lion and leopard.

It's All Just Nuts

Diana always made egg and bacon sandwiches for the journey and Beth never bothered to stop the car to munch the feast but pouring tea from the thermos flask was a risky business. She'd hold the flask between her legs to unscrew the top then pour the tea holding the cup at 12 o'clock on the wheel. The roads were invariably quiet and her eating antics on the move were quite safe in her estimation.

She turned off the main Bulawayo-Victoria Falls road a few miles past Gwaai River to visit a customer at the Hwange game reserve Main Camp, a five mile drive from the main road. The area was entirely natural where any of the game could be seen on that five-mile journey and one had to peer carefully in to the bush to spot the animals. Trees were frequently torn down by elephants often out of sheer boredom but primarily to gain access to the sweet tender foliage that might otherwise have been out of their reach.

There were fresh elephant droppings on the road just ahead then she saw them, a small herd of about eight elephants picking green leaves off the bushes with their long grey trunks, unhurried and elegant. It was a young herd about fifty yards off the road, some youngsters barely visible through the bushes.

Beth saw the buyer at the curio shop and talked over sales and estimated tourist levels in the coming months and it all sounded positive. She went back to the car with briefcase and sample case in hand, pleased with the order they'd received. The camp was busy with open safari landrovers entering the camp, some stopping off at the curio shop and restaurant loaded with life-giving tourists for the industry. The camp was well laid out with stone rondavals with thatched roofs dotted between the trees.

Shiny starlings cooed from the top of the thatched entrance to the camp and thorny acacia trees and bushes with their delicate leaves stood motionless in the background. The sun was strong and there wasn't a cloud in the sky and it looked peaceful and inviting.

It was an hours drive to the Falls from Hwange. The road was straight for miles and the trees provided interesting scenery with their branches like umbrellas shading the road from the midday sun high in the sky. Troops of monkeys sat on the edge of the road nibbling wild fruit whilst others sauntered around aimlessly on all fours some with babies sitting perilously on their back, all with not a care in the world.

Beth reduced speed when she encountered a herd of cattle and goats on the road. They were a menace and she knew that goats were far more intelligent and traffic conscious than cattle. She stopped the car and had to hoot when the animals surrounded the car. The goats were alert and reacted and moved off but the cattle stood and stared at Beth like morons. A cow put its head up to the car window and stared gormlessly at Beth as it chewed the cud.

"Go on. Scram. Get out of it." Beth clapped her hands at the dozy beast trying to peer in the open window. It blinked its huge brown eyes at her and Beth laughed. The beast looked like Molly, one of Diana's friends. It chewed slowly on the lump of grass in its mouth then strolled away from the car.

It was early afternoon when she drove into the car park at her usual stamping ground, the Sprayview Motel in Victoria Falls with its comfortable rooms and hospitable friendly staff. The humidity hit her as she got out of the car but she thrived in the heat and loved it. She walked up the steps to the reception desk set in an open foyer with ceiling fans flying around at hurricane speed. Water circulated in a fountain in the middle of the foyer, provided an artificial feeling of coolness. She was greeted by the staff she knew so well and they shook hands and talked like long lost friends.

She drove around to her room and off loaded her suitcase and samples in the clean comfortable room with a French door and veranda that overlooked lawns, huge evergreen trees and the swimming pool. She turned on the air conditioning and ordered a pot of tea from room service. There was time to unwind with the first appointment scheduled for the morning.

She found her way to the village and made an informal call on one of their big customers, a friendly PR visit and confirmed she'd see them in the morning. She hadn't been down to the Falls themselves for a few years and thought a visit was overdue. It was a few minutes drive from the village to the big dusty car park at the entrance to the Falls area and she walked along the cobbled pathway to the western edge of the gorge.

The mass of water plunged over the precipice a mile across, the longest plummeting sheet of water in the world and it never ceased to amaze Beth as she stood near the statue of David Livingstone, the English missionary and first white man to see the Victoria Falls. The mighty Zambezi River flowed through a fairly narrow portion between an island and the western edge of the Falls creating the most violent raging gush of water along the entire width of the Falls and was aptly called the Devil's Cataract.

The gigantic river rose in the Congo where good rains had fallen, the results evident at the Falls as the river pounded powerfully and relentlessly over three hundred feet into the narrow gorge below. The spray from the thundering crash rose hundreds of feet into the air, the strong sunlight forming permanent rainbows of varying intensity in the swirling mist and spray and indeed, as Livingstone wrote, "A scene so beautiful it must have been gazed upon by angels in flight."

There were tourists on the pathways and vantage points along the length of the Falls and in the rain forest, incongruous with their umbrellas and raincoats in dazzling sunshine. Beth knew she would be back and would leave the rain forest for the visitors and as she walked back to the main entrance the thunderous sound of the river was still audible, the local people aptly naming it 'Mosi oa Tunya,' the smoke that thunders.

Beth made a few more PR calls and went back to the motel, ordered more tea and wondered down to the main motel building for supper. The lawns and pool surrounds with miniature bougainvillea and tropical plants were gently lit with lantern-shaped lights and the swimming pool with its underwater lighting yards away from the veranda used as a dining area made it a perfect tropical paradise. Diners enjoying a candlelit meal occupied most of the tables. Exuberant tribal dancers arrived on the patio, bare-chested with skimpy leopard skins around their waists and heads as they danced in perfect unison to the beat of their traditional music, singing and humming in tune to the drumbeats and marimbas.

A successful day was had meeting the buyers from the curio shops in the village and the top class hotels. The shops exuded their familiar smell, a mixture of leather goods and woven basket-ware of grass and reeds and it lingered pleasantly in Beth's nostrils for most of the day.

Boat rides on the river, the late afternoon 'Booze Cruise,' made the perfect ending to the day. Beth drove down to the river and followed a narrow footpath through the thick vegetation and undergrowth to the boat tied to the jetty. A number of passengers were already onboard, seated at the tables on deck enjoying their sundowners. Beth found a table and ordered a long cold beer. The boat was almost full when the rumble of the diesel engine started and the boat vibrated into life. Staff threw the moorings onboard and it accelerated away from the jetty and westwards up river, the gentle throb of the engine adding to the excitement. The boat was long and low in the water like a pontoon, one almost able to touch the water rippling alongside the boat.

"Elephant!" shouted a crewmember and pointed to a well worn clearing on the southern riverbank.

Cameras flew into action as passengers stood at their tables or moved to the side of the boat, Beth aware of a variety of nationalities confined to such a small area; Germans, English, Americans, Japanese. There were at least a dozen elephants drinking from the river with four warthogs standing quite wisely to one side, also sipping the Zambezi.

They travelled west towards the setting sun. Puffy clouds appeared above the Zambezi Valley in the late afternoon heat, the moisture from the mighty river condensing into majestic cloud formations above the desolate escarpment through which the river meandered. The sunset was spectacular, the deep orange sun with its golden rays peeped out from behind grey and white clouds shaped like unfinished sculptures, and as the sun visibly sank lower in the sky, the shades of orange and gold changed with the burning sphere's movement behind the clouds.

"Hippo!" came another shout from the crewman. The boat was turning now for its return journey down river and as it did so they neared the heads of three hippopotami, their shiny black heads and snouts protruding from the water. They were still and near the middle of the river, the only movement came from their small ears flicking on their enormous heads. The boat throbbed nearer to them as it continued its turn and almost as an act of showmanship one of them disappeared momentarily under the water then shot its head out of the river, expelling jets of water from its cavity-like nostrils accompanied by a monstrous groan, much to the delight of the trigger-happy spectators.

In those few minutes the sky had changed dramatically and the sun had changed to a gigantic red ball hanging above the trees upriver, the rays had given way to endless shades of mauve, plum and crimson splattered across the skyline silhouetting the deep violet static clouds. It was peaceful and serene, the call of a lone Fish Eagle adding to the beauty and mystery of Africa.

Beth visited Jill, Nora and Emily on a regular basis and they got on well together, but it seemed a little one sided with Diana, William and Beth receiving far less visits from Jill and her two friends. That was generally the case with Jill preferring to remain with her two friends of over twenty years but all six had been on a roll for a while, each household exchanging invites and meals on a regular basis.

Emily and Beth were sitting on garden chairs on the lawn at Nora's house, Beth having arrived for a friendly visit on a Sunday afternoon. They were joking and nattering in the sun when Nora came out of the house with a tray of tea and a plate of hot fat pancakes covered in melting butter. Nora was the size of a house, a very big round woman with her fair hair bundled into a scruffy lump at the back of her head. Her huge tent-like dresses made her bigger than she was but they were cool for her and she would waddle around her garden content with her size. She loved cooking cakes, scones and pancake and she swore blind she never ate any herself but her weight was a give away. Old Nora had a heart of gold sometimes but often had the 'poor me' syndrome, forever indicating she was broke and no one really knew if this rubbed off from Jill or visa versa. Jill was still working as an accountant as was Emily, but Nora ran a not so successful business from home. Jill and Nora were forever broke. Finances were a grey area in their household and not talked about much but when odd things were mentioned it only left Beth and her parents scratching their heads.

Nora, Emily and Beth were having their tea on the lawn when Jill appeared from her barn. She dressed immaculately for work but at home she wore old holey clothes and had no qualms about the way she dressed.

"Hi Roe-Roe," said Beth.

"Hi," said Jill sleepily and sat down in a canvas camp chair.

Jill used to be quite well covered though never fat, but she was much thinner now. She had short mousy coloured hair that invariably hung loosely over her forehead. Jilly had a small face with a permanent suntan on her slender arms and legs. She looked tough and walked with a positive step.

"How come you're always sleeping when I come here?" asked Beth.

Emily chipped in. "We never see her. She's always in that bloody barn, sleeping."

"I'll be dead before I'm fifty," said Jill seriously.

"Oh don't talk such rubbish Jill," said Nora and gave a belly laugh. "You talk such rubbish."

"I will. You wait and see." Jill had a macabre sense of humour sometimes.

Jill got up and walked over to an old wooden bench on the veranda, with leather cushions. "Come," said Jill looking at Beth. "Come and lie down on the bench."

"We've decided we're going to psychoanalyse you. We want to find out why you're so anti your father," said Emily light heartedly.

"Oh come off it," said Beth.

"Come," said big sister again. "I want to know why you're so rude to Pa."

"Well that's too bad. He just drives me up the bloody wall. You try and live with him," said Beth earnestly.

"That's why I live here," said Jill. "It's my choice not to live with him."

"Who's helping them financially since Pa retired?" Beth was almost sorry she'd asked such a stupid question. It wasn't a matter Beth talked about because what she did for her parents in that regard she did very willingly without any thought. She was living with them anyway and had to pay her way.

It's All Just Nuts

Beth's last comment put paid to any psychoanalysing. Jill went off to do her chores and Emily pottered in the garden, her short black hair neatly in place. Beth stayed a while longer then left. They had their ups and downs but Beth enjoyed their company. She drove home knowing how much she really loved her home but very conscious of the fact she had a serious attitude problem towards her father. She wished he had a job to go to.

Beth was having water works problems and was passing blood-tainted urine. She ignored it for a week hoping it would go away but it didn't. As close as she was to Diana she found it difficult to talk about personal matters and kept it to herself. Into the second week there was no let up and she thought a visit to the doctor was necessary. He referred her to a surgeon who wanted an examination under anaesthetic. Beth told Diana about her problem and understandably she was concerned.

The examination was done and the surgeon took a sample from the bladder for a biopsy and she had to see him a week later.

"Hello Mr Solomon," Beth greeted the surgeon.

"Hello, please come in."

"I've had the result of the biopsy and the lab report indicates the tissue has been affected by a chemical," said Mr Solomon.

"What do you mean?" asked Beth.

"Have you taken a chemical of any sort?" he asked.

"Heavens no!" said Beth.

"Are you still passing blood?"

"Yes, it hasn't stopped."

"I'm going to give you some tablets which should stop the bleeding and I want you to see me in a week."

Beth told the story to Diana.

"What did he mean asking you if you'd been taking a chemical!" Diana asked anxiously.

"I don't know what he's talking about. He's mad," said Beth.

Beth took the tablets for a week and Diana kept quizzing Beth.

"Is there *no* improvement?" Diana was getting concerned.

"Nope," said Beth casually, not wanting Diana to worry or make an issue about it.

Beth saw the surgeon again and told him the bleeding hadn't stopped.

"I'd like you to have a kidney x-ray. They'll inject a dye into your system which should show up any abnormalities," said Mr Solomon.

He looked through the papers on his desk. "Are you *sure* you haven't been taking a chemical?"

Beth thought he was round the bend. "No, I can assure you I don't make a habit of swallowing *chemicals*!" She thought his questioning so absurd, she answered with sarcastic overtones.

The x-ray didn't show anything specific and Beth was referred to a specialist physician and she was pleased to be out of the clutches of the mad surgeon. Nearly three weeks had passed since the symptoms started and her visit to the physician was brief. He phoned a urologist in Harare and made an appointment for four days later.

Beth hired a car at Harare airport and drove into the city. She liked Harare; it was more vibrant than Bulawayo but Bulawayo was home. She booked in to Meikles Hotel, a five star hotel in the city centre and ranked as one of the top ten hotels in the world.

She arrived at the specialist's rooms in the avenues the next morning and explained the problem to him.

"I'd like to do an examination under anaesthetic tomorrow morning," said Mr Tilbury.

"Well I was due to go back to Bulawayo tonight." Beth was disappointed.

"I think we should resolve your problem and I have a theatre booked for tomorrow."

"Fine," said Beth. "I'll just have to change my flight."

She drove herself to the hospital the next morning and was given a general anaesthetic lasting only twenty minutes and understood from the surgeon he would send samples to the laboratory and she should phone his rooms the following week.

Beth seemed to thrive on anaesthetics and was fully awake and rearing to go a few hours later. The staff didn't ask her if she was being collected and she didn't tell them how she was getting back to the hotel but she walked out of the hospital with her car keys in her pocket and drove back to the hotel feeling on top of the world.

"I've just phoned Mr Tilbury's rooms," Beth told Diana the following week. "They say the test was negative, whatever they were looking for, and he wants to do another examination tomorrow."

"Hasn't he given any indication what's causing the bleeding," asked Diana.

"Nope. The whole thing's crazy, but I'd better make a booking for tonight."

Beth repeated the process and spent another night at Meikles Hotel, drove to the hospital the next morning, had another examination under anaesthetic and flew back to Bulawayo that evening, having been told to wait a week for the result.

Beth had been passing a fair amount of blood in the urine for about five weeks now but had no other symptoms and felt perfectly well. She continued to manage the business and life continued as normal oblivious of what lay ahead.

Diana and Beth were in the kitchen a week later and they heard car doors slamming.

"Sounds like the girls are here," said Diana as she took a homemade sausage and egg pie from the fridge.

It was a Sunday morning and Jill, Nora and Emily were coming for lunch. It was a perfect day with not a cloud in the sky, so normal for sunny Bulawayo. They sat on the patio in their perfect setting, the swimming pool nearby with extensive lawns, rocky outcrops and plants and trees of every description as a backdrop.

"Mrs Maynard, you always put on the perfect spread," Emily told Diana as she helped herself to the food laid out on the dining room table on the bridge. It was a hot day and Diana had made a mixture of hot and cold dishes, a pie, cold chicken with salads, a scrumptious lasagne and garlic bread.

"Why don't you make a noise," Beth said to William when he sucked the end of a chicken bone. Her tone was offensive and abrupt and needless to say William didn't answer but threw the bone onto his plate and was for once, openly annoyed with Beth. There was no reason for her outburst but she was unjustifiably anti her father once again. She knew it upset Diana and that was the last thing she wanted but she couldn't stem her onslaught.

"Stop talking to your father like that." Diana sounded cross.

"Well he's just a fart," said Beth and walked into the house, hating herself for her absurdity. Jill and her friends had seen it all before and tried to shrug it off.

Diana had taken a message from the surgeon's rooms in Harare and she phoned Beth at the factory.

"Mr Tilbury wants to see you again Beth," said Diana. "Apparently the results were negative and they want to speak to you."

"Bloody hell," said Beth, "Meikles are doing well out of us. I'll phone his receptionist and find out what they want. Thanks Ma."

"Mr Tilbury wants you to have a CT scan. When can you come back to Harare?" asked his receptionist.

"Day after tomorrow?" asked Beth.

"That'll be fine. You'll have to drink a special liquid the morning of the scan so can you call at the surgery and I'll give it to you?"

Beth flew to Harare again, had the scan and returned home and was told to wait for the results. The symptoms remained the same and Beth was feeling fine. It was a mystery to everyone.

"Can't we just leave it now? Whatever it is, it'll probably disappear as quickly as it appeared." Beth was talking to Mr Tilbury's receptionist who had told her the

CT scan was clear but they wanted her back in Harare for another examination under anaesthetic.

Beth didn't win and she returned to Harare. They wheeled her into a small operating theatre and Beth saw the surgeon standing in the room.

"Hello Mr Tilbury. What sort of tests are you doing and what are you looking for?" She knew it wasn't the right time to talk to him but they never had the chance to talk.

"We've been doing what's known as a 'renal wash.' The urinary system is flushed out and the laboratory checks for any abnormalities." Mr Tilbury was obviously explaining in layman's terms.

"What are you looking for?" Beth continued her questioning as she transferred herself from the trolley to the operating table.

"Well, I've got a few ideas up my sleeve but let's have another look first."

Beth woke a few hours later in the ward, had a cup of tea and was raring to go with the routine becoming old hat to her now. She jumped in her hire car and spent the rest of the morning visiting customers in Harare assuring them she'd be visiting them in a few months time with a new range of jewellery.

Diana had an interesting message for Beth on her return to Bulawayo.

"We had a phone call from the Safari Den in Hwange yesterday and they want to see our range. They sounded very interested," said Diana.

"We've been trying to get a foot in there for years. They're very big and a good outlet. Yes, it sounds good!" said Beth. "Do you want to come with me, just for a change of scenery? Pa can look after Choo-Choo and the house," suggested Beth.

"No darling. Why don't you ask the girls to go with you but shouldn't you wait to hear from Mr Tilbury?" said Diana.

"Ugh, I'm sick and tired of going up there every five minutes. It can't be that serious and they'll only be phoning in a week or so with the results." Beth foolishly wasn't concerned with her problem.

"Phone Jill and suggest they go with you," said Diana.

"They won't come with me. They like to do their own thing. They've never asked us to go with them to the bush so why should they come with me now." Beth knew Jill too well.

"Just phone her and ask. There's no harm in asking," said Diana positively.

Beth phoned Jill that evening. "Hi Roe-Roe. Listen, I have to go to Hwange to see someone. Do you guys want to come with and perhaps we can all stay at Gwaai River?" asked Beth.

"No, we're too busy." Jill never wasted time making up her mind.

"Go on, you guys love Gwaai and Hwange. We can go at the weekend and perhaps do a bit of game viewing at Hwange as well? It could be….." Beth was cut short.

"No. Forget it. We can't come," said Jill. "Anyway, what did Tilbury say?"

"Oh, nothing, just more tests. I'll live. Don't you want to change your mind?" Beth persisted.

"*No*! Look, I've got to go. See you." When Jill made up her mind she seldom changed it.

"They won't come," Beth told Diana. "They're a pain. I know, I'll tell them the company will pay for their accommodation. Bet you they won't say no to that! Shall I suggest that to her?"

"Yes, why not. We can afford it." Diana backed her suggestion. "Give her a ring again."

"Hi Nora. Is the rodent there?"

"I think she's just gone out to the barn. Hang on Beth, I'll call her."

Beth held on for a few minutes and she heard someone pick up the receiver.

"What." Jill was in a bad mood now.

"What, what," joked Beth. "Listen, will you guys come if the company pays for your accommodation at Gwaai River?"

There was silence from Jill for a few seconds. "I don't know. I'll have to ask the others." Jill was weakening.

"Can you let me know just now?" asked Beth.

"*No way.* I'll phone you tomorrow."

Jill phoned the following evening. Diana answered the phone and Jill had a long chat with her before speaking to Beth.

"Hi. Yes, we'll come but we'll have to leave here on Saturday and be back on Sunday night," said Jill.

"That's good. I'll be able to see the buyer and we can get in a game drive. Good! It should be fun." said Beth.

Beth went to see Diana in her workshop – the kitchen. "There you are, they're coming! Probably because we're paying eh?"

"That doesn't matter darling. You'll all enjoy it." Diana never looked negatively at any situation, especially relationships, and if she did, there would be good justification. She was a sincere honest woman.

"It's the first time I've been away with all of them in over twenty years. Oh well, they've always preferred to do their own thing I suppose," said Beth.

Beth had a 4x4 pickup not suitable for carrying four passengers so they went in Emily's sedan. The girls loved the bush and had been to Gwaai River and Hwange dozens of times on their own over the years. They booked into the small family owned hotel at Gwaai River late on Saturday morning, Beth saw her buyer at the Safari Den near Hwange game reserve shortly after and secured a good sized order of jewellery.

"Right, the time's yours now," said Beth.

"Let's go to Main Camp, grab something to eat then look at game?" said Jill.

"The Nyamandhlovu pan will be worth visiting late afternoon. The elephants drink there in the afternoons." Nora knew Hwange well.

They drove through the main entrance into the reserve and through the big granite stone pillars with the thatched roof. The game are totally wild and dangerous and visitors are not allowed out of their cars except at designated areas like the Nyamandhlovu pan and it was certainly a hit and miss affair whether one saw any game at all. One just had to have a keen eye and be vigilant.

Rough dust roads meandered through the bush and elephant grass, varying in density sometimes with areas of open grassy plains. Nora and Jill were good at spotting game.

"Buffalo!" whispered Nora and pointed to a grassy area near a cluster of trees. There was a herd of about fifty beasts grazing in the mid afternoon sun, their squat horns used as landing pads for the tickbirds that were swarming ravenously about, probing the animals for bloodsucking parasites.

They drove off slowly and a few hundred yards ahead a herd of warthog crossed the road. They were on the move, apparently on a mission, the adults trotting convincingly ahead with the youngsters and babies taking up the rear, nature strangely placing them in order of size and seniority. There were eight grey scruffy animals and they stopped in the short grass and stood like statues dauntless and bold, the grizzly male snorted from beneath his dirty yellow tusks protruding from his jaws, while the progeny waited patiently and innocently in line. They were off again trotting purposefully through the short grass with eight periscope-like tails at ninety degrees, bobbing comically through the grass.

They didn't see anything for a while other than a herd of kudu with their long curly horns and waterbuck, easily identified by the light coloured ring of fur around their rump.

"Shall we go to Nyamandhlovu pan?" asked Nora.

"I'm easy," said Beth.

"The elephants should be there now," said Jill.

There were a few cars and a safari Landrover parked next to the mammoth wooden viewing platform. The pan was a natural waterhole for the animals set in a huge barren clearing of clay soil. It was barren from constant use and trampling by the destructive elephants. They climbed the steep steps to the platform and joined the tourists looking at a handful of elephants wallowing in the muddy water. Five zebras were drinking at the edge of the waterhole keeping their distance from the elephants that had taken control, nonchalantly oblivious to the other animals trying to share the water.

A lone giraffe nibbled the leaves high in a thorny acacia tree on the edge of the clearing, the dry dusty air drawing it to the water. It too drank a distance away from the delinquent elephants, sprawling its front legs to reach the water with its long neck.

Excitement flared at the waterhole. A crocodile whipped its jagged jaws out of the muddy water, the genteel zebras and giraffe frantically twisting and turning their lanky legs and fleeing to avoid the jaws of the carnivorous reptile. Two elephants looked cautiously at the crocodile, wisely left the waters edge and strolled to the edge of the clearing and sucked dust into their rubbery trunks, exhaling it over their wet bodies, content and at ease with their languid lives.

The air was still and dusty as the girls made their way back to Main Camp, the shadows lengthening across the bush in unison with the sun setting through the trees.

"Look, look!" said Jill quietly. They had turned a corner and saw a spotted cat ambling slowly into the thick grass to the right of the car. Nora stopped and turned off the engine.

"Well spotted!" whispered Nora.

"Excuse the pun," said Beth seriously.

They could just hear the rustling grass as it made its way deeper into the bush.

"Pity we didn't see it earlier. Not sure if it was a leopard or cheetah," said Nora starting the engine.

Nora and Emily shared a room and Jill and Beth had another. The hotel was old but clean and laid out in various blocks of rooms a short distance from the main building, more like a motel. Big trees with twisted gnarled branches adorned the lawns and bush beyond, while the hotel displayed colourful bougainvillea in a fine show of topiary neatly positioned around the hotel swimming pool.

They sat on the long veranda outside their rooms after supper taking in the serenity of the place, the dim hotel lights throwing ghostly shadows into the garden. They devoured copious quantities of tea and Emily spoke after a long silence.

"So what's happening about your problem Beth?"

"Ugh, I dunno. I'm waiting for more results but I'm not fazed. If I ignore it long enough, it'll go away." Beth really wasn't concerned about the blood in her urine that had been incessant now for nearly two months.

"You'd better get to the bottom of it," said big sister wisely.

Beth was woken at 4.30 the next morning by a noise. Jill was looking in her bed with a torch.

"What the hell are you doing?" asked Beth.

"I think I've eaten an earplug," said Jill seriously.

"Are you crackers? Put the light on."

Jill turned on the small light above her bed. She always wore earplugs when she slept and that night she'd put some small sugar coated jelly sweets on her bedside table.

"I dropped a few sweets in my bed earlier on and I ate them in the dark and I think my ear plug was amongst them," groaned Jill quietly.

"You're a real arse!" joked Beth.

Jill found a sweet in her bed and popped it in her mouth. She looked under the pillows and on the floor but there was no sign of her missing earplug.

"Shit," said Jill, still looking. "Hey, let's go in the kitchen and I'll cook everyone egg and bacon." Jill was a superb cook and loved cooking on the open fire when the three went camping.

"We can't just go in the kitchen and anyway, everything will be locked up now," said Beth.

"Nora and I know the owners. We've done it before and they won't mind. I know where they keep the key at night. Come, let's go!" Jill was serious with her suggestion.

"Hmm, you cook lovely fried eggs. OK, I'm game."

They slipped on their shorts and T-shirts and went along the narrow dimly lit pathways in the garden towards the kitchen in the main building. Jill knew where everything was and in no time had a pan full of bacon sizzling on the gas stove. Jill was so comical at times, a real clown and the two sisters had a good rapport. Beth wished she knew Jill better and saw her more often but she had her life with Nora and Emily, and although Diana, William and Beth were family, they were secondary in her life and that's how Jill wanted it.

Beth answered the phone. It was Mr Tilbury's receptionist.

"We've had your results back Miss Maynard. They have found cancerous cells and Mr Tilbury needs to remove your right kidney."

"Oh that's great," said Beth casually.

The receptionist was keen to continue. "Mr Tilbury is going away in a weeks time and he'd like to do it on Friday."

It wasn't what Beth was expecting. "Can I think about it?"

"He's anxious to get it done and you shouldn't delay it," explained the receptionist.

Diana wanted to accompany Beth to Harare but she wanted to go it alone and Diana reluctantly agreed she'd fly to Harare a few days after the operation.

Beth woke momentarily with someone wiping her arm with a flannel. She looked around the room and saw other beds and patients and she knew she wasn't in her private ward.

A nurse spoke to Beth. "You've had your operation and you're in Intensive Care."

When Beth woke again she was back in her ward and Sarah, an old family friend, came in and sat in a chair next to the bed. The sunlight from the window behind Sarah irritated Beth and she closed her eyes and it was evening when she woke again with a nurse fiddling with the saline drip. Beth was a wiry sturdy individual with an indelible heavy-duty air about her, the concept of hospitals and infirmity a fervent abhorrence to her. She was now, fortuitously, oblivious to the copious volumes of pipes, tubes and drains dangling repulsively about her, justifiably unwilling, at least in Beth's preposterous opinion, to have Diana observe her in that reduced state.

"Hi Ma, Hi Molly," Beth was sitting in a chair and greeted Diana and her friend as they came in her room.

"Hello darling." Diana gave Beth a kiss.

"Molly's just collected me from the airport and we came straight here. How are you darling?"

"It's my first day out of bed. Yup, I'm fine." Beth gave the standard Maynard answer. She was strong physically and emotionally, except when it came to her father. "Tilbury did two operations on me apparently and chopped out something in the bladder region as well, but I'm fine. How are *you*?"

Beth was out of hospital on the seventh day and they had a room at Meikles Hotel for the day before flying back to Bulawayo in the evening. She told Diana she was fine but in reality was in a lot of pain, Diana obviously aware of it by the way she walked. She hated displaying her feelings to Diana, that old enigma still dogging her.

Beth was up late the next morning and Diana had a message for her.

"The office called earlier with a problem and they want you to phone them."

"Hmm, no peace for the wicked," said Beth. She made the call and although the problem was resolved she wanted to visit the factory and see everyone.

After lunch Beth told Diana where she was going.

"You can't drive," Diana told her.

"I'll be fine Ma. I'm not pushing the car, just driving it. It'll be alright, I promise," Beth assured her.

"You have to think of all the stitches and repairs *under* the skin. It's too soon to drive. Let me take you," said Diana.

Beth was as stubborn as a mule and wanted her freedom. "No Ma. I'll drive carefully."

"What if you have to brake suddenly or take evasive action?"

Beth wouldn't listen to Diana's wise advice and took the car. She had driven barely a hundred yards and she realised how right Diana had been. Every bump, every movement gave excruciating pain on her right side but she was determined to drive to the factory six miles away. She didn't realise how many muscles were used just steadying the body on a bend in the road and she had to hang on to the car door with her right hand and steer with her left to steady her torso and reduce the pain.

Diana stood on the patio when she arrived home. "Every picture tells a story," said Diana sympathetically. Beth was walking very slowly and gingerly.

"OK, you were right. That was bloody painful."

"You're a naughty girl. Come inside and sit down," said Diana. Beth obeyed her for once.

The following day Beth felt awful and stayed in bed, which was quite out of character and it transpired she had an acute infection with a temperature of 102°F, apparently put down to her pig-headedness the day before. Diana wasted no time in phoning the specialist and an antibiotic knocked it on the head in a few days.

There was a lot of work to do at the factory and Beth realised, reluctantly, that she had to take it easy for a while and let everything heal. William did a sales round for the company and enjoyed every minute and secured above average sales, William believing customers had taken a sympathetic approach to Beth's situation and immobility.

Jill was very good and agreed to take a few weeks unpaid leave and took over Beth's role.

They were doing very well and Beth was pleased she was able to assist her parents, not to say they wouldn't have managed on their own. They would merely have downsized their lives, moved into something smaller and would no doubt have managed quite amiably without Beth, but they were all able to remain in their house with the lovely garden that gave them such serenity except when Beth unleashed her vile tongue on William.

A few months passed and Beth went on another sales trip around the country. Their sales were particularly good having incorporated the Christmas period as well and things were looking quite rosy for the company.

"I saw an advert in the paper today. The Elephant Hills Hotel is putting on an extravaganza with overseas artists and I'd like you and Pa to see it and stay there over a weekend. I'm forever going to the Falls and I thought it would be nice for you to go for a change," suggested Beth, as she wondered around the garden with Diana. It never bored them and it was a truly beautiful haven.

"Oh I don't know. You know we're quite happy to stay here. I'll discuss it with your father," said Diana.

They were both happy to go to Victoria Falls and Jill went with Beth to Bulawayo airport to see them off.

Beth rattled around the house on her own that night with only Choo-Choo for company. She sat in the sitting room and watched TV but Choo-Choo look disturbed.

"What's the matter my baby? Where's granny and grandpa?"

Choo-Choo looked hard at Beth and gave a quiet meow as though she understood. She jumped on Beth's lap and kneaded her arm, consoling herself.

The following evening Beth was locking up the house, preparing for bed when the phone rang. It was nearly 11 o'clock and she wondered who it could be, unaware that the news she was about to get would change their lives forever.

"Hello Beth." It was William. He would never ring her out of the blue in the middle of the night and Beth wondered why in heavens name he was phoning her.

"Hi Pa," said Beth, waiting to hear what he had to say.

"Your Ma has had an accident," said William quietly.

"What's happened?" Beth envisaging a car accident.

"She fell at the hotel and we think she's broken her leg. She's in the hospital here."

Beth's heart pounded and she felt a rush of blood to her head. "How is she? What are they doing for her? How did it happen?" Beth was full of questions.

"She went to the loo before the show started and she slipped and fell on the floor. I've just left her and I'm back at the hotel. She's comfortable and they'll have her flown back to Bulawayo on the next flight tomorrow. They haven't got x-ray facilities here but the doc. is sure it's broken."

"I just can't believe this. Are you sure she's all right?"

"Yes cock. She was talking to me and insisted I come back to the hotel. I'll see her in the morning and fly back with her," said William.

"Alright Pa. I'll see you tomorrow."

It's All Just Nuts

Beth couldn't believe what she had heard and wondered around the house in a daze. She thought about driving up to the Falls there and then. She could be with Diana in four or five hours. Perhaps she should send a private ambulance up there from Bulawayo but that would mean an uncomfortable journey for her by road. Beth didn't know what to do. She couldn't sleep and paced the house and at 3 o'clock she decided to phone the Victoria Falls hospital to enquire how she was.

The hospital staff said Diana was awake. They must have told her who was on the phone.

"I'm so sorry darling," were Diana's first words to Beth.

"No Ma darling, it's not your fault, don't worry. How are you feeling?"

"I'm alright. I'm just so sorry to have done this to you." Diana sounded strong and was concerned for Beth.

"Don't worry Ma-Ma darling. It's *my* fault for letting you go up there." Beth was feeling devastated.

"They say they'll fly me back on a stretcher tomorrow."

"OK Ma. I'll be at the airport to meet you. Now don't worry. Just relax and try and get some sleep," said Beth.

"I'm alright. I promise. Don't *you* worry."

Beth stood on the balcony at Bulawayo airport and saw an ambulance on the apron, beside herself and in disbelief that it was waiting there for Diana. She saw the Boeing in the distance reducing altitude as it neared the airport. It seemed to be coming in fast and a puff of smoke flew up from the tyres as it hit the runway, it bounced off the ground for a second and hit the runway again. "Shit.

Bum landing," said Beth out loud to herself hoping Diana hadn't experienced any pain.

The staff brought her down the aircraft steps on a stretcher and put her in the ambulance. So near and yet so far; Beth wanted to go down there and see her but it was a restricted area. Ambulance staff were attending to Diana for about ten minutes but Beth wasn't able see what they were doing and she decided to wait at the exit to the apron area where she might be able to see her when they leave.

She waited another anxious five minutes until the ambulance eventually appeared. She waved it down and went straight to the partially open sliding window on the side of the ambulance and saw Diana lying inside.

"What were they doing to you in the ambulance?" queried Beth.

"Putting a splint on my leg," said Diana.

"I'll follow you to the hospital," said Beth as the ambulance drove away.

Diana was in hospital for a week and seemed to recover quite quickly after the operation to insert a pin in her upper leg to repair the break. Margaret, Diana's oldest daughter, arrived for a visit from South Africa whilst she was still in hospital and everyone thought Margaret's arrival boosted Diana's recovery. To everyone's dismay, Margaret had to return to South Africa before Christmas and Jill had made Christmas arrangements with Nora and Emily, leaving Diana, William and Beth spending Christmas Day on their own.

As Beth wrote out her messages on the parcel labels for Diana and William her usual fear came to the fore but stronger than ever before, her fear that it might be the last time she'd write her Christmas message to them. They weren't getting any younger with William at 78 and Diana 74 and she perished the thought of them dying, especially Diana.

Diana's accident hit her harder than any of them realised because she just wasn't the same again. She walked with a limp and lost a fair amount of weight. She was never again the strong vibrant woman she had always been. Diana knew Beth had a strong bond with her and Diana was concerned about the consequences when she did eventually die and the impact it would have on Beth. Her accident made everyone more aware of life and death and Diana would try and lessen the blow on Beth by telling her she wouldn't be around forever.

Diana was also concerned with Beth's attitude to her father and Diana dreaded the thought of dying before William and the consequential torture the two would go through without her being there for both of them. The pain she encountered after the operation and probably those concerns she had for her family all took their toll on Diana's health and she had to contend with high blood pressure and then emphysema. Although they both had a little while to go, Diana was always of the opinion that when one reached 80 that would be the end of the line and ones health would decline after that age. She had seen it happen countless times to many of her older friends and it was her true belief.

It took nearly nine months before Diana felt sufficiently strong enough to agree to go on holiday with William to visit Barbara and her husband in South Africa. They were looking forward to their holiday having had a rough road during the year with Diana's ups and downs in her health. Diana was to accompany William to the bank one morning to get their travellers cheques for the holiday and as she walked down the steps of the patio to go to the car she lost her balance and fell to the ground, falling on her right leg, the leg she had broken nine months earlier.

Diana didn't break anything but after that second fall she suffered a great deal of pain in the region of her original break and didn't feel well enough to go on holiday and everything was cancelled. She consumed painkillers almost continuously after her second fall and despite numerous visits to the specialist nothing eased the pain.

Beth helped as much as she could and helped with her bathing until she felt strong enough to manage on her own but even so she couldn't get up from the sitting position in the bath. Bathing aids weren't available on the market and Beth found a small heavy-duty plastic container that was placed in the bath as a seat, not ideal but the best they could do in the circumstances.

William and Beth were very aware of Diana's slow down and it worried them constantly. She spent a lot of her time sitting in her chair on the bridge and Beth tried to interest her in the garden or encourage her to invite her friends for a dinner party, the things she loved to do so much but Diana wasn't interested. She seemed not to have the strength and the pain got her down.

Diana was willing to have Jill, Nora and Emily for meals but one day Jill declined an invitation and then all subsequent invites and they never came to have a meal with the family again. Diana and William never said anything but it must have hurt them. Beth, as forward as she was, tried to get to the bottom of it and wanted to know who out of Jill, Nora and Emily was unwilling to take up the invitations. In a lot of ways they were in a world of their own and despite Beth's many visits to them she often felt like an outsider. Beth asked Jill a number of times why they had declined Diana's invitations and Jill would give a vague excuse. When Beth still queried the excuses Jill told Beth they were too embarrassed with Beth's rudeness towards William. Beth knew Jill could be dishonest in so many little ways and she believed Jill had used that as an excuse for some other reason. Jill still visited the family on her own but without Nora and Emily.

Although William owned the house Beth financed a number of improvements to the property and over the years extended a high stone granite wall around the property and had the driveway paved, including parts of the garden near the house, adding to the charm of the location.

Diana and William mentioned many times over the years that they intended leaving their house and possessions to their three girls. Beth willingly financed the improvements to the property knowing that one day it would be to the benefit of Margaret, Jill and herself although Beth asked her parents on a few occasions to consider a fifty percent share to herself and the remaining half in equal shares between her two sisters and they were in agreement.

Diana and William never envisaged or realised the consequences of their wishes and undoubtedly they would not have expected and certainly would not have wished or intended that their house or possessions might inadvertently wind up with a beneficiary not of their choice. Despite Beth's closeness to her parents and their belief in justice, such a scenario was not discussed or anticipated and Diana and William were never to know the mental anguish Beth was to encounter as circumstances unfolded.

Over several months Jill had suffered pain in the abdomen and was being treated for a stomach ulcer. She was very committed to her work and despite the pain would still go to work but it took a toll on her strength and health. It was discovered many months later that she had gallstones and Jill was advised to have an operation. Beth finished work late on the day of Jill's admission but went to the hospital to wish her well for the operation the following day. Nora and Emily were visiting Jill and Beth couldn't understand why the two friends were so surprised to see Beth. She often wondered why they took that approach only to assume there had been some unjustified conniving disparagement between the two, recalling their refusal to accept invitations to the house. Beth thought this was treacherous.

Jill managed the operation well and despite having a drain tube in the wound, she joked with Beth on her visits and they would go onto the veranda to have a cigarette, Jill carrying her draining apparatus with her. She was a breath of fresh air for Beth and had so much spunk in comparison to Diana and Beth so wished Diana had been like that.

The business continued to grow, Beth travelling to the tourist resorts and committed at the factory and William involved with chores and errands for the business and for Diana. Diana's accident had brought Beth closer to her father for a while but her rudeness reared its head again and it became par for the course.

Beth was standing on a high wall in the garden one Saturday afternoon cutting back a bush and removing a creeper when she lost her balance and fell. She knew she was going and could do nothing about it but managed to land upright and on her feet. She suffered excruciating pain in her right foot and sat on a low stonewall in the garden devastated by the pain and as usual was reluctant to show her feelings to Diana, preferring to retain her image as the tough tomboy. The pain forced her to abandon any further work and hopped inside on one foot.

"What have you done," exclaimed Diana, when she saw Beth in her moment of weakness struggling to walk.

"I lost my balance and fell off the wall at the back of the house." Beth sat in a chair on the bridge with Diana. "Shit it's painful," Beth had to admit.

"I'll get you a couple of painkillers."

"I'm a real wimp. Thanks Ma," said Beth as she took the pills and glass of water from Diana. "You've been through so much and I fall on my foot and I'm whining like a drip."

An x-ray at Diana's insistence revealed the bones in the heel had been cracked and the foot and lower leg were immobilised with a plaster cast much to Beth's annoyance and not to be housebound or reliant on anyone she managed to drive safely even with the cast in place.

A week later Beth had a call from a customer at Victoria Falls complaining about the quality of a few pieces of jewellery. She couldn't understand what could have happened due to their high standard of workmanship.

Beth spoke to Diana and William about it in the evening. "I think I'd better go and see them."

"Are you going to fly?" asked William.

"The flight goes on to Harare and not back here so I'll go up by car," said Beth.

"You *can't* drive all that way with your foot like that," Diana said adamantly. "Anyway, ask them to return the goods."

"No." Beth had made up her mind. "It'll be a good bit of PR if I see them personally. They're really pissed off and I want to soothe their feathers."

"Well let me come with you then," said Diana. She really wasn't up to it but wanted to see Beth would be alright.

"I'll be OK Ma, I promise."

Diana got up and went to the kitchen. "You're as stubborn as a mule."

"You, Pa and Jill are Taurus's and I'm just following in your footsteps," joked Beth.

Beth *was* concerned about driving for nearly five hours with her foot and ankle in plaster and then there was the return journey too and she wondered how uncomfortable it would be but she'd made up her mind to go and nothing would change it.

Victoria Falls was at least ten degrees hotter than Bulawayo and being in the Zambezi Valley it was often humid and could be uncomfortable. Beth was about fifty miles from the Falls and her foot was already aching, a dull throbbing pain like a nagging toothache that wouldn't go away. It was hot and it felt as though her foot was on fire and she was mesmerized at the thought of dipping her foot in a bucket of cold water.

She drove in to the Sprayview Motel car park and was frustrated at having to climb the steps to the reception area on her crutches. She was a tough individual, wearing her khaki safari shorts, a cool T-shirt and a leather sandal on her left foot. She was tanned and wiry and combed her fingers through her short hair to lift it off her wet forehead. She looked at the steps and knew how she could run up them two at a time but she fiddled with the crutches and limped up the steps one by one. "Damn and blast," she muttered out loud to herself.

"Hello Miss Maynard," the receptionist greeted Beth. "Oh my goodness, what has happened to you?" he asked. Staff gathered around Beth to show their commiseration and enquire what happened. They talked and joked for too long and Beth was glad to get to her room and put her foot up for a while.

After resting for half an hour she was ready to go again and drove down to the village to see their customer. She walked into his shop and was met with that familiar mingled smell she loved so much, the pleasing aroma of leather, reed basket-ware and polished woodcarvings. Despite the heat the shop had no air conditioning and the ceiling fan had little effect as it flew around circulating the hot air.

"Hello Mr Van Lukan!" Beth greeted their unhappy customer. He always made large purchases and Beth had to look after him. She had to explain to him too why she resembled a war zone relic.

"Now you've made me feel very guilty," said Mr Van Lukan. "You mean you've come all this way just to sort out my complaint!" he exclaimed.

"Good, I'm pleased you're feeling guilty!" said Beth and continued. "I'm only joking. If a customer has a complaint about our quality I take it very seriously and that's why I'm here."

"Well I'm very impressed Miss Maynard and I do appreciate it. Can I show you what you sent us?"

"Yes, please do."

Mr Van Lukan took Beth through to their stockroom and showed her the poor quality jewellery.

Beth took one look at the pieces he showed her and knew something had gone horribly wrong. "These are rejects and I really don't know how they went out with your order and I can only apologise and assure you it won't happen again. If we have any in stock we'll replace them immediately if not we'll make up a special order for you."

"As a gesture of my appreciation for your effort I'm going to double our order and I'd like to repeat it again for another delivery next month."

"That's great! Thanks very much." Beth was ecstatic.

Beth had the rest of the day free to make unexpected PR visits to customers and in so doing obtained additional orders, which she assumed was probably 'compassionate buying' but nevertheless very welcome and unexpected.

Outside one of the shops was a traditional African grass hut with a large wooden board leaning against the side of it. Primitive lettering in hideous bright colours, painted seemingly with a tar brush and thick oil paint, caught Beth's eye. 'Have your fortune told by a genuine Nyanga.' Beth was a horror when it came to fortune telling and she would often ask Diana to read her teacup. She'd never been to a Nyanga before. There's a first time for everything she thought. She was swearing at the plaster cast on her ankle as she hobbled across to the grass hut on her crutches, her skin burning under the plaster and as she neared the small opening in the hut she looked inside. She peered hard into the darkness and as her eyes adjusted she made out a figure sitting in the middle of the small round hut.

"Yebo sir!" came a deep voice from the darkness.

Here we go she thought. "No, I'm not a *sir!*" replied Beth jokingly. She knew she really needed to grow her hair or wear pigtails with ribbons.

She heard movement in the hut and the figure got up and came outside. An old man with a protruding round bare belly looked at Beth and beamed at her, his white teeth contrasted against his black shiny face. He clapped his hands together slowly, a greeting gesture in African custom.

"Yebo madam!" The old man corrected himself, beaming from ear to ear.

"Yebo Baba," replied Beth clapping her hands gently and calling him 'father,' a traditional sign of respect. "You can tell my fortune?" asked Beth.

"Yes, yes," said the old witch doctor, wearing leopard skin draped loosely over his shoulders and around his waist and a hat made from some poor animal that Beth couldn't identify. "Come inside."

Beth had to bend down to enter the narrow doorway and avoid the thatched overhang of the roof. It smelt smoky and musty inside and as Beth's eyes adjusted to the semi-darkness she saw a reed mat on one side of the floor and the old man invited Beth to sit on the mat and he sat opposite her with a well worn hard mud floor between them. A small pile of unidentifiable objects were positioned in the middle of the floor and as the witch doctor picked them up Beth realised they were small animal bones and he was to literally throw the bones to tell her fortune.

The Nyanga shook the bones vigorously in his clasped hands making a monotonous humming sound and gave a deep grunt as he threw the bones on the hard mud floor.

"You will go far away to another country but you will come back here."

The witch doctor shook the bones, hummed again and his body shook as he grunted and threw the bones. He moved the bones around with his forefinger, beads of sweat appearing on his face. He spoke again. "You will meet someone in the far away country but he won't be good. You will come back alone."

Thank heavens for that thought Beth, cherishing her single life and freedom. The little hut was hot and stuffy and she could feel the perspiration running down her chest.

"Do you have any questions?" asked the Nyanga.

Beth was hoping he'd ask and she had a specific question. "Do you see any illness for my parents or are they going to be well?"

The old man repeated the process and threw the bones. He moved them around with his fingers for a long time and said, "Right now they're not too good but they live a long time."

"That's good!" said Beth hearing the news she wanted to hear. Beth had to ask the Nyanga for a hand up, pleased to hobble outside into the cooler air.

She drove back to Bulawayo the next day and went home past the specialist's surgery. The skin was itching under the plaster from the heat and perspiration and the discomfort was driving her mad. She insisted he cut off the cast, which he did and assured her it would be alright providing she didn't walk heavily on the heel for a few weeks.

When Beth got home Diana had some news for her.

"Jill came around yesterday and told us about a freckle on her leg which has got bigger. She's been to see a surgeon and he's going to remove it next week. Poor Jilly, she's had one thing after another," said Diana.

"You're not doing too badly yourself Ma-Ma. You've both been in the wars," said Beth. "Everything seems to be going wrong, hey?"

"None of us are getting any younger darling." Diana always looked at things logically. "We're not going to be around forever."

"I'll pop off before any of you," said Beth.

"I wouldn't be too sure about that. You'll miss me when I'm gone," said Diana.

"You'll miss me when *I'm* gone!" Beth hated the thought of losing Diana. "Anyway, I went to a witch doctor at the Falls the other day and he said you'd both live for a long time."

"You didn't waste your money on that did you? They talk a lot of mumbo jumbo." Diana got up from her usual chair on the bridge. She had lost a lot of weight and still walked with a limp. It upset Beth to see her like that and she cherished the prospect of her getting well and strong again. She looked at Choo-Choo lying on the lawn in the shade of a pot plant, blissfully unaware of the changes talking place with the family and Beth pondered about her life and where it would take her. She knew Diana was right about the Nyanga but hoped his prediction was right.

Beth visited Jill every day in hospital. "Ma sends her love and said she's sorry she can't come and see you. She's not feeling strong enough."

"That's OK," said Jill. "She hasn't been well since her fall. Pa came in this morning which was nice."

"So tell me. What's happening with you?" asked Beth.

"I told you what the surgeon said, didn't I?" Jill was a bit confused with the sequence of events.

"What?" asked Beth.

"That freckle was malignant – a melanoma. Do you know what a melanoma is?" asked Jill.

"Well, a cancerous growth isn't it?"

"Yeah, but they say it's the most aggressive form of cancer," said Jill quietly, "but he tells me he's got it all."

"Is it covered up?" asked Beth.

Jill looked soulfully at Beth and pulled back the blankets and exposed her skinny suntanned leg with a dry dressing just above her left knee.

"Why are you looking so worried, come on you big fart, where's your usual spunk?" Beth tried to make light of Jill's concern.

Nora and Emily came in to Jill's private ward and Beth greeted them and went onto the veranda to have a cigarette. Jill joined her minutes later with her two friends, limping, her left leg bent. Like Beth, Jill was wiry and strong but Beth thought she'd lost too much weight.

Beth visited Jill regularly at home after her operation and she regained her strength and went back to work. Beth continued with her business, working long hours and helped Diana in the house. Life seemed to be boring for Beth and she knew she was under Diana and William's feet.

"Why don't you go out and meet new friends?" asked Diana. They were having their Saturday afternoon tea on the patio. Beth, as usual, had been ridiculing William and she knew it upset Diana.

"*You* never go out and that old fart just pisses me off." Beth was ridiculing her father again.

"We're quite happy as we are," said Diana. "You're bored stiff and you've got nothing better to do than attack your father."

"Do you blame me. He's just a big nerd." Beth was wearing a short pair of denim shorts and had her bare feet up on the chair with her teacup resting on her knee. She was looking at the swimming pool and ignored her father sitting next to Diana.

Diana was upset and frustrated at Beth's persistent nagging at William. "I just hope I don't go first. I hate the thought of you two left together. Your father will be 80 next year so just show a little respect please," said poor Diana.

"That's a new one. What's a 'nerd'?" asked William jokingly, changing the subject.

Beth wasn't particularly annoyed but just felt like poking fun at her father. "You. You're a nerd, an idiot." Beth felt like a fool sometimes talking to her father like that but she couldn't help herself and didn't seem to care. She got up and went back to the lawn mower on the lawn. She put her bare foot on its base to steady it and pulled hard on the cord to start the petrol engine. It didn't start. She pulled again on the cord but the engine didn't respond. She kept pulling but the engine wouldn't turn over. She waited a moment and gave a good long pull and the engine spluttered into life but died again.

"*Pa!*" called Beth. She knew she was such a beast to her father and although it may well have hurt him, he was gentlemanly enough to shrug it off and she knew he was always there to help her.

William got his toolbox from the car and went over to Beth, still pulling unsuccessfully on the cord.

"Hang on my girl, you'll flood it. Let me have a look." Poor William was always willing and helpful despite the way she treated him and deep down she loved him for that. Beth left him to it and went back to Diana for another cup of tea. Nearly ten minutes later Beth heard the engine burst into life and it turned over gently. "Good, it's fixed," Beth said to Diana.

"Thank you!" Beth shouted above the sound of the engine.

Diana stood on the edge of the patio looking at the lawn. They had had good rains and it was looking particularly green; the rocks, paved paths and rose drums enhancing the neatly mowed lawn.

"Shall we cut some roses?" Beth wanted to entice Diana into the garden. She never went outside anymore, except for visits to the doctor.

"No, not now." Diana seemed so reluctant to venture into the garden now and it upset Beth to see her slowing.

They heard the phone ringing and Diana limped inside but William had answered it.

He talked for a few minutes and Diana knew he was talking to Barbara. Diana stood next to him waiting for him to finish and he handed her the phone.

"Hello Barbara darling! Yes, I'm getting stronger by the day but still in a lot of pain."

Beth went to the kitchen and listened to one side of the conversation.

"That would be lovely, yes, lovely to see you. Oh I don't know Barbara. I don't know if I could manage it. Yes I suppose so, if I took it easy."

Beth was itching to know what she was talking about and as soon as she put the phone down she asked Diana what it was all about.

"Barbara and John are coming up next month and they want Dad and I to go with them to Vic Falls for a little holiday," said Diana.

"Hmm, you and Vic Falls don't go together. Where will you stay?" asked Beth.

"They've got a time-share. There I suppose. It'll only be for a few days apparently," said Diana.

"You deserve a holiday but you'll have to be extra, extra careful not to fall again Ma-Ma," said Beth.

"That's what I was concerned about but Barbara assured me she'd look after me!" joked Diana. William came in the kitchen and Beth left and she heard Diana putting the proposition of the brief holiday to him.

Barbara and John came up to Bulawayo from South Africa and they drove Diana and William to the Falls. Beth was very apprehensive and although Diana had got marginally better, she wasn't right by any means and another fall would have grave consequences and everyone knew that.

Beth went to visit Jill. She spent a lot of time in the barn and seemed to be on her own a lot with Nora and Emily spending time together in the main house but Jill seemed happy with that arrangement. Beth felt sorry for Jill in a lot of ways and thought she was lonely but Jill was content with her own company.

Beth went straight to the barn assuming Jill would be in there. "Hi Roe-Roe." Beth called out to her at the door.

"Hi," came Jill's voice from the barn and Jill's Rottweiler, Angie gave a greeting bark.

Beth sat on Emily's bed. "What are you doing?" asked Beth casually. Angie was whimpering with excitement and Beth made much of her.

Jill was sitting on her bed writing on a sheet of paper. She was often wrapped up in herself as though deep in thought and would often ignore Beth, or anyone else for that matter, when someone spoke to her.

Beth looked at her as she wrote. "Hey?" Beth reminded her.

"What?" asked Jill casually, still not looking at Beth.

"What you do – ing." Beth was messing around to attract Jill's attention.

"The household budget," said Jill, still writing on her piece of paper.

Jill and Emily paid most of the household bills and they paid the rates and upkeep for a few years whilst Nora fiddled with her partly successful business despite Nora owning the house. Beth knew that Emily and Jill had asked Nora for a part ownership of the house because of the money they were putting in to it but it never happened.

"Chancellor of the Exchequer eh?" Beth knew the conversation wasn't going anywhere but it was the normal chat between the two of them.

"Ah ha," said Jill.

"The folks are coming back tomorrow," said Beth and patted Angie.

There was no response from Jill but Beth knew she was listening.

"I'm really worried about Ma. She's not well and I'm terrified she'll fall again."

Jill was still writing and Beth sat on the bed, quietly contented with Jill's company. They were like the terrible twins in their T-shirts, Bermuda shorts and leather sandals.

"They're old now," said Jill quietly.

"No they're not." Beth didn't want to accept it.

Jill didn't respond for a while. "Pa's 80 next year and Ma's 75 now."

"So? They've got a long way to go," said Beth, still watching Jill writing.

Jill put her pen and sheet of paper down on the bed. Angie was standing next to the bed looking at Jill and wagging her tailless rump. "Hello puppy." Angie was a whopping great three year old Rotweiller but Jill called her 'puppy.'

"Have you finished?" asked Beth.

"No, not yet," said Jill yawning. "Do you want to see something?"

"What?" asked Beth enjoying Jill's company.

"Look." Jill pointed to the three inch scar from the operation to remove the malignant freckle.

"What?" asked Beth and sat next to Jill on her bed looking at her scar. "What?" giggled Beth.

"There's a lump under the scar," said Jill.

"Oh come off it Jill, it can't be!" said Beth.

"Feel." Jill took Beth's finger and put it on the scar.

Beth felt a distinct lump under the scar. "So what does that mean?"

"He didn't get it all out and it's growing again," said Jill casually. "I don't want you to tell the folks. Ma's got enough on her plate."

"Blast the bastard. Shit Jill." Beth was concerned and annoyed at the surgeon's blunder. "What now?"

"I suppose I should have it looked at but Emily wants to go to South Africa in a few months and I might wait until we come back. Are you listening? I don't want you to tell them," said Jill.

"I wish you'd be honest with them, but OK I won't tell them if that's what you want but you should have it looked at chop-chop Jill," said Beth.

"I'll see. I might have it done before then. Bad news eh?" said Jill.

"I hope not." Beth was quiet for a few seconds. "Are you coming for Christmas?" she asked, changing the subject.

Jill didn't answer and Beth knew that was a good sign.

Everyone sighed with relief when Diana and William came home in one piece. Diana was unsteady on her feet and there was a real fear of her falling again. Beth was so accustomed to dashing around the house at full pace, she had to make a concerted effort to slow down in fear of bumping into her and knocking her over. Diana was so thin now and getting quite fragile.

Beth had such mixed feelings about this particular Christmas that was just around the corner. They loved and cherished the festive season but this year Beth was apprehensive, trying desperately to shove the resurgence of her annual fears behind her but the gut wrenching thoughts kept haunting her, ricocheting around in her mind.

Diana wanted to have her hair done and Beth and William drove her to town and parked near the hairdresser. It was only a short walk to the shop but it seemed to take her forever to walk the short distance, Beth holding her as she limped along the pavement.

She looked a hundred times better with her hair in a neat perm but she looked pale and tired when William and Beth went to fetch her. To their dismay Diana found it difficult to walk to the car and the hairdresser brought a sturdy chair onto the pavement for Diana and she was carried in the chair like an African queen to the waiting car. It was a horrific experience for them as they recalled how Diana had, just a few years earlier, been so strong and vibrant, dashing around her garden and her beloved Bulawayo.

They were pleased Jill joined them for Christmas Day and Beth wondered if Jill shared her thoughts although they never discussed them. Beth as usual showered them with gifts and it crossed her mind occasionally if she did it out of a sense of guilt but she had a genuine deep love for her parents and she always dispelled such a morbid concept. She gave Diana and William a pedicure one evening over Christmas, her oblique way of showing her love and concern for them, something compelling her to lavish as much affection upon them as she could.

At the end of January Beth was off on another sales trip, this time flying on a round trip from Bulawayo to Victoria Falls then to Harare and back to Bulawayo. It was such a regular occurrence now she'd drive herself to the airport and leave the car there and drive herself home when she returned, saving Diana and William the upheaval of travelling to the airport.

Victoria Falls from the air was spectacular, the massive expanse of the dark Zambezi River shimmered sporadically like pieces of quicksilver in the bright crisp afternoon sun then burst into a white cascading sheet over the mighty chasm and into the narrow gorge. The bulbous mountain of spray hung majestic and proud along the length of the gorge, appearing lifeless and still in sympathy with the ageless wonder below it.

Beth gazed out the port window of the aircraft as it headed southeast to Harare, hypnotized by the sights below which she'd seen so often but never ceased to astonish her.

"Excuse me." A voice brought her thoughts back into the 'plane. "Would you like something to drink?" asked a wide smiled airhostess.

"Yes, thank you. A Lion Lager please." Beth seldom drank at home but enjoyed a sundowner on her business trips.

The strong African sun was hot on Beth's arm and she revelled in it. She was mesmerised by the desolate arid bush lying in grand silence as far as the eye could see, beautiful in its remoteness yet that deep sense of enjoyment was not the same this time. A dark cloud hung low over her, nagging incessantly, enveloping her deepest thoughts.

Beth phoned home every day whenever she was away and she spoke to Diana on her last night at Meikles Hotel. She was pleased Diana sounded well and assured her she'd be home the next day.

William was standing in the garden when Beth arrived home and he approached her when she got out of the car. She momentarily thought it unusual but what he had to say was urgent. He was round shouldered and appeared dejected and wasted no time in speaking to Beth.

"Hello my girl. Your Ma had a fall last night."

Beth felt a deep hollow inside her, a deep swirling horror engulfed her. It was something she never wanted to hear. "Where is she?" asked Beth.

"She's in hospital. She broke her left leg this time. They operated today and put a pin in the leg." William was talking quietly and was as devastated as Beth.

Beth couldn't believe what she was hearing. It was worse than a nightmare. "How is she? How did it happen?"

"I was with her this afternoon. She's alright but sleepy." William was trying to be strong and was managing well. They were a strong family, strong physically and emotionally and they never burst into tears at the drop of a hat. They all shared the same problem, hiding their innermost feelings. Beth never cried and would let things build up inside, a trait she inherited from her parents.

"What happened?" asked Beth again.

"She was standing in the sitting room last night and turned around to do something and fell over. It all happened in seconds. Your Ma insisted we didn't call anyone last night so I got her into her chair and she sat there for the night. I called the doctor this morning and he called an ambulance."

"But that's crazy. Why didn't you get her to the hospital last night?" asked Beth.

"Your Ma was adamant we didn't call anyone."

"I'm going to see her," said Beth and returned to the car.

Beth hated hospitals and especially when she was visiting family. She found Diana's ward and went in. She was sharing a ward and she knew Diana always preferred a private ward. Beth went up to her bed. She was awake but she looked wan and different and gave Beth a little smile.

"Hi Ma," said Beth sympathetically and hugged her, burying her face in Diana's pillow. "You weren't supposed to do that. *Why* didn't you call the doctor last night?"

"Oh darling, it all happened so quickly. I was going off to bed and got up from my chair, turned around to straighten the cushion and in a split second I was on the floor. Dad got me into the chair again. I just didn't want to worry the doctor."

"But Ma, that's what they're there for. Is the surgeon happy with everything?"

"I think so. It was my left leg this time." Diana sounded tired.

"Oh Ma. Why this. You were battling to get well again from the last fall."

Beth stayed with her for a long time but she saw she was tired.

William had cooked supper when Beth got home. They barely spoke, not from Beth's awkwardness towards her father, but it was just their way of handling their dreadful ordeal, a way of commiserating with each other.

William and Beth visited Diana twice a day, each under their own steam during her five days in hospital. Beth thought she was being discharged far too soon as she was very weak and had great difficulty in walking. She insisted on walking along the pathway at home and pulled herself up the steps onto the patio, using the handrail specially installed for her.

It's All Just Nuts

Diana spent the next two days in her chair unable to get into her kitchen, her 'workshop.' Beth noticed Diana's left leg was swollen and called the doctor. He suspected a thrombosis and immediately had her re-admitted to hospital. She had her own room this time and she looked far happier.

"You look very bright today," said Beth as she walked into her room. She gave Diana a kiss.

"I feel much better today thank you darling. I hope to be home in a day or two."

"Don't be in too much of a hurry, just get yourself right first. Have you done any walking today?"

"I've been told to stay in bed, no walking around allowed," said Diana.

Jill visited Diana in hospital, which pleased them. Jill, being the progeny of Diana and William shared the same genes and needless to say inherited the family trait of concealing her feelings and never showed her grief but she was very sympathetic.

Diana was home again after another week in hospital. Beth obtained a metal walker and it helped with her walking and gave her more confidence. She was in her chair as usual on the bridge when Jill came to visit her.

"Hello Ma," said Jill kissing her. "How are you?"

"Oh coming along, just frustrated being in and out of hospital. The spirit is willing but the flesh is weak," said Diana.

"Emily has to see a family member in South Africa and we're going down in a few weeks," said Jill.

"How long will you be away?" asked Diana.

"Only a week. Are you going to be alright Ma?"

"I'll be fine. Don't worry about me," said Diana trying to be positive.

Beth went out to the car with Jill when she left. Diana stayed in her chair, Beth desperately saddened that Diana wasn't able to wave goodbye to Jill from the patio as she did for so many years.

"So you didn't tell Ma and Pa about my lump?" said Jill.

"Nope, you told me not to but I wish you'd tell them."

"*No!*" Jill was adamant. "Not now. Look." Jill raised her left leg to show Beth.

"That lump's visible now," said Beth.

"Feel it," said Jill.

"No. Sis! I wish you'd see someone about it," said Beth.

"I have. The surgeon's taking it out when I get back."

"Good. About time Jill."

The following weeks were very difficult for Diana finding walking painful and strenuous. Walking a short distance down the passage tired her and seemed to take forever. One evening she was feeling particularly weak and breathless and Beth phoned the doctor. She had to take Diana to his house and they had to go through the front door to get to his examination room. Beth saw her stop for a moment and look towards the dining room and noticed he and his wife were hosting a dinner party. Beth knew she was reminiscing on the many occasions she and William hosted their own perfect dinner parties and Beth had a sickening feeling of despair in the knowledge she might not have those wonderful parties again. As unwell as Diana felt she apologised profusely for the interruption and carried on to his examination room. Despite asking him what was wrong, he gave an inconclusive answer but prescribed some tablets for Diana.

Diana was seeing a specialist on a regular basis and a few days later William took her to see him. Having to go out, getting in and out of the car and visiting his surgery always exhausted Diana and on this occasion he wanted her in hospital everyone believing she had high blood pressure.

When Diana was admitted again she appeared to be alright for a few days, trying to be strong and positive but she started bringing up her food. Her specialist Dr Pollard couldn't give an explanation and to compound that Diana started to pass black stool. She was in hospital for a few weeks and had been prescribed, in Beth's view, far too many drugs. Beth was beside herself and got no satisfactory answers from Dr Pollard. They eventually did an endoscopy and everyone was concerned how she would manage it and a few days later she had a bowel x-ray involving a barium enema, a dreadful procedure for the fittest of individuals.

When Beth went to visit Diana on the morning of the x-ray, the staff were returning her to her room in a wheelchair. Diana looked thoroughly washed out and she looked at Beth and had a look of total despair and sorrow in her eyes. Neither of them spoke but Beth hugged her tightly.

The two procedures only weaken her further and Mr Mitchell, the surgeon, told Diana they only found an enflamed oesophagus. Beth went to see Mr Mitchell at his rooms for a more detailed explanation but got no satisfactory answer and they continued pumping her with a multitude of drugs.

"You had your perm just in time. Your hair still looks good." Beth combed Diana's hair as she sat up in the hospital bed. Diana stretched her lips as Beth put on her lipstick as best she could. The lipstick enhanced Diana's stunning blue eyes but she looked pale and weak. Beth felt so helpless she wanted to die.

A nurse came into her room and was impressed with what she saw. "Your nightie matches your blue eyes!"

"You can tie me with a ribbon and throw me in the deep blue sea," said Diana a faint smile appearing.

Everyone, including the hospital staff, were surprised when Dr Pollard said she could go home. She was too weak to walk to the hospital entrance from her room and had to be taken in a wheelchair. She wasn't strong enough to walk up the patio steps at home and William and Beth had to carry her in a garden chair. She remained in bed most days, just managing to get to the bathroom and the sitting room in the evenings, walking with great difficulty with a walker and with the assistance of William or Beth.

A few days after her discharge from hospital she again started bringing up and complained of abdominal pain. They arranged for a district nurse to visit her daily, taking her blood pressure and keeping an eye on her. Everyone was distraught, even the nurses puzzled over her symptoms and condition. Diana had always been a strong wiry woman and had a high pain threshold and if she was complaining about an abdominal pain, William and Beth knew it must have been agonizing. Beth spent some time with Diana in her bedroom but Diana didn't talk much and was very weak. It would upset Beth terribly and she'd wonder off and do something else, leaving William to spend more time with her.

Beth helped her to the sitting room in the evening.

"I won't be kept down for long," said Diana as she struggled to walk to the sitting room, trying to be strong and positive.

Diana wasn't hungry that night, still suffering from the abdominal pain and retired early. The district nurse visited the next morning and Diana wasn't able to sit up in bed and felt unwell. The nurse phoned the doctor who wanted her admitted to hospital again and the ambulance was called to the house. The sight of Diana in her beloved garden on the ambulance trolley wrenched Beth's heart. She was in Diana's private room when they took a multitude of blood samples and she heard from the staff that all her medication was to stop.

Once again Beth went to see Dr Pollard for an explanation and again didn't get a satisfactory answer. She returned to the hospital in the late afternoon to find Diana sleeping and William sitting quietly in a chair next to her bed. Beth paced the veranda and corridor not knowing what to do. She saw Mr Mitchell in the passage and she stopped him.

"My mother has been admitted again. What in heavens name is wrong with her? No one's telling us what's wrong." Beth was desperate.

"I saw her again when she was admitted earlier on. She's just old," said the surgeon.

"*Just old?*" repeated Beth. "What's causing the pain she's been having?" Beth wanted to wring his bloody neck but miraculously remained calm.

"I'm sorry. These things happen when one gets older," persisted Mitchell.

Beth knew she was bashing her head against a brick wall. She had *no* time for the medical fraternity after the last few frustrating months. She went back into Diana's room and found William sleeping in the chair and Diana hadn't moved and was in a deep sleep. Beth sat in a chair and looked at the parents she loved so much, wanting to do so much for them but feeling devastated and helpless.

William and Beth were advised to go home with the reassurance Diana would be alright. Beth kissed her on her cheek but she didn't waken. Once more William and Beth barely spoke, wrapped up in their emotions not wanting to accept or believe how sick Diana really was and believing that she would recuperate.

The next morning Beth was at the hospital. It was becoming routine and she hated going there, hated walking along the corridor, hated the noises and smells and hated the moment of entering Diana's room fearing what she might see.

A nurse who knew Beth from all her visits, approached her. "We've moved your mother upstairs and you can see her there."

Beth walked up the stairs, found Diana's room and popped her head around the door. She was sitting in a chair but Beth felt her heart sink into a grievous pit. They had a special empathy between them; an umbilical bond of understanding and Beth knew there was something seriously wrong with Diana. Her precious blue eyes were dull, a far away look with barely a hint of recognition. Beth kissed and hugged her and her beloved mother hardly responded. Her speech was slurred and very quiet and she could barely hold a conversation with Beth. Beth was totally devastated and tried, tried so hard to talk to her normally as though she was alright. She couldn't bring herself to ask Diana what was wrong; Diana always tried to be as strong as she could for her family and never wanted to complain and what Beth saw in her mother was clearly the best her mother could do for her and Beth knew she had to be strong and accept it.

She visited Diana again in the afternoon and brought her some flowers. Beth and William were in the room when Jill came in, having just returned from her trip to South Africa. She hadn't seen Diana for a few weeks and the change in Diana came as a shock to her. Jill gave her mother a kiss and hugged her and asked William to go out of the room with her. Beth knew she wanted to ask William what had gone wrong and what had happened to Diana in those few weeks.

They stayed with Diana for a long time and Beth and Jill spoke on the veranda outside Diana's room. No one knew what had happened but Beth told Jill she thought their mother had had a mild stroke. She hardly talked and when she did it was hardly coherent. They were devastated at the change in her condition.

Beth and William stayed beyond visiting time and again the staff told them they should go home. Beth put her fears to William and he wondered too if Diana had suffered a mild stroke.

Choo-Choo noticed the difference at home and had a puzzled look on her face.

"Where's Granny darling? Hey? Granny will be home soon and you can see her." Beth got on the floor and stroked Choo-Choo, trying to convince herself Diana would be alright. Her purr sounded like a diesel engine, not knowing the gravity of the situation.

Another day dawned and Beth woke with a feeling of grief and emptiness and she hoped Diana would be looking better; she wanted to see a glimmer of hope in her eyes. She went through the hospital entrance, up the stairs, along the corridor, her mind blank, the process automated. She went into Diana's room but the bed was made up and the room empty. She went to the nurse's office.

"Where's Mrs Maynard?" asked Beth.

"The doctor wanted her transferred to the high care ward," said the nurse.

"High care? What's happened, what's wrong?"

"It's just a precaution."

She hated the vagueness exuded by hospital staff and had a venomous hate for those brainless morons that had the audacity to call themselves doctors. Beth found her way to the high care ward, walked inside and scanned her eyes around the ward until she saw Diana. She was lying on her back, her eyes were closed and she looked pale. Beth stood next to the bed and touched Diana. She opened her eyes but that brightness she had hoped for wasn't there. Diana said hello but nothing else. Beth felt a huge hole, a gigantic cavity in her chest as though her heart had been ripped out of her ribcage.

"It's Pa's birthday tomorrow. Eighty hey! Eighty years young." Beth didn't know what to say or how to react but she was so happy to see Diana give a small nod.

She didn't want to stay too long; it upset her too much to see Diana lying there and she had something to do.

"Pa needs a new pair of shoes so I'm going to town to get them now and they can be from you. Is that all right?" Beth felt such sorrow and emptiness.

Diana gave another nod. "Thank you darling," her voice was weak.

"OK Ma-Ma. I'll come back this afternoon."

Beth returned in the afternoon and there was no change in Diana. Beth showed her the shoes but Diana found it hard to be receptive.

"I've got a card. Can you write in it? I'll get your specs so you can look at it." Beth looked in her locker and put Diana's glasses on her nose. "Hmm, that looks good," said Beth and gave Diana the card.

Diana had the same dazed, far away look in her eyes and she tried to look at the card but she didn't respond. Beth put a pen in her hand and held the card up for her against a magazine. "Do you want to write something?" asked Beth, so wanting everything to be normal. She wanted to tell Diana how devastated she felt but believed it would upset her. She was never to know if Diana needed to hear that, needed to know how she cared but the empathy and bond between them undoubtedly sufficed.

Diana tried to write but it was illegible.

William and Jill came in to the ward and Beth went onto the veranda finding it too difficult to cope with the circumstances. They stayed again as long as they were allowed. When Beth was leaving Diana asked her to bring a specific bath soap from home and Beth said she'd go home and come straight back with it.

She foolishly phoned the nurses when she got home to say she was returning with the soap but they convinced her not to bring it that evening. Beth had a mind of her own and she could have taken the soap but she left it.

They returned to the hospital the next morning. It was William's 80th birthday and although Diana was reminded of it she wasn't able to acknowledge it and gave no response but lay quietly on her back, her eyes dull and glazed yet with an expression of despair, needing and longing to communicate shared thoughts and feelings but her illness had worn her strength.

William and Beth were distraught yet William sat quietly next to Diana. He always kept a small diary in his top pocket for his chores and shopping lists and he paged through it as though to distract his thoughts. Beth spent a lot of time on the veranda grieving and praying Diana would get better.

They left at lunchtime promising to return in the afternoon. Beth kissed Diana and Diana said quietly and weakly, "I'll screw Pollards balls off."

"I know Ma." Beth didn't know what to say. She hated the medical fraternity as much as Diana and she just wanted Diana to get better. "I've seen the shit head but got no conclusive answers. Just rest and we'll see you a bit later. Love you Ma-Ma."

At mid afternoon the phone rang and Beth answered it not expecting any bad news but it was the hospital and they wanted them there right away. Beth phoned Jill's house and spoke to Nora and told her the news. William was in his bedroom and she related the news to him. They were calm and there was no reasoning, no conversation, just overwhelming silence.

Diana was wearing an oxygen mask, her breathing laboured, her eyes closed. William and Diana sat either side of the bed and Jill, Nora and Emily arrived shortly afterwards. They hardly spoke, each grieving silently, praying she would waken, speak to them, breathe freely and be well.

The phone rang in the ward and a nurse called Beth to the phone. It was Margaret phoning from South Africa and she wanted to speak to Diana but Beth told her she was too weak and wasn't able to talk. Margaret burst into tears but Beth remained calm, the intensity of the moment clouding her ability to focus realistically not able to tell Margaret that Diana was fading. Margaret wanted to know why they hadn't phoned her earlier but they had believed Diana's condition was temporary, not wanting to believe or accept the consequences.

Beth went back to Diana's side. "Margaret's just phoned Ma and she sends her love." Beth found it so hard to talk to her. She wanted Diana to respond and answer but knew her strength wouldn't allow.

Diana's eyes remained closed but she gave a slight nod of acceptance and took a deeper breath as though wanting to respond.

The pastoral nun from the hospital came in and threw the Holy water on Diana as William and Beth sat next to her not believing the gravity of the moment and truly believing Diana would recover. She was their wife and mother and she was always positive, always strong and always there for them. What they saw now was only temporary and she would recover and come home again.

Diana faded and gently sank away and the nun, with her vast experience, comforted them with the knowledge that it was the most peaceful passing she had encountered.

Beth left the room oppressed with grief. That moment, that event, that nightmare, that awful fear that had haunted her all her life had finally happened and she wanted her friend, her mentor, a part of her soul to come back. Nora was standing in the corridor and the big round woman opened her arms and Beth flung her arms around her and cried like a baby.

When William and Beth returned home the house was in darkness and although they turned on the lights and floodlights in the garden to welcome Jill and her friends for tea and sandwiches, the brightest shining light was extinguished from the house.

Beth remembered attending the funeral service of Emily's father with Diana and William at a little chapel in a funeral parlour and recalled Diana saying that was all she wanted and she didn't want anyone to attend her funeral. That was the only time they ever discussed the aftermath of death and Beth wanted to honour her wish.

Jill and Beth visited the funeral parlour together and chose a coffin together and somehow, miraculously, their emotions remained intact believing and openly discussing that Diana was with them and comforting them in their time of despair. Their local priest insisted that the service was held in their church in the leafy suburbs and not in a funeral parlour's chapel and William and the family were in full agreement knowing too that Diana would have been content with the arrangement. The service wasn't advertised as Diana had wished and only the family and a handful of close friends attended.

CHAPTER 13

William enjoyed cooking but never interfered in Diana's 'workshop'. Diana knew what she was doing and didn't want anyone under her feet and when Beth had spare time in the evenings, she would talk to Diana in the kitchen and William was wise to give Beth a wide berth in fear of the caustic remarks she would hurl at him.

William took over the kitchen and the cooking the day after Diana's passing, not suggesting it to Beth or wondering if he should or shouldn't do the cooking. He just seemed to slip into the role and revelled in it, partly because he liked it and he probably felt a sense of nearness to Diana being in the kitchen that had been her domain for so many years.

They never spoke about Diana to one another, the pain was too hard for them to bear. They loved her so much and she had been such a precious vital part of their lives, her not being there was just too unbearable for them and they tried to carry on as though nothing had happened, with an atmosphere of unspoken empathy.

Months later Beth bought books relating to near death experiences, wanting to know what Diana would have experienced and where she would be now. They were a Christian family and although their separation was real they knew it was temporary and that one day they would be together and that gave them consolation. The books helped Beth, learning about tunnels of bright lights, family and friends on the other side waiting to greet newly departed loved ones and above all, those who had temporarily visited the other side and had found it so beautiful and peaceful they didn't want to return to their earthly bodies. Beth mentioned the books to William but he said he couldn't read them, saying it was 'too soon,' perhaps having his own way of handling his loss and grief.

Jill had delayed her second operation to remove the lump in her leg but eventually plucked up the courage to have it done. Beth never wanted to visit that hospital again but found herself walking in the entrance feeling cold and empty.

The incision to remove the lump had been deep and Jill was in a lot of pain but in true family form tried to be cheerful and positive but she did have an eccentric, sometimes comical character.

"Do you know I died on the table?" said Jill with a humorous twinkle in her eyes.

"Oh come off it Jill!" said Beth, quite sure Jill was in one of her weird outlandish moods.

"I'm telling you! I was looking down on the table and I could hear the surgeon saying 'I've got to get it all, I must get it all out.'"

"And did he get it all? What has he told you?" asked Beth.

"He said it was very deep and had penetrated the muscle," said Jill.

"So what's the prognosis?"

Jill shrugged her shoulders and didn't answer and knowing Jill as she did, Beth wasn't sure if Jill *did* know or if the surgeon hadn't fully briefed her.

William and Jill seemed to be competing with hospital admissions because a few months later William was admitted for a hernia operation. He had been suffering with a lower abdominal pain for a few months, unrelated to the hernia, and it had worn him down but the surgeon was adamant the hernia operation was needed. Beth visited him twice a day and was concerned that he was quite weak and looked pale but the surgeon assured her he would be fine and he had handled the operation well for an eighty year old.

He recovered from his operation but continued visits to the doctor and it was decided he needed a prostate operation, the doctor recommending a specialist in Harare. Beth flew to Harare with William and saw him safely admitted to the hospital, happy he had a private ward with en suite bathroom. They knew the medical aid would cover most of it but she wanted him to have the best and she was happy to have met any shortfall. Beth had to return to Bulawayo the same evening to take care of Choo-Choo and the house and she knew their Harare friend Molly would be there for him. Dear old Molly looked so like that brown-eyed cow Beth had encountered on the Victoria Falls road.

Although William's lower abdominal pain continued he went to Dublin in Ireland some months later, to visit his sister and family. He thoroughly enjoyed the trip but in his letters to Beth he complained of the pain and occasional times of feeling unwell.

On his return home he continued to help Beth with the business and although he had slowed down he tried to remain positive and focused. Beth now had a good rapport with her father, so aware of Diana's desire that she should be more tolerant towards him. She loved William in a very different way to Diana, respecting his high ideals and his gentlemanly approach to life and people. He always made wise decisions and seldom had a bad thing to say about anyone.

Beth was business minded and was concerned about William's will and the awkward legal implications with the house in his will. Diana's passing had given them a greater awareness of life and death and the consequences brought about by a death. She suggested to William that he donated the house to his three daughters whilst he was alive and shared it between the girls as everyone had always assumed would happen. William did it very willingly but Beth would always remind him that it was still *his* house although he had donated it to his girls and that's how Beth sincerely felt about it.

William and Beth visited Jill on a regular basis but they felt, as they did so often over the years, that it was a one sided affair. Beth and William would phone them and visit them but Jill and her two friends very seldom phoned and Nora would never pop in for a visit, although Emily did so a couple of times after Diana died. Sometimes Beth and William made a concerted effort not to contact them, sometimes for weeks, just to see if they would phone or call around but they never did yet they were generally pleasant and receptive when they did make contact which always puzzled William and Beth.

Jill hadn't been well and was working mornings only after her operation, even the morning work was exhausting her. She started to look drawn and tired and would sleep most afternoons until she felt she couldn't cope with work. She was off sick for months and virtually never got out of her bed but would tell everyone that she *would* be returning to work, would give a date when she wanted to return but she was never able to honour it. Jill just wasn't well enough. Although Jill had stopped drinking some years earlier she would sometimes have her 'highs' by taking codeine-based tablets, an ingredient her system couldn't tolerate and the more she had the 'higher' she'd get. When Beth visited her she'd have slurred speech on occasions or be very dopey and if she was confronted about pill popping antics she'd deny it emphatically. It was as though Jill had given up. She spent most of her time in bed sleeping and had become a recluse.

Jill would keep a lot of her thoughts and problems to herself but on one of Beth's visits, Jill told Beth the surgeon had suggested she contact the hospice. The news worried Beth and when she told William what Jill had told her it came as no surprise to him and merely indicated that Jill wouldn't be with them for much longer.

Easter came around and they had been through a spell where they hadn't contacted Jill or her friends for a couple of weeks and although William and Beth stayed at home over the Easter holiday, busy with numerous things to do they were disappointed the girls hadn't contacted them despite the holiday.

On the last day of the holiday it was apparent that the girls weren't going to make contact so Beth decided to visit them. She parked outside the gate and hooted to allow one of them to unlock the gate, which was the normal routine. She waited longer than usual until she saw Nora and Emily walking to the gate, not in their usual casual way but with a sense of purpose.

"Your bloody sister has been bombed out of her mind all bloody weekend," said a highly annoyed Emily.

"We've had to put up with all her crap and nonsense and had no time to ourselves," said Nora.

"And *you* don't do a damn thing. You don't help out or come and see her." Emily sounded bitter and angry.

"I don't see why we should be landed with all this and have the responsibility of looking after her when she's so bombed out." Nora was just as bitter.

"We're on the end of a telephone. Why didn't you *phone* us for heavens sake?" said Beth, controlled, but shocked at their attack.

"Why should we? Why don't you….." said Emily.

Beth interrupted, annoyed now and surprised at their attitude. "Come on now. Get real. Pa and I are always here, always phoning and we never hear from you people so don't start please," said Beth.

"She's your sister and you should take more of an interest," insisted Nora.

Beth couldn't believe what they were saying. "You've all lived your independent lives here for over twenty years and it's the life Jill chose and we visit and contact her when we can." Beth got back in the car. "I'll visit again when you've all cooled off."

Beth told William of the venomous attack, so out of character and like a pack of wild dogs but he was a wise man of few words and wasn't unduly shocked at the revelation.

William and Beth spent a lot of time together in the garden and would often go for a walk in the late afternoon, William in his shorts and cotton shirt and his wide brimmed Aussie-style hat and Beth in her usual Bermuda shorts, T-shirt and sandals. They would discuss what new plants to put in and where to build new retaining walls for flowerbeds. They loved pottering around together knowing the garden was so much a part of Diana and they felt a sense of peace and oneness with her. William had slowed down and was now a little bent and he had lost a lot of weight and that concerned Beth. He used to be a tall, well-postured elegant man and it upset her to see him ageing yet he wouldn't allow himself to succumb to the use of a walking stick. He would carry his 'stick' as he called it, a well-worn straight tree branch almost as tall as himself and resembling a staff and he'd use it to help him over rocks and rough ground or to poke the soil in a flowerbed to see if it was moist.

They had had the entire property walled with stone granite, done in sections over the years as and when they could afford it and they now decided to fit an electric gate. Their entrance wasn't visible from the house and was some distance away and Beth and William believed it would enhance the property. They were ecstatic with it, especially William, being able to press his remote control to drive in and out of the property and not have to climb out of the car with his abdominal pain.

It was now over three years since Diana had died and William and Beth seemed to muddle through with their lives, Beth keeping busy with the business with William helping and also doing his own chores. She knew she had a commitment to Diana to tolerate William and avoid her vitriolic remarks but she was finding it difficult now. She was beginning to feel cracks in her tolerance and sometimes had difficulty maintaining her equilibrium, a state of ambivalence starting to tear at her emotions. Slowly but surely she returned to her old ways showing no respect for her father, unleashing her tongue on him, his physical and mental slow down playing havoc with her emotions.

He still enjoyed cooking the evening meals and like a gentleman, still wore his collar and tie in the evenings and tolerated Beth's rudeness like no one else would. Beth would hear him in the kitchen some evenings giving a long pitiful groan, like the groan of a wild animal grieving the loss of a mate and she knew he was grieving for his mate, the mate who had been part of his life, his being, his core, his soul for fifty seven years. The loss of Diana tore him apart but he remained constant in his resolve to be strong for Beth yet she began to tear his emotions apart with her abuse.

It hurt her to see him walking so bent and slow yet she found it hard to show him sympathy; she knew it was a beastly, dastardly thing to do but she found it hard to do otherwise, yet she knew how Diana would have disapproved. She was torn and angry and she knew what she was doing was so wrong but she didn't let up.

Some evenings she wouldn't sit with him at the dining room table, leaving him to dine alone whilst she ate in the sitting room but would throw abuse at him for no reason at all, only to vent her own selfish anger and frustration.

She would clear the dining room table still hurling foul language at him and once when she lost it altogether, she threw the placemats on the floor in a rage. A few twisted as they flew violently to the ground and she swore and bellowed even more because they were Diana's placemats, her precious mats over which they had enjoyed so many delicious happy meals, content in their togetherness. Poor William would be distraught and slink away and take refuge in the kitchen, distressed and alone with no one to console him and Choo-Choo would scuttle away to the sanctuary of the garden, petrified by the commotion.

Beth went on to visit Jill despite the abuse that had been thrown at her by Jill's friends and it was clear Jill was still taking her codeine-based tablets that made her sleep a lot of the time. Nora and Emily seemed more civil towards Beth and they had obviously had a particularly bad day with Jill on the day of their attack.

A few months later Beth had to go on a business trip overseas and would be away for three weeks. She was concerned about William but he assured her he would be alright. Beth asked Nora and Emily if he could have supper with them most evenings or when it suited them and that would give him company and ensure he ate properly. They agreed to help out and Beth paid them to cover the cost of the food.

Beth's 'plane landed at Bulawayo Airport, the end of her three week trip. She looked out of the window, her eyes automatically scanned the end of the terminal balcony where Diana and William used to stand. She saw a figure standing alone, away from the crowd, thin and bent and that lump jammed in her throat, her eyes burnt as she forced back the liquid welling up around them. He looked so lonely and she knew how he missed his Diana.

She went through immigration and customs and carried her case into the waiting area. William was sitting on a bench and stood up gingerly when he saw Beth. He looked so different from three weeks ago, thin and pale, his bent back accentuating the indentation in his midriff as though a sculptor had steadily chiselled a grievous hollow in him. Beth felt an agonising sorrow bursting inside her.

"Hi Pa," said Beth cheerfully. She dropped her suitcase to hug him.

"Hello my girl. Here, let me take your case," said William.

"No no. I'm used to carrying it. I'll take it," insisted Beth.

Beth drove them home catching up with their news.

"Choo-Choo went outside the other morning and she didn't come in until after eleven that evening and I've never felt so lonely. She was great company for me," said William.

"Did you eat with the girls?"

"Yes, but they piled my plate with food and I could hardly manage it. Anyway I'm pleased to see you; I've been waiting for you to get back," said William quietly.

Beth wondered what he meant by that.

William always had his bath in the early evenings before venturing into the kitchen but he was getting so slow and finding such difficulty in dressing Beth had to take over his chores. One evening he was particularly late after his bath and on investigating Beth saw him sitting on a chair in his bathroom, his trousers up to his knees.

"What's wrong?" asked Beth.

"I know I'm slow," said William. "I'm just tired at the moment."

Beth went in the bathroom and helped him put on his socks and to stand to put his trousers on. She felt so sorry for him but tried to be strong and not show her emotions.

"Anyway I'm cooking supper. Just come when you're ready," said Beth.

"All right my girl. I won't be long."

Beth always burnt the midnight oil and after William said he would be going to bed she went into his room some time later to check on him. He was on the floor next to his bed.

"Now what?" asked Beth in a friendly tone.

"I was sitting on the edge of the bed and I slipped off and now I can't damn well get up," said William.

Beth helped him onto the bed. "Hey you're a weight!"

"I've got so slow. I don't know what's wrong," said William. "I'm finding it hard to get in and out of the bath, even with your Ma's seat in it." He sounded so worried and concerned.

"Well I'm not going to bath you. Let's get a district nurse in to help you. Shall we?" Beth wanted his approval.

"Yes, I think that might be a good idea Beth. Yes, all right."

Beth arranged for her to come each day and she helped William to bath and dress.

"Your father is delightful, a true gentleman," said the nurse.

"Yes, he is." Beth knew all about that.

A few days later Beth arrived home early in the evening and she pressed the intercom bell at the gate. She knew it was a pointless move because she had her remote control to open the gate but she wanted to chat to William before she drove in.

"Hello." She heard William's voice on the intercom speaker at the gate.

"Hi. Just checking!" said Beth and as she spoke she heard a loud clatter through the speaker. "Hello?" Beth spoke again. There was no response and she assumed there was something wrong with the system.

She drove up the driveway, parked the car and walked through the garden, across the patio and into the house and she saw William lying on his back on the floor. The intercom handset was dangling on its cord, a coffee table was on its side and his chair had moved a couple of feet.

"What happened?" asked Beth as she went up to William.

"I was talking to you on the intercom and I lost my balance and here I am," said William, trying to get up.

"Bend your knees and roll onto your side," said Beth and she put the chair next to him. "I won't be able to lift you. Can you hold onto the chair and get on your knees, then we're half way there." William was very slow, confused and weak and Beth could hardly believe the dreadful change in her father.

She was concerned about him falling and worried about him when she was at work and away from the house. He was still driving but he hadn't driven into town for over a week having indicated he wasn't feeling very well. William never complained and Beth knew that if he said he wasn't feeling well there was something very wrong. She took him to the doctor on a few occasions but nothing conclusive was diagnosed much to the annoyance of both of them.

The following Sunday morning Beth noticed his car wasn't in the garage and she assumed he had driven to the nearby shops. She kept looking out for him and on one of her peeps through the window she saw he had returned and she signed with relief but several minutes passed and she noticed he was still in the car.

Beth went out to the car and before she reached it William had got out of the car. He staggered, lost his balance and fell to the ground knocking his forehead against the side of the car. Although the wound wasn't serious it was bleeding profusely.

"Bloody hell Pa," said Beth and tried to help him up but it was pointless. He had no energy and he was too heavy for Beth to manage single-handed.

"You were waiting for me to fall," said William as he sat on the ground leaning up against the car.

She was surprised at his comment as it was so out of character. "Don't talk crap. You fell before I could get to you." Beth was concerned about him and his wound. "I'm going to phone Nora and Emily and ask them to come over. Don't try and get up. I'll be back in a minute."

Beth was back in minutes with paper towels to hold on the wound. "They're coming over to help. Let's wait 'til they get here," said Beth knowing she couldn't handle him alone.

Nora and Emily were there in less than ten minutes and between the three of them got William inside and into a chair despite him being dreadfully weak and unsteady on his feet. Beth got the first aid kit and big round Nora, an expert with injuries and accustomed to injecting their animals, got to work on William's wound that fortunately was superficial.

Beth got a walking frame for William to help him walk on his own but even lifting the lightweight aluminium frame was tiring for him. A few weeks went by and William didn't drive the car, knowing he wasn't well enough. He ate very little and he was a constant concern for Beth.

Some days he would sit in the garden beneath the June winter sun as though quietly reflecting the garden parties he and Diana had hosted, the blood sweat and tears they'd shed to arrange and built their extensive garden. It was all a dream now, his strength, his life, his memories on the wane, sinking gently away like the setting sun and unstoppable as nature intended.

They sat together at the dining room table one evening but William didn't want his supper. He loved his food and never left a scrap but tonight he couldn't touch it. He was pale and distressed, more so than usual. She helped him to his bed breathless and tired as he struggled with the lightweight walking frame.

"I'm calling the quack," said Beth. She had no respect for the medical fraternity and thought them unworthy of a respectable title.

William lay on the bed fully clothed and didn't respond and Beth assumed he was in agreement.

Beth left the doctor to examine William and she waited in the sitting room.

"What's wrong with him?" Beth asked him after his brief examination.

"He has heart failure. Don't be surprised if he doesn't survive the night," said the miserable doctor.

"Can you admit him to hospital?" asked Beth.

"There's nothing that can be done," he said coldly.

"I'd rather he be there than at home," insisted Beth.

"I can't. There's nothing we can do," he said.

Beth ignored him as he walked to his car, not bothering to thank him for his visit, hoping he'd trip over a rock in the garden and break his bloody neck.

William struggled on for a few days and Beth was preparing for a sales trip that needed her full time and concentration.

"Pa, I'm going to be so tied up in the coming week, then I've got to go on a sales trip. How about staying in a nursing home for a while?" asked Beth.

Beth knew straight away he wasn't keen on the idea. "Do I have to?"

"I've got too much to do and when I go away you *can't* stay here on your own," Beth assured him.

"Why can't I go in when you're away? Why before then?" Beth knew he wasn't happy with her decision.

"Pa, I'm going to have so much on my plate and I can't afford to have the worry of you as well. You take up all my time and energy." Beth tried to be light hearted. "It'll only be for ten days or so, it's not permanent. You'll probably enjoy the break from me anyway!"

William was quiet and Beth knew he still disapproved.

"I've got no choice Pa. You know you can't manage here on your own. It's not forever. I'm going to phone the quack and see if he can arrange it."

The doctor was in agreement and arranged William's admission into the nursing home.

Beth packed a small suitcase and toilet bag for him. "It's not forever Pa! I really need time to get my work done before the trip. You know what it's like."

"All right Beth, as long as I don't have to stay there too long."

Neither of them knew that the circumstances in which William left the house made his departure less traumatic for him and they'd never know if it was Diana guiding and influencing the events.

William walked very slowly into the nursing home and Beth knew they'd made the right decision. He went into his room with Beth. "Do you like it? It's got an en suite bathroom as well." Beth wanted her father to be comfortable and have the best facilities available. "I've arranged for 24 hour nurse aide cover as well, so you won't be falling again."

"Thanks my girl. I need to sit down." William was weakened from the short walk and had lower abdominal pain again.

Beth visited him twice a day when she could and in a few days his condition deteriorated. He became weaker and breathless and complained of abdominal pain. She was in constant contact with the doctor and he decided to admit him to hospital.

"It'll be better for you to be in hospital Pa. They can keep an eye on you there," Beth told him as she drove him to the hospital.

He hated wheel chairs but he needed one, the walk through the hospital and along the corridors too much for him. "It's the same floor Ma-Ma was on," Beth told him.

"Yes," said William, his voice weak, almost confused.

She saw him into the ward and settled down. "Sorry it's not a private ward. I did ask for one but there aren't any apparently."

Beth visited him in the evening. He was in bed and didn't look happy. She learnt from the staff that he had become incontinent with loose bowels. The hospital wouldn't clean his pyjamas and as much as she wanted to help her father, she drew the line and couldn't clean them herself. She and William had become friendly with a nurse aide from Diana, Jill and William's previous admissions and she kindly offered to do the ghastly chore.

"Hi Nora," Beth was phoning Nora. "I've got to go away on a sales trip for a few days. Pa's in hospital as you know and I was wondering if you and Emily could feed Choo-Choo for the few nights I'll be away?"

"Yes, sure. How's your Dad?" asked Nora.

"Not too good this evening. He's incontinent at the moment so perhaps he's in the right place," said Beth.

"Now, how are you getting to the airport?" Old big Nora could be very helpful.

"I'll drive out and leave the car there."

"No, that's not nice. We'll take you there and fetch you when you get back," said Nora.

"OK Nora. Thanks." said Beth. "How's Jill?"

"She sleeps all day and she's very down," said Nora. "When are you going away?"

"Day after tomorrow. Hope that's all right with you?"

Each time Beth visited William he was lying in bed.

"Hi Pa," said Beth.

"Hi Beth."

"You look fed up."

"I wouldn't mind getting out of here," said William quietly.

"I'm glad the nurse aide came with you from the nursing home," said Beth smiling at the nurse near William's bed.

"Can do without them," grunted William. He was so independent and Beth knew he would hate anyone having to toilet him.

"Well Pa, it can't be helped for now. Just get strong and you can come home when I get back. I'm leaving for Victoria Falls tomorrow, then on to Harare. I'll be back in three days."

"What about Choo-Choo?" asked William.

Beth was glad he had remembered her. "Nora and Emily said they'll feed her and they've offered to take me to the airport and collect me *and* they said they'd come and visit you, so you've got nothing to worry about. Just get strong!"

"I've been looking for my diary." William looked towards the locker next to his bed. "I need to update it." He always kept a diary of important events and made detailed notes when Diana was ill and in and out of hospital.

"You and your diary!" joked Beth. She found it in his locker and handed it to him with his pen.

One of William's friends came in to see him and he stood at his bedside. William was pleased to see him. "Hello my boy," said William and gave him a soft punch on the stomach.

His friend, Beth thought, must have been in his late sixties or early seventies and she was pleased William had a bit of spunk. It gave her confidence that he'd be well soon.

She stayed for as long as she could. "I've got to meet the girls at home and show them the ropes with Choo-Choo."

A couple of nurses came to the bed. "We need to change Mr Maynard."

"I wonder what that means," Beth said to William. "Anyway, let me get out of the way." Beth kissed and hugged William as he lent on his elbow. "I'll phone from the Falls and let you know how things are going."

"All right my girl. Good luck." As he always did, he didn't say good-bye.

"Thanks Pa." Beth stood in the corridor and waved to her father.

The nurses were around his bed and he had a look of concern on his face as he looked at Beth still leaning on his elbow. He didn't smile but gave a 'thumbs up' and Beth did likewise and waved to him. "Bye Pa."

For a fleeting moment she wanted to go back to him but she hesitated. The nurses were busy with him. He looked worried and she wanted to go back but she left it, knowing she'd see him in a few days.

Beth phoned the hospital from Victoria Falls and spoke to a nurse. "Please tell Mr Maynard that Beth phoned. Tell him we had good sales and I send my love. Are you sure you'll tell him? How is he?" asked Beth.

"Yes, yes, we'll tell him. He's comfortable," said the nurse.

Beth put the phone down. "He's comfortable," Beth repeated the nurses comments. "Standard bloody answer."

She flew to Harare enjoying the flight as usual but with confused muddled thoughts, worrying about her father but with the belief he would be all right.

Beth checked in to the hotel in Harare, her second night away from home and she phoned Nora and Emily.

"We saw your Dad this afternoon and he's not looking at all well Beth," said Nora.

"What do you mean Nora?" asked Beth.

"He's *very* pale, quite confused and he's got that glassy far away look in his eyes. He's not good Beth and we think you should come home tomorrow and not the day after tomorrow." Nora sounded concerned and Beth had confidence in her judgement.

"It's too late now for the morning flight. I'll come back tomorrow evening. Can you meet me?"

"Yes, fine. We'll be there," Nora assured her.

Nora and Emily met Beth at the airport the following evening. "Your father really isn't at all well Beth and I'm pleased you came back today," said Nora.

Beth knew Nora had a sixth sense with these things and she knew her father's condition must be serious. "Can we go to the hospital?" asked Beth.

"Yes, we're going there now," said Emily. "Visiting time is over but they'll let you see him."

Emily parked in the hospital car park. "We'll wait in the car while you see him."

Beth so hated that hospital and each time she had to force herself into the building. She knew her way blindfolded up the stairs and along the corridor. The florescent lighting in the corridor was bright and reflected against the ghastly white walls. She looked in her fathers ward and his bed was empty, the bed neatly made and she went to the nurses office and was directed to another room.

Beth went in and she knew his move to a two-bedded ward was a bad sign. The lights above both beds gave a subtle light in the room. Her father was lying in the bed nearest the door, the bedding neatly tucked around him with only his head and shoulders exposed, his arms under the blankets. A nurse aide standing on the far side of the small room smiled briefly at Beth, a sense of concern expressed in her eyes.

Beth sat in the chair next to William's bed. His face looked thin and pale and his breathing was shallow. His eyes were closed and he seemed to be in a deep sleep. Beth nudged his side. "Hi Pa." There was no response. She thought he looked peaceful but she wanted to say hello. Beth sat with him for about ten minutes and somehow felt a sense of peace with him, their unspoken empathy, yet not realising how ill her father really was. She didn't want to believe or accept the gravity of his condition and she believed that tomorrow he would be feeling better, as she believed with Diana.

"Hi Pa." Beth nudged her father again but he didn't stir. She stood up to leave. "I'll come and see you tomorrow Pa." Beth's voice was shaking and she could feel tears welling up inside her, tears of sorrow and guilt and she hated herself. "See you tomorrow Pa," she said again and left the room. She walked down the corridor wanting him to be better tomorrow.

The phone rang at 7 o'clock the next morning and Beth knew it was the hospital.

"Can you come down right away," said the voice.

Beth phoned Nora and Emily and told them the hospital wanted her there.

Once more Beth found herself in the hospital. She walked passed the ward where her mother had been and she looked straight ahead. Four years had passed since they were in that ward with Diana and she was still unable to glance at it. Her head was spinning with despair as she went into her father's room, just three rooms away. Two nurses were in there. "We're very sorry, he's passed away."

Beth put her hands over her face and she saw her father lying in the same position as he was the previous evening. She couldn't believe he had gone; when she left him yesterday she was sure he'd be all right. His face was white and Beth was accustomed to his permanent bright ruddy complexion. Her sorrow and grief were asphyxiating her and she exploded into tears and fell onto her father's chest, crying, resentful, guilty, regretting past issues and she hated herself. The nurses eased her off the bed and she saw Nora, Emily and the priest behind her, Jill too weak to come.

"Thanks for coming," said Beth trying to control herself.

Unlike Diana, William never mentioned what send off he would have preferred and Beth took that as a green light to go the whole hog. Nora and Emily came to the fore and helped with the funeral service arrangements including big Nora's forte, the eats. The church was packed and Jill, although weak and unwell, attended the service. She and Beth, Nora and Emily sat in the front row and Beth was saddened that Jill looked so thin, fragile and small, her rounded shoulders accentuating her sorrow and grief.

Beth became more engrossed in the business taking her mind off the events but she was soon thrown back into reality when, about a month after William's passing, she received a phone call from the firm of lawyers holding his will.

"Hello. Could I speak to Miss Maynard please," came the voice on the phone.

"Speaking!" said Beth. She knew the voice but couldn't put a face to it.

"I'm Mrs Hawkins from Burtt, Hamilton and Masey. I'm sorry about your fathers passing."

"Thank you," said Beth, remembering she'd met her when William donated the house to his girls. "Hang on, let me put my glasses on so I can think," joked Beth. "How did you know?"

"We check the condolences in the newspaper then contact relatives when we think it's appropriate for them," said Mrs Hawkins.

Beth was asked to find a mound of documents and letters, including building society passbooks, pension fund and medical aid details and endless other documents. It was a nightmare for Beth having to go through William's personal documents, constant reminders eating at her conscience.

Jill had to move from her much loved barn and sanctuary into a spare room in the main house, too weak and unsteady to manage walking to and from the two. Beth and the girls would encourage her to take walks each day to build up her strength but she always declined and spent her time in or on her bed, smoking like a chimney as she always did. There were many times when they thought she needed to see a doctor but Jill would refuse to go and it was as though she had given up the will to live. She hadn't been back to work for several months yet told everyone she would be returning but her strength didn't allow.

Beth arrived at Jill's house one afternoon, on one of her many visits to Jill and Nora approached her.

"We're wondering if Jill's had a mild stroke. She can barely speak and when she does, her speech is slurred, more so than usual," said a concerned Nora.

Beth went in to Jill's room and she was lying on top of the blankets as she usually did. She was wearing a pair of Bermuda shorts and a T-shirt full of cigarette holes. Jill was seldom without a cigarette and if she was taking her codeine tablets she'd be in a drunk-like state and drop her 'fags' as she called them, anywhere and everywhere inflicting cigarette burns and holes on her casual clothes and bedding. But Jill didn't care; it was her domain, her life, her clothes, her blankets, her lungs and if she wanted to puff away and drop her fags in a drunken stupor that was her problem and woe betide anyone who even *suggested* otherwise.

"Hi Roe-Roe. How are you?" said Beth cheerfully and wanting to gauge Jill's reaction.

"I'm fine," said Jill looking dazed.

"I thought you'd say that. Your standard bloody answer eh?" said Beth, sitting on Jill's bed. "Come on, what's wrong?"

Jill had a cigarette burning in an ashtray next to her bed and reached over to pick it up but her hand missed it, landing instead in the ash.

"Here." Beth picked up the cigarette and handed it to Jill and she took it, looking dazed and stupid, her hand unsteady. "Stop messing around," said Beth. Jill could be a clown sometimes and act like a fool and Beth seldom knew if she was serious or monkeying around.

"What have you been doing today?" asked Beth, hoping Jill would talk to her.

"I'm waiting for Paul," said Jill. Paul was Jill's accountant friend cum financial advisor who Jill spoke about occasionally but Beth had never met him. Jill's throat sounded congested, her speech indistinct and her mouth slightly lopsided.

Beth called a spade a spade with Jill. "What's wrong with your speech? You're not talking properly."

Jill stared briefly at Beth with her wide-eyed innocent look and shrugged her shoulders. "Stroke," said Jill barely coherent.

"Who said?" asked Beth.

"Me," said Jill poking her chest with her finger.

Jill always appeared as strong as an ox when it came to handling her own difficulties and was never afraid of health problems that came her way. She would openly discuss death and was never afraid of the prospect of dying. If she had had a stroke, it didn't perturb her.

"I think you should see a quack," said Beth but she knew she'd said the wrong thing.

"*No way!*" Jill's words were slurred and weak and she held up both hands defiantly. Jill had spoken. "I'm not going near them." She spoke slowly and with difficulty.

"You're bloody impossible. Just let them check you over," suggested Beth.

"*No!* Forget it." Jill was adamant.

"OK, OK, don't have a wobbly," said Beth.

"Why is Paul coming?" Beth changed the subject. Jill had never discussed her finances in depth with the family and she wasn't expecting her to do so now, but it provided some small talk for them.

"I've got shares that he handles," said Jill almost incoherently.

"Are those the ones you showed me years ago?"

Jill looked at her vaguely and shrugged her shoulders, seemingly not wanting to commit herself or perhaps not remembering she'd shown Beth her unit trust account.

Jill hadn't worked for several months now and no doubt had no income in that time and Beth assumed Jill was financing her expenses with the money she had in the unit trusts.

Political moves in Zimbabwe were affecting the economy, the value of the currency and importantly for Beth, tourism. She was a perfectionist and wanted the business to run efficiently but she found it unsustainable, unable to cost the products effectively or hold prices quoted to customers. Sales fell dramatically with the decline of tourist arrivals and about six months after William died she decided to suspend trading.

Although she had sufficient finances to sustain herself and maintain the upkeep of the house and business, she had to pull her horns in dramatically but she was prudent and managed surprisingly well. She spent a great deal of time in the garden she loved so much and in which she felt so at peace but she missed William tremendously, reminiscent of the many times they had walked through the garden, William with his 'stick' and wide brimmed hat, discussing what improvements they could make and what to plant. The peace the garden gave her consoled her in the belief that Diana and William were there with her, guiding and protecting, forgiving, wanting her agonising guilt to subside.

Beth got the lawnmower from the storeroom. The rains had started and the grass on the driveway was long and messy.

"Hello Choo-Choo," said Beth. Choo-Choo had appeared from nowhere. She would hear Beth in the garden and would crawl out from one of her numerous hidey-holes under a bush or a hedge and join her on her walks or 'help' Beth with whatever she was doing. Beth filled the mower with petrol and got ready to pull the starter cord. "Mind Choo-Choo. There's a big noise coming," said Beth as she pulled the cord and grateful the engine fired first time, knowing William wasn't there to attend to it, well not physically, she thought. Choo-Choo ran off and lay on a low granite wall, shaded from the burning afternoon sun by a saringa-berry tree, her yellow eyes slit open sleepily as she watched Beth.

It took Beth nearly three hours to mow the driveway and surrounding areas between rocks and walls, her bare legs and arms a ruddy brown from the scorching sun. She cleaned the mower and put it away and walked down to the gate to take in the scenery.

"Come on Choo-Choo. *L-e-e-e-t's* go," said Beth. Choo-Choo knew what that meant and jumped off the wall and followed Beth down the driveway still believing she was a dog.

"*Shit*! Damn it," said Beth to herself. She was wearing her designer-ware shoes; a worn out pair of canvas shoes with no laces, her big toes protruding gracefully through jagged holes in the dirty canvas. She'd stood on a multi-spiked devil thorn and it went right through the old thin soles into her foot. "*Come* Choo-Choo. *Come.*" Choo-Choo had stopped to sniff the leaves on a bougainvillea bush.

Beth stood at the gate and looked along the length of the driveway and thought it looked good, really good. The green grass was neatly cut and contrasted beautifully against the two strips of rust coloured paving on the driveway, complementing a long high granite wall along one side and bougainvilleas, succulents and a variety of aloes strategically placed in rockeries and between pathways on the other side. The sun was setting at the far end of the driveway and the lengthening shadows gave an air of coolness in the stifling afternoon heat.

Choo-Choo was lying down now on the freshly cut grass to cool herself and Beth left her, knowing she'd prefer to find her way back to the house in her own time as she would catch tasty grasshoppers and sniff at the plants for signs of other animals.

Beth went to visit Jill, having not seen her for a few days. "'Allo. Hi," said Beth as she went in her room. She was lying on her bed with an electric fan whirring noisily on a chest of drawers near the bed. "How are you?" asked Beth.

"Fine." Jill virtually mimed the word, a croaking mumble coming from her mouth.

"Bloody liar," said Beth. The two sisters had an unwritten law as to how they could communicate with one another. "Your speech is worse, do you know that?"

Jill shrugged her shoulders as though not particularly bothered and reached for her packet of cigarettes on her bedside table.

"Can I have one of yours? Is it doctored?" asked Beth. Jill put menthol crystals in her toasted cigarettes to give them an extra kick and Beth enjoyed one occasionally. "I don't want one too strong."

"Front," said Jill, Beth only just deciphering her mumble.

"Are the ones at the front weaker?"

Jill nodded and lit up and coughed heavily.

"You know you're a bugger," said Beth standing next to her bed, lighting her cigarette. She went over to the window and sat on the arm of a chair, conscious of the smoke in the room. "Everyone's concerned about you and you're not helping yourself. I wish you'd go for a check up."

If Jill could have bellowed at Beth, she would have. "*Don't start!*" Beth just made out Jill's comment.

"You're a fart," said Beth. She drew on her cigarette and blew the smoke out of the window. They sat in silence for a few minutes.

Jill mumbled a sentence to Beth but she couldn't understand what she said.

"Say again," said Beth.

Jill repeated herself, trying to talk slowly.

"Shit Jill, I can't understand you. Write it down," suggested Beth.

Jill was getting agitated and she repeated herself again.

"Sorry, it's no good. Here, write it." Beth found some neatly cut pieces of paper and a pencil on her bedside table. "Have you been writing messages on these?"

Jill ignored her and snatched the pencil from Beth and wrote on a piece of paper.

Beth read her note. 'I'm running out of money.'

"So?" asked Beth. "What do you want me to do about it."

Jill looked at Beth with a forlorn look, shrugged her shoulders and put her hands in the air.

"Shit Jill. I hope you don't want me to finance you. I just can't do it at the moment." Beth was to the point. "What's happened to all that money you had in those shares or whatever? You had mounds of it."

Jill shrugged her shoulders again and brushed her hand away from her mouth, indicating it had gone.

Beth saw Emily drive into the garden presumably back from work and a short while later Nora and Emily came into Jill's room. They were concerned that Jill wasn't walking enough or getting into the garden.

"We're still giving her a lot of natural therapy tablets to boost her immune system to try and strengthen her. Hey Jill? We have to get you strong again," said Emily.

"I'm glad the stubborn madam had agreed to take them. They're pretty costly aren't they?" said Beth. "Sounds as though you're paying for them?"

"Yip," said Emily. "Shall we all go to Matopos on Saturday?" asked Emily, changing the subject.

Matopos was a national park about twenty miles from Bulawayo, famous for thousands of square miles of spectacular granite outcrops and kopjes and a sanctuary for wild game. Jill, Nora and Emily had camped there many times over the years and they loved the beauty and sanctity it provided.

Jill shook her head. "No," she said with a rough voice.

Emily seemed annoyed. "Well I'm going. I don't know about you. There are other people living in this house you know." Emily was notably frustrated.

"Come on Jill. It'll do you good. We'll set you up nicely in the back of the car," said Beth.

"No!" mumbled Jill. It was clear she wasn't going to change her mind.

"I'll come. It'll be a nice change," said Beth.

Big round Nora stood in the middle of the room with her hands on her hips or rather where her hips should have been and looked at Jill. "Hey my friend," said Nora sympathetically. She knew how stubborn Jill could be and she wasn't going to argue with her. "I'll ask Liz to keep an eye on you on Saturday." Liz was a neighbour.

"No," mumbled Jill again, waving her hands in the air.

Nora wasn't arguing and she'd get Liz to help out.

Nora, Emily and Beth headed for Matopos on Saturday, Jill still refusing to join them. Nora and Emily were more familiar with the area than Beth.

"Shall we go to Malemi Dam?" suggested Emily.

"Yes, there're good facilities there and shady trees," said Nora.

They drove through the Matopos national park on their way to the dam and looked out for game.

"Giraffe over there." Nora had a keen eye for game.

Emily stopped the car on the narrow tarred road and they watched the five graceful mottled beasts standing lifeless, their horned heads looking suspiciously at the car.

They drove past monstrous granite-packed kopjes dwarfed by huge craggy rock formations as though some had been carved into motionless upright statues, others balancing precariously one on top of the other unmoved and desolate for millions of years. It was eerie yet peaceful and beautiful, troops of baboons and monkeys inhabiting rugged rocky structures, wary of the leopards sharing their silent caves and craving their meat.

"This'll do," said Nora. They'd found a camping spot with a heavy cemented table and matching benches under some trees. The site was on the shores of Maleme Dam with high rocky kopjes nearby. They got out their folding chairs and Nora put the insulated picnic box on the table. "We'd better keep an eye open for those thieving baboons," said big Nora, terrified at the prospect of the flea-infested kleptomaniacs pilfering her food.

Beth found a sunny spot nearby and sizzled in the midday sun, clad in her denim shorts with frayed edges and no longer resembling the trousers of their youth. Her light brown short-cropped hair was bleached from the sun and her wiry arms and legs indelibly tanned from years of outdoor life.

Nora and Emily sat in the shade, Nora in her big tent-like dress and floppy cotton hat covering her full head of hair that she'd bundled into a mass on the back of her head. She'd been overweight for as long as Beth had known her but she was strong and active with it, her big round cheerful face matching her character.

Emily wore cool cotton trousers and a sleeveless blouse, keeping Nora company with similar headgear. She was fairly slim and tall with short black hair, which could be wavy and wiry given the opportunity but Emily kept it under strict control, neatly cut and combed against her head. Like Jill would do, she dressed impeccably for work and unlike Jill she maintained a good dress sense away from work.

"When are we eating?" asked Emily casually.

"That's a good question," said Beth from her roasting spot.

"Do I take it everyone's starving?" said Nora.

Nora enjoyed being 'mother' and piled their plates high with salad, cold meat and bread rolls. Poor old Nora was probably accustomed to eating copious quantities of food and her servings matched her state of hunger, forgetting Emily and Beth were small eaters in comparison to her.

Two grey warthogs appeared from nowhere, clearly accustomed to human company. The smaller of the two strutted right up to Beth nonchalantly scavenging around her for any pickings.

"Bloody cheek," Beth was amused. "Excuse me," said Beth slowly and concisely, looking right at the little warthog sniffing in the short bush grass near her feet. She'd never seen one at such close range, with sparse coarse lengths of wiry hair on its grey wrinkled skin and its little black eyes glancing everywhere in a bumptious carefree way. It had filthy yellow tusks protruding viciously from either side of its jaw. "Who invited *you* to the picnic?" It rubbed its hairy body roughly against Beth's leg and she tried to push it away with her hand but it turned around and in a flash had bitten her hand with its loathsome dirty teeth. "*Aaah!*" Beth made a noise to frighten it off. "Go on, bugger off," and the dirty little animal moved away slowly, still sniffing the ground and unperturbed by Beth's language.

The broken skin turned mauve as the blood oozed to the surface then welled up and overflowed from the gouge in her hand.

"Damn it," said Beth and placed a paper napkin over the wound.

"You'd better have an anti-tetanus injection for that," said Nora.

"Aah. I'm not bothered. I'll live," said Beth, as casual and as anti the medical fraternity as her sister.

"Hi Roe-Roe." Beth greeted Jill in the kitchen on their return from Matopos. "Nice to see you up and about."

Jill mumbled something and Beth only picked up the word 'puppy' as she prepared the evening meal for her huge black Rotweiller.

"Anyway we had a good time. Saw some giraffe."

Jill ignored her as she mixed the dog food. Beth had found an old cloth in Emily's car and had wrapped it around her hand.

Jill pointed to it and mumbled. "What's that?"

Beth giggled. "A warthog bit me."

Jill opened her eyes wide and looked surprised and made the motion of having an injection in the arm. Jill was a real bush pig and knew all about the bush and bush craft.

"Huh! Speak for yourself!" laughed Beth. "I'll make a deal with you. *You* go to the quack then I'll have an injection." Beth knew she was wasting her breath. She saw the lump on Jill's leg and it looked bigger than usual. It was like a plum, red and bulbous and had developed over her scar. Jill walked with a limp, her knee bent to reduce the pain, her permanently tanned lean legs protruding from her Bermuda shorts dotted with cigarette burns. Beth changed the subject. "That lump looks really angry and painful."

"Ah huh," said Jill in agreement as she hobbled outside to give Angie her supper.

"Now listen Beth," said Nora as she came in the kitchen. "Can I clean that bite?" Big Nora was a good first-aider and didn't mind the sight of blood and guts.

"Thanks Nora, but I've got to go. I'll sort it out at home with antiseptic and a dry dressing. OK Roe-Roe, I'll see you tomorrow or in a few days and look after your bod."

When Beth got back to the house it was almost dark but everything was visible in the fading light and she could just make out a little black object coming towards her on the lawn. Well it's not a warthog thought Beth.

"Hello my cottage pie, my pumpkin pip. What have you been doing? Did you miss me eh?" Beth stopped to greet her and Choo-Choo rubbed herself against Beth's legs.

They were grateful for each other's company and Choo-Choo followed Beth onto the patio. She had mixed the chlorine for the pool before she went out that morning and she picked up the large opaque plastic bottle on the patio, gave it a good shake and walked around the edge of the pool pouring in the diluted chlorine. She dipped each foot in the water to cool off and remove the dust from her filthy feet and as she turned off the pool pump that whirred incessantly in the background a sudden hush engulfed the garden, such peace, such serenity. Beth watched the trees silhouetted against the pale silver sky with Venus shining brightly above the western horizon, the Goddess of Love, reflecting her lustrous affection on Diana and William's exquisite garden.

Choo-Choo was sitting patiently on the lawn for Beth. "Come. Supper time," Beth told her cat and she gave an acknowledging purring meow as though talking to Beth and followed her inside.

Shortly after lunch the following Saturday Beth drove over to visit Jill having made a few visits during the week. It was nearly seven months since William died and Beth was surprised how well she was managing although she desperately missed her parents. Her visits to Jill provided company for both of them as they silently grieved the loss of their parents.

There was a sense of emotion as Beth walked into the house, a feeling she couldn't grasp for a moment and as she walked through the passage she heard voices outside and Beth went to investigate. Jill was lying in the garden at the back of the house.

"Jill's just fallen this minute," said Nora, concerned and out of breath. "I think she's broken her leg. I'm calling an ambulance."

"Oh shit Jill," said Beth and she knelt down next to her sister. "That's all you need."

Jill lay quietly on the lawn, a little dazed and confused.

"We'll get you sorted out, don't worry," said Beth trying to reassure her.

"Honestly, she's so unsteady on her pins she literally fell over and we couldn't get to her in time," said Emily.

Nora, Emily and Beth sat in the waiting room at the casualty department, Jill behind the curtains in a cubicle in a nearby room. They heard her groaning and crying.

"Bloody hell, what are they doing to her?" said Beth. Jill wasn't a moaner and they knew she must have been in a lot of pain.

"I'm going to see her," said Nora positively and big Nora waddled down the corridor and into a side door.

"Come, let's go and see her," Beth told Emily.

They went behind the curtains and no one was attending to Jill but she was pointing to her lower back.

"What is it Jill?" asked Nora. "I think this table's so damn hard and you're a bag of bones. Is there pressure on your spine?" Nora asked Jill.

"Hmm," said Jill emphatically and nodded.

A nurse and doctor came through the curtain and as Beth and Emily did a quick exit, Nora explained the problem to the doctor.

It was over an hour before she was wheeled to a ward with confirmation from an x-ray that she'd broken her upper leg whilst Beth, Nora and Emily were asked to go to reception and have Jill officially admitted.

Emily completed the necessary forms. Nora's business was registered with a medical aid society and she had Jill on it and she was able to submit claims for Jill's hospital visits and prescription claims.

"I'm not signing that," said Emily. "The hospital wants a guarantor."

Beth thought her comment strange because Emily, Nora and Jill had been an inseparable team, the closest of friends for over twenty years and there for each other but Beth wasn't going to make an issue out of it.

"I'll sign it," said Beth. She knew it had to be signed and got on with it although she was concerned she didn't have an income at the time. Beth had a fair amount of company capital that she was living on and if there was a shortfall from the hospital she knew she'd have to handle it somehow.

The surgeon was visiting Jill when they got back to the ward and he called them in.

"She's very weak and I'm reluctant to operate right now. We're going to monitor her for twenty four hours," said the surgeon. He pulled back the blankets to examine Jill and saw the red plum-like bulge on her leg. "What's that?" he asked.

Nora told him she'd had a melanoma removed and the red lump had appeared over the months.

"It's giving her hell. It's very painful," said Beth for Jill.

"Yes I see that," said the surgeon. "We'll remove that for you."

Beth went home that evening, the surgeon still undecided when to operate. Jill's condition worried Beth and she started thinking about William's donation of the house and her thoughts were in a whirl. What would happen if something happened to Jill? Beth wanted to think it through logically. *If* Jill died her quarter share of the house would go to whoever the beneficiary was in her will and if Beth knew Jill as she did, Jill certainly wasn't leaving anything to Beth, not that worried her one iota; poor Jilly never had much to her name anyway, then on the other hand thought Beth, Jill was such an eccentric character she'd go and do something weird that no one would expect. That was Jill's prerogative and fine by Beth too.

What *did* concern Beth was Diana and William's wish all through their lives that their three daughters would share anything they owned. So hypothetically thought Beth, if Jill died her share of the house would probably go to Nora and Emily or one or other, assuming they would be her beneficiaries.

Beth was in a dilemma and she knew it was a scenario that Diana and William wouldn't have envisaged. But on the other side of the coin thought Beth, it was Jill's share to do whatever she wished with it. Beth thought the whole thing was crazy. She wanted to honour and uphold her parent's wishes *and* she had to consider Jill's wishes.

Beth was cooking her supper as she tried to be judge and executioner. She'd write out an agreement, where Jill would donate her share of the house to Beth and she'd show it to Jill. It'll be up to Jill if she elects to go along with it. Yes thought Beth, that's fair enough.

Jill was lying on her back in her hospital bed and looked sleepy.

"Hi Roe-Roe," said Beth quietly. "So they still haven't done anything?"

Jill shook her head.

"How are you feeling?" asked Beth.

Jill shook her head again and Beth wished she could talk.

"Shame Jill. Listen, I've been thinking about your share of the house." Beth didn't know how to word it without Jill knowing her thoughts of Jill's possible demise. Damn it thought Beth, knowing she had to be poignant.

"I'm just a bit spooked that if something happens to you, your share would probably go to someone outside the family and I know that's not what the folks would have wanted *so*," emphasized Beth, trying to make light of it, "I've written out an agreement with you donating your share to me. You *don't* have to sign it but it's my suggestion and it's up to you to decide if you want to do it. And *don't you dare* go and bloody well pop off on me," Beth finished off on a note she knew Jill would appreciate.

Jill made no attempt to talk and she seemed to have difficulty in swallowing but she made a motion with her hand as though writing something.

"Do you want to sign it?" asked Beth.

Jill nodded briefly and Beth took the handwritten piece of foolscap paper from her pocket and read the brief contents to Jill. Jill gave a motion with her hand as though signing and Beth handed a pen to her.

"I've put Nora and Emily's names down as witnesses. I think you should wait until they're here," said Beth but Jill, as stubborn as she was, ignored Beth and started to sign the agreement and as she did so Nora and Emily came into the room.

"That was good timing," said Beth and she explained to them what she had done, showed them the agreement and asked them to sign it as witnesses. Beth was a little surprised that they made no comment but they signed it. "Thanks guys," said Beth.

They were still there when the surgeon came in to see Jill and he said he would operate the following day to repair the break.

"It has to be done Jill," said Nora. "The leg's broken and you can't lie there forever but he's obviously happy with your condition," said Nora, reassuring Jill.

Jill had the operation the following afternoon and when Beth went to the hospital Jill was in the operating theatre. Nora and Emily were sitting on a bench outside the theatre waiting for her to come out. Beth could handle death, post mortems and any morbid aspect of life but when it came to her family it was a different story. She had never been able to wait outside an operating theatre for *any* family member as it would upset her too much. She stayed with Nora and Emily for about half an hour and said she would visit Jill the following day.

Beth was dreading her visit the next day wondering what state Jill would be in. She had found it hard enough to come to terms with Jill's stroke, her difficulty in talking and her weakness and had tried to believe that Jill would recover and would be well and strong again, but she knew that her fall would affect Jill's health greatly. She'd seen it over and over again with Diana and Beth tried to come to terms with the fact that Jill was in for a rough time.

A nurse was carrying a bedpan in the corridor and Beth gave her a wide berth holding her breath instinctively and shuddered at the thought of what was in it. She hated the sight of anything that was expelled from any orifice in the human body and it gave her the screaming heebie jeebies but scraping brains off the road was as easy as falling off a log for her.

Beth stuck her head around the door of her room and she saw Jill lying on her back, her eyes closed. She looked so tiny and thin under the blankets and it broke Beth's heart. She reflected how strong Jill used to be, how they had walked through the bush together and how she had run over those rocks and through dense bush to rescue her from those revolting spiders.

"Hi Roe-Roe," said Beth quietly wondering if Jill just had her eyes closed or if she was sleeping.

Jill opened her eyes and looked at Beth but gave no sign of recognition. Beth went in the room and stood next to Jill's bed. "Hi Roe-Roe," she said again and Jill opened her mouth but no sound came out and she tried to swallow. "You've been through the mill hey? Anyway Nora and Emily said the op. went alright." Jill showed no intension of responding and lay still, her eyes dull, her face thin and pale.

"Are you in pain?" asked Beth.

Jill responded at long last and nodded and closed her eyes momentarily.

"Are they giving you something for it?"

Jill looked over towards her bedside locker and made a writing motion with her hand. Beth found some neatly cut pieces of paper and a pencil on top of it. "I see Nora has brought your communication equipment for you," said Beth and she handed Jill a wad of paper for her to lean on and the pencil. "Here, let me put your specs. on your nose."

Jill wrote on the piece of paper and handed it to Beth. 'Need painkiller,' read Beth.

"I'll see the nurses and see what they can do," said Beth. "Don't run away," she joked.

Beth found a nurse and told her Jill was in pain and needed another painkiller.

"I'll check her notes," said the nurse and disappeared into the office. Beth waited outside, too familiar with nurses' antics, and knew she'd have to keep on her tail before something was done.

Beth had waited patiently for over five minutes, when the nurse came out of the office and walked off down the passage, ignoring Beth. "Typical," muttered Beth to herself, "operation normal."

"Excuse me," said Beth loudly.

The nurse turned around. "Oh, she's due a painkiller in half an hour. I can't go against doctor's orders."

"I'll remind you!" said Beth.

Beth went back to Jill. "You're only due one in half an hour," said Beth.

Jill closed her eyes and shook her head.

"I know. It burns my bum but they've got to follow the rules. Just lie quietly and the time will pass soon enough," said Beth.

To the relief of Beth, Nora and Emily came in and she hoped their presence would boost Jill's morale.

"Hi Jilly," said Nora quietly. "How are you feeling?"

Jill rolled her head from side to side on the pillow.

"She wrote a note to me just now and she's in a lot of pain but she's not due a painkiller for about twenty minutes," said Beth keeping an eye on the time.

"You look really bombed out," said Emily. "You'll be having your highs on your painkillers!" said Emily.

They knew Jill couldn't tolerate painkillers at the best of times and she was obviously having strong doses in hospital and they'd have her flying high on cloud nine, a state Jill loved to be in.

Beth went onto autopilot and was in and out of the hospital visiting Jill for the two weeks she was there. They were all concerned that she hadn't done any walking or exercise; she was just too weak and it was always a mystery for Beth why patients had to be in such high beds when they had difficulty getting on and off the bed. Jill had been able to sit on the edge of the bed to have her meals but she would choke on the tiniest piece of food that would send Beth running off for a member of staff.

At the end of her two week stay it was decided there was nothing further the hospital could do but she had to regain her strength and Jill was admitted to a nursing home with a full time nurse aide. She was thinner than ever before but she tried to strengthen her skinny legs with short walks each day and they were short walks; about five yards from her bed to the veranda outside and that was all she could manage. Her repaired leg was now inches shorter and she had to walk on the ball of her foot, unable to place her foot normally on the ground. Poor Jilly was having great difficulty walking and couldn't manage without a walking frame.

Beth would keep her company on the veranda talking to her and trying to get her to improve her speech but it was impossible. Jill would have to talk slowly and distinctly and even after the effort it was difficult to grasp what she said and Jill would invariably have to resort to writing notes to Beth or anyone else that required one.

Beth received numerous calls from Mrs Hawkins of Burtt, Hamilton & Masey, the executors handling William's estate, still requesting a number of documents in order to winding up the estate and Beth dealt with Mrs Hawkins on a number of occasions.

"I have an appointment with Mrs Hawkins," Beth told the receptionist.

"Yes she's expecting you, please go through to her office."

"Hi Mrs Hawkins," said Beth.

"Hello Miss Maynard. Please come in and sit down," said Mrs Hawkins with her strong Dublin accent. Beth liked her and her Irish accent and she was pleased Mrs Hawkins had met William and had had the opportunity to appreciate his impeccable gentlemanly manners. Beth was proud of her father and he was popular with a great number of people.

"I've got the letter and address you required from the pension fund," said Beth and handed her the letter. "On another subject, my sister fell and broke her leg some weeks ago. As you know my father donated his house to his daughters…"

"That's correct," interrupted Mrs Hawkins.

"Anyway, before Jill had her operation I asked her to donate her share of the house to me just in case, heaven forbid, anything happened to her. She was willing to do that and she signed an agreement I drew up. I'd like you to place it with the title deeds, just for the record," said Beth and handed Mrs Hawkins the agreement.

Mrs Hawkins took the agreement and read it. "I'm not a lawyer. I only deal with the estates and I think you should have this verified with Mr Hamilton who was your father's attorney. Let me see if he can see you for a moment." She punched in an extension number on her phone. "Hello Betty. I have Miss Maynard here who needs to have an agreement verified. Is Mr Hamilton free for a few minutes?" Mrs Hawkins covered the mouthpiece and whispered to Beth "She's just checking." She held on for about a minute. "Yes Betty. Right-o, thank you."

"He'll see you in about five minutes," said Mrs Hawkins and handed the agreement to Beth.

"Will it be long before my father's estate is wound up and do you have any idea yet what the three daughters will be paid out?" asked Beth.

"Oh, it'll be some time yet. This is a slow process and we need our estimator to visit his house and value the contents. I'll have to arrange a day with you on that one," said Mrs Hawkins, almost talking to herself as she paged through William's file.

"My sister Jill, I gather, is running short of money and any monies due from the estate would be useful to her right now," said Beth. "If I was to give her an advance could the estate reimburse me from her share?" suggested Beth.

"That would be very messy," said Mrs Hawkins.

"I thought so. I'll have to make another plan to help her out," said Beth.

Mrs Hawkins placed her elbows on her huge solid wooden desk with her hands clasped under her chin. "You know, your father loved you very much."

It was the last thing Beth wanted to hear. William's connections with Dublin and Mrs Hawkins melodic Irish accent only accentuated the lump in Beth's throat. "Yes I know," said Beth, "and I was a bastard to him." Beth had such pangs of guilt she had to punish herself by openly acknowledging how horrid she had been to him. "But I loved him too and I miss him terribly."

"Hello Mr Hamilton." Beth went into Mr Hamilton's office and he closed the door behind her. His massive heavy desk was piled high with folders and a desk under the window was bending under the weight of more folders, neatly stacked and labelled.

"Please sit down," said Mr Hamilton, a tall thin man with white hair and ruddy complexion. "Mind if I smoke?" he asked.

Beth had no choice but she had no objection. He picked up a pipe lying in an ashtray on his desk and placed it in his mouth. He re-ignited the sweet smelling tobacco with a gold lighter. He pulled heavily on the mouthpiece and bellows of smoke added to the existing smoky haze in his office.

"Thanks for seeing me at short notice. I'll be brief," said Beth. She repeated the story to him and handed him the document. "I wanted Mrs Hawkins to place it with the title deeds but she wanted you to verify it first."

"Who drew this up?" asked Mr Hamilton.

"I did," said Beth.

"Well it's all right but the wording is not quite correct. Can I write on it in pencil?"

"Yes, certainly," said Beth. "I lived in the house with my parents for thirty odd years and I'm still living there and have no intention of selling it, so none of us will really benefit from any sale. My parents always said it was the family home and my father used to say one should never sell the roof over ones head. I asked Jill to donate her share to me, so if anything did happen to her, heaven forbid, it would remain within the family, with the two remaining daughters. Do you think I've done the right thing?" Beth was seeking confirmation that her request was justified.

"If your sister was willing to donate her share to you then that's her prerogative but I would suggest you word it as I've suggested," said Mr Hamilton.

It's All Just Nuts

"Thank you. I'll re-do it and ask her to sign it," said Beth.

Jill's stay at the nursing home didn't strengthen her, which was the main purpose of her stay there. Her food had to be liquidised to avoid her choking and poor Jilly looked so pathetic as she sat in her chair on the veranda; she looked old, thin and wizened and Beth felt so desperately sorry for her.

"I took that agreement thing, your donation of the house, to the lawyers recently to have it filed with the title deeds but they said the wording wasn't quite right so I've re-done it," said Beth handing the agreement to Jill. "It'll need your signature again. Can I get your specs.?" asked Beth.

Jill mumbled something that Beth couldn't understand.

"Shall I get them?" asked Beth.

Jill nodded and pointed towards her room.

Beth found her glasses in her locker and gave them to Jill.

"Hey, you look smart with your glasses on. You look switched on and with it. It's your bod that's not switched on yet!" joked Beth.

Jill read the agreement and signed it unconcerned with her little sister's comments.

"I'll get Nora and Emily to sign it when they come," said Beth. "I've noticed they don't talk to me much these days. I hope they're not pissed off because I've asked you to donate your share to me. What do you think?" asked Beth.

Jill shrugged her shoulders and made no attempt to say anything or write a note to Beth. Jill coughed and had difficulty in swallowing then wrote a note using her bits of paper and pencil on the table next to her. 'Did Pa die in here?' wrote Jill.

"He was in that private room over there," Beth pointed in the direction of his room, "right next to your bed. En suite and all. Spoilt eh? He was there for a week or so before they transferred him to hospital and he died in there. You were too bombed out to remember," said Beth.

Jill nodded slowly. Beth felt sorry for her skinny sister.

"You worry me. Do you know when you'll be able to go home?" asked Beth.

Jill shrugged her shoulders again and Beth thought she looked down and depressed.

"Do you want to go home?" asked Beth. Jill's inability to talk was frustrating for both of them.

Jill's little face screwed up and she started to cry.

"Hey Roe-Roe, what's the matter!" Beth wondered if she'd hit a nerve and why.

Beth saw Emily's car drive into the car park and Nora was with her.

"Here come the girls," said Beth.

Jill made a groaning sound.

"What's that meant to mean!" asked Beth jokingly.

Nora and Emily sat down with them on spare garden chairs on the veranda.

"Before I forget," said Beth. "Could I ask you guys to sign this agreement again as witnesses. Apparently I hadn't worded it properly and the lawyer wanted me to re-do it."

Nora and Emily signed the form and again made no comment to Beth. Were they having devious talks about it between themselves? She wished they'd be open about it; if they had something to say, just say it. She wanted to discuss the donation with them to clear the air although it had nothing to do with them. Well, thought Beth, perhaps it did have a lot to do with them; Jill's donation negated Nora and Emily's share of the property.

Beth's thoughts were in a spin again. Nora and Emily knew damn well the house was intended for the three girls and not outsiders and Beth was annoyed that they seemed to want a share of the family home. It was obviously an issue with them and they were probably annoyed with Beth's request. Then again, thought Beth, Jill elected to donate her share so what was she supposed to do? She knew that discussing it with Jill's friends wouldn't be the answer.

Beth had a strong suspicion, in fact she was damn sure, that Jill wanted to go home but Nora and Emily were balking for some reason and Beth wanted to find out if she was right.

"I think Jill wants to go home," said Beth, jumping in at the deep end. Now she'd put a cat amongst the pigeons.

Jill nearly had a heart attack and mumbled loudly "*No!*" She waved her hands in front of her and looked angrily at Beth.

"What's wrong?" asked Beth amusingly, but she knew something wasn't right. "You've been here for nearly two months and I'm sure you're ready. Don't you want her home?" Beth looked at Nora and Emily.

Neither of them answered and Beth had her answer. What the hell's going on thought Beth.

Poor Jilly responded again angrily and mumbled "No. Stop it."

"We don't think she's ready to come home," said Nora.

"She's as ready as she'll ever be," insisted Beth. Beth had a feeling they probably felt they couldn't cope with her and if that *was* the case, they should bloody well say so, thought Beth. "If you feel you can't manage I'd like to pay for a nurse aide for her for a few months until everything settles down."

Nora and Emily didn't take up Beth's offer and Jill was insistent that she dropped the subject but all Beth learnt was that Jill's homecoming was an issue with them and but she didn't know why.

Beth continued to visit Jill at least once a day and for some reason seldom bumped into Nora and Emily on their visits although Jill said they were visiting her. Beth talked to Jill about getting a special shoe made for her to make up for her shortened leg but Jill wasn't interested. She lived in sandals or better still she was barefoot most of the time and having to wear a bulky shoe was a non-starter for Jill. Beth offered, and surprise surprise, Jill agreed, that she should take Jill's sandal home and make an attempt to build up the sole.

To attain the additional height of three inches and have stability and some flexibility, Beth cut up an old towel and folded it tightly to the required size and tied it to the sole of her leather sandal. It turned out to be a hideous monstrosity and Beth saw Jill try it on once probably out of politeness and never saw her use it again, still preferring her bare feet.

Some two weeks after the flare-up over Jill's return home she did go home and Beth's offer to pay for a nurse aide wasn't mentioned or taken up. Almost every late afternoon Beth visited Jill at home and she'd be on her bed, some days looking quite perky and others she'd be feeling down.

"Hi Roe-Roe." It became Beth's usual greeting. Jill looked perkier than usual which pleased Beth but Jill still had a problem communicating and she had volumes of paper at her bedside to write her requests, thoughts or answers and Jill was surprisingly patient with her afflictions.

'Surgeon said I died on operating table,' wrote Jill on a piece of paper and handed it to Beth.

Beth read the note. "Not again! That's the second time you've died. Will it be third time lucky?" joked Beth.

Jill gave Beth a big smile and nodded and mumbled "yes" quite cheerfully.

Beth opened Jill's box of cigarettes. "Piss off. I'm only joking. Shall I light two?" asked Beth.

Jill looked at Beth and nodded and Beth gripped both cigarettes tightly in her lips and lit them then handed one to Jill. "You're a macabre creature. I think you want to bloody well die," said Beth opening the window to exhale her smoke.

Jill smiled widely again and drew on her cigarette, inhaled and started coughing, patting her chest with her hand.

"So what did the surgeon do? Did he resuscitate you?" Silly question thought Beth but Jill nodded.

Jill put her cigarette on the ashtray and wrote another note. Beth read it. 'Don't tell the others.'

"Why not!" asked Beth.

Jill shook her head and mumbled "no."

"I don't know what difference it makes. You're nuts," said Beth going back to her open window.

Beth and Jill had a good rapport and most of Beth's visits centred around nonsensical casual communication but they both enjoyed it. Jill made an effort for a few months after her return home to walk to the sitting room and watch television in the evenings and late into the night but that declined after a while and she'd spend most of the time on her bed.

Finances were becoming tight for Beth and with tourism and the economy still on the decline it still wasn't feasible for her to resume production. For several months she was living on drawings from the company. Finances had to be handled very cautiously ensuring there was sufficient for annual business commitments, returns, secretarial and accountancy fees and the upkeep of the house.

There seemed to be financial issues in Jill's household as well. Emily was bringing in a good salary; Nora now had a permanent job having given up her own partially successful business and, as far as Beth could gather, Nora had a minimal income and Jill hadn't worked for about two years due to her cancer and then her mild stroke.

Jill could be very cagey sometimes and all too often Beth didn't know how to take her. Beth would ask her how she was managing financially and she would either shrug her shoulders or point in the direction of Emily's bedroom.

"I just don't know how you went through all that money you had Jill," said Beth one day. Beth knew it was none of her business to know about Jill's finances but Jill had been making subtle hints over a number of weeks indicating that she needed money and Beth wanted to know what was going on.

"How much are you paying Nora and Emily every month?" asked Beth.

Jill indicated a figure using the fingers on her hand.

"*What!*" said Beth. "That's *far* too much. You're mad. You eat bugger all and lie here all day".

"And you told me the other day your money was used to pay for the satellite TV licence and who watches the bloody thing? You watch bugger all!" Beth was getting annoyed but she, Diana and William always knew that finances were a grey area in their household and if Beth had her way she'd rather have *nothing* to do with it. "Your only expenses here should be the teaspoon of food you eat each meal and any medical aid shortfalls. If your friends are making you contribute to the running of the house or domestic staff wages, then I think it's bloody mean of them Jill. It's the very least they can do for you. Anyway, Emily said she paid for all those natural therapy tablets. I'm wondering now if she did or did she use your money? You guys can't be straight for one minute."

Jill looked at Beth and rubbed the tips of her fingers against her thumb.

"What does that mean?" asked Beth, still annoyed. "Do you want money?"

Jill nodded slowly.

"And where am I going to get it from?" asked Beth.

Jill put on her silly look and opened her eyes widely.

"I don't know what you're on about Jill. You'd better write it down," said Beth.

Jill lay on the bed and made no attempt to write a note for Beth.

"So what's this? Twenty questions?" asked Beth.

Jill nodded again and grinned.

"You're a shit head Jill," said Beth knowing Jill wouldn't take umbrage at her comment. "Are you waiting for your share from Pa's estate?" asked Beth.

Jill nodded.

"Heaven knows when that's coming. I've seen Mrs Hawkins who's handling Pa's estate and she reckons it'll take a while yet. For your information, *madam*," said Beth jokingly, "I *did* suggest to Mrs Hawkins months ago that I give you an advance against your share but she said it would be very messy and advised against it."

Jill was listening but gave no response, reached for her cigarettes and offered one to Beth.

"I'll have one of mine," said Beth and took her box of cigarettes out of her shorts' pocket. "Do you want one of mine?" asked Beth but Jill had already lit hers. "Anyway, I bought you a few cartons of fags a while ago so that's better than a kick in the bum eh?" said Beth.

"I presume you're still happy with your donation of the house to me?" asked Beth.

Jill didn't respond again but held her cigarette between her thumb and forefinger and started to draw on it slowly, watching the tip glowing as though deep in thought. She inhaled and started coughing, taking short breaths of air between her coughing fit.

"Die you bugger die," joked Beth again, Jill still unperturbed by Beth's fun intended comments. "I'm not bloody psychic, why won't you give me an answer?"

Jill lay on the bed in her usual Bermuda shorts and holey T-shirt, looking blankly at her cigarette. That awful angry looking red lump on her leg had gone, removed by the surgeon when he repaired her broken leg, the skin puckered into a six inch scar on her bony leg above the knee.

"I suppose you want me to pay you out for your share of the house?" asked Beth. "Now I'm thinking 'Jill style,'" said Beth.

Jill rolled her cigarette in her fingers, shrugged her shoulders and gave Beth a wide-eyed look again.

"You're dreaming girl," said Beth. "You can forget that one. I certainly don't have that kind of money. I get that feeling your friends are pushing you over your finances. Honestly Jill, that's bloody unfair of you. We never had to pay for the house; it was *given* to us. The folks always said it was the family home and they wanted us to share it. We'll probably never sell it, so Margaret and I may never realise the financial rewards of the sale so why the hell should you?"

Jill's face was expressionless.

Beth went on, wishing Jill would reason. "The only way I could ever pay you out for your share, would be for us to sell the house. Do you *want* us to sell it?"

Beth got a response from Jill and she shook her head adamantly and mumbled "no."

"Well thank God for that. Honestly Jill, I wish you'd say something or write something down. You lie there pulling faces and I don't know what and I don't know what you want out of me," said Beth. "Here comes the lady of the house."

Emily drove into the garden from her day at the office. Nora was in the house somewhere and would pop in periodically to see Jill but Beth hadn't seen her that afternoon.

"Hmm." Jill made a noise to attract Beth's attention. Jill pointed outside then twirled her forefinger in the air near her right temple.

"Who's mad? Emily?" asked Beth amusingly.

Jill grinned and nodded.

"Why?" asked Beth again.

Jill mimed the word 'wait' and held up the palm of her hand.

"The plot thickens. I'm in suspenders," quipped Beth.

Jill fiddled on her bedside table and picked up the box of cigarettes.

"You're smoking too much," said Beth.

"Tough," gurgled Jill.

"Get outside you bloody dog. Look at the bloody mess you're making in here," came Emily's voice from the passage. "I'm sick and tired of living in a bloody tip."

Beth looked at Jill and pulled a face with a surprised look and Jill nodded.

"What's her problem?" asked Beth.

"Hi Emily" Nora greeted her in the passage, trying to calm her.

"I suppose nothing's new or changed in the household?" quizzed Emily with a tone of sarcasm.

There was a sound of something falling that came from the direction of Emily's bedroom. "Shit, damn it," said Emily and it sounded as though she kicked something.

"I see what you mean," said Beth. "Huh, having a bit of a tant."

It's All Just Nuts

Jill wrote a note and gave it to Beth. 'This goes on every day,' wrote Jill.

Beth and Jill listened to Emily having her tantrums around the house and things went quiet for a while.

"I've been thinking over the last week or so," Beth sat at the open window cooling herself in the stifling humidity, "about going overseas to work for a couple of months. I've got a bit of money, yes, company funds, but I'm drawing on it all the time and it won't last forever. But I can't just lock the house and go. I'll have to get someone to house sit and look after Choo-Choo. If I go, rather *when* I go, because I'll have to, then I'll be able to help you out."

Jill opened her eyes widely, obviously in approval and mimed 'when.'

"When? When I find a suitable house sitter," said Beth.

Emily came into Jill's bedroom. "Hello," she said coarsely, her greeting not aimed at anyone in particular and clearly she wasn't at ease. "How are you?" she said, looking at Jill.

Jill looked at her and shrugged her shoulders.

"Huh, looks like I'm the only one who does any work around here," said Emily sarcastically.

Beth and Emily had never exchanged harsh words in twenty odd years except for the occasion when Emily and Nora attacked her like a pack of dogs a few years earlier but Emily's comment annoyed Beth and she wasn't going to be walked over. "There's no need for that comment," said Beth sternly.

"Oh and *who* do you think you are?" asked Emily sarcastically again. "I'll say what I like."

"Just cool it please," said Beth and Emily left the room and went down the passage muttering to her self.

"Boy, she's hyped up," said Beth and they could hear her swearing in the kitchen. "Shame Roe-Roe, don't let them bully you."

Nora came in the room a little out of breath and looked at Jill with a look of concern on her face. "All right my friend?"

Jill nodded. It seemed they were accustomed to it.

"Anyway, I'm going to disappear and I'll see you tomorrow," said Beth and kissed Jill on the head.

Jill waved at Beth and mumbled "Thank you," her voice croaky and thick.

The weeks slipped by and Emily's moods, according to Jill, continued. Jill had fallen on a few occasions going to the bathroom in the night and she'd cut herself on the leg and she was battered and bruised. Beth had given Jill a battery-operated buzzer, which Diana had used, so she could call Nora in the night. Jill was too proud and stubborn to use it and she'd continue to get up on her own at night and would invariably fall. Jill was on morphine that helped the pain but she couldn't tolerate it, putting her in a drunken state and causing her to fall more frequently.

It was a cruel cycle, a vicious circle that upset and tormented the household and Beth. Jill's condition deteriorated and she got weaker and refused any medical attention. Beth was so worried about her at one time she asked a doctor to see her at the house. He was quite blunt with Beth, Nora and Emily and said it was only a matter of time. Jill refused any form of treatment from him and his hands were tied.

'Why did you call the doctor?' Beth read Jill's note.

"*Because*, dear loving sister, we *care* about you and we're *worried* about you. Any objection? asked Beth.

Jill scribbled another note. 'DON'T do it again.'

"You're worse than impossible. You've got to think how others feel as well Jill," said Beth.

Jill put her hands in the air.

"Yeah, who cares eh? Well *we* care, madam. To change the subject; can you manage a little walk onto the veranda? A little exercise will do you good," suggested Beth.

"No," gurgled Jill. Her throat was thick and she was still having difficulty in swallowing.

"Thought you might say that. I think Nora and Emily are out there and I'm going to have a fag."

Nora and Emily were on the veranda having a late afternoon cup of tea. "There you are," said Beth.

"Jill's not too good," said Emily. "I saw her when I came home."

"She's really up and down these days. I keep telling her to call me at night if she wants to go to the bathroom but she won't. She says she doesn't want to disturb me and then she falls. I'm not sleeping properly because I'm listening out for her," said Nora.

"She's as stubborn as a mule," said Beth.

Big Nora laughed. "She's not a Taurus for nothing."

"If she breaks a leg again she's had her chips," said Beth.

"My poor poor friend," said big Nora sadly, her outsize backside squeezed tightly into a garden chair. She sat quietly with her eyes closed and her hands clasped on her huge belly, thinking and meditating.

"Nora and I are going to stay at the rest camp at Maleme Dam next weekend. Will you come with us?" asked Emily.

Beth loved the bush but now wasn't the time. "No, thanks. Would be nice but the timing's not right," said Beth.

"Of course we'd *love* Jilly to come," said Nora calmly, still sitting with her eyes shut like a Buda. "You know how she loves the bush, especially Matopos."

"Sure, it was your old stamping ground for years. You were always camping out there," Beth recalled.

"Jill would be up before dawn – she loved watching the sunrise. She'd make the fire and wake us up with a cup of tea," said Nora.

"Yes, then she'd make a full breakfast for us, fried eggs, bacon, tomato, the whole tootie," said Emily.

They sat in silence on the veranda for a while watching the afternoon shadows lengthening across the garden and the bush beyond. There was a special peace, a special aura about Africa not found anywhere else in the world. The air was always crisp and clean though sometimes alluringly dusty, unpolluted by raging money-spinning industries, the skies refreshingly blue for most days of the year, often not a cloud in the sky from one week to the next.

Emily broke the silence. "Which sister do you prefer out of Margaret and Jill?"

Beth wondered what Emily must have been thinking about to come out with such an odd question. "That's a strange question. Neither actually." Beth didn't have to ponder on the question. "Why?" asked Beth.

"Just wondered," said Emily.

"It burns my bum seeing her like this. I must go and say cheerio to her; I've got to get home," said Beth.

"OK Roe-Roe, I must run away. Are you all right?" asked Beth.

'Thanks' mimed Jill.

"Oh, I forgot to tell you. I've been hunting around for a house sitter and someone's coming to the house tomorrow afternoon to see the place. So I'll probably see you day after tomorrow?" said Beth.

Beth went home thinking about Jill and her finances. She wanted to help her and had the finances to do so but she couldn't afford to be short for the company commitments. She felt in some ways she should pay Jill for her share of the house but then thought she and Margaret would probably never benefit financially from the property, so why should Jill? Beth was wondering if she had a guilty conscience having asked Jill to donate her share of the house to her, but she knew Jill could have declined. She did after all sign that agreement twice. Beth decided she wanted to speak to Mr Hamilton again about it.

Beth phoned Mr Hamilton's secretary first thing the following day and got an appointment to see him at 2.30, which suited her fine as the potential house sitter was coming to the house after 5 o'clock.

"Come in Miss Maynard." Mr Hamilton stood at the open door to his office. "I saw you a few months ago was it?"

"That's right. It's about the same matter. You'll recall my sister donated her share of the house to me. I feel guilty in a way for having asked her to do that and what I'd like to do is pay her out her quarter share of the property, at the value at the time of her donation," said Beth. "It's the rampant inflation here that might make it possible but I can't help that," said Beth, "but I believe I have a moral obligation to do it."

"Why would you want to pay her out?" Mr Hamilton sounded surprised. "You're under no moral *or* legal obligation to do so. She agreed to donate it to you and I'd advise you to put it to bed."

"Oh boy!" said Beth feeling more undecided. "I just feel I've let her down and I feel inside," Beth thumped her chest lightly, "my heart tells me I should do it."

"I can only advise you against it, unless you had a gun to her head when she signed it!" said Mr Hamilton jokingly.

"She signed the agreement *twice* if you recall. I had to re-word it and she signed it again," said Beth.

Mr Hamilton held up his hands and smiled. "I rest my case."

Beth sighed. "All right, but I would still like to do it! I'd like to give it more thought if I may."

"Let me know what you decide."

Beth was in town and had time to spare before her meeting at home. She had wanted to talk to William's doctor about his illness but it had been too painful for her. She felt she could handle it now and she decided to go home via the doctor's rooms.

There were so many memories in Bulawayo that reminded her of Diana and William. There had to be; they had lived together there for over thirty five years. It was a young city, started in the 1890's by pioneers and settlers and consequently had a mixture of Victorian and modern architecture which blended perfectly with its very wide and beautiful tree-lined streets and avenues, history confirming they were made wide enough so as to turn a span of sixteen oxen. The city's tourist attractions made Bulawayo a popular tourist destination and visitors described it as a 'Jewel Beneath the Zimbabwe Sun.'

The shops, the restaurants, the industrial areas and almost every street Beth drove down bought back such happy memories for her. There was one block in the avenues Beth couldn't drive past for a number of years after Diana's passing. It housed Diana's doctor's rooms; a place she visited so often with Diana and her problems and Beth would travel any other route to avoid that dreadful building. They all loathed the place and unanimously knick-named it the 'snake pit.'

Beth parked outside the surgery housing William's doctor, grateful it wasn't the infamous snake pit. She sat in her 4x4 and wondered if she was doing the right thing. He probably won't tell her anything anyway; that doctor/patient confidentiality thing she thought.

"They're all a pain in the arse," said Beth out loud to herself. She got out and alarmed the pickup with her remote. "Jill's got the right idea. Avoid them like the bloody plague," Beth was still talking to herself.

She braced herself and walked into the surgery. How she hated those places.

"Hi Miss Maynard!" The receptionist greeted Beth cheerfully and remembered her from her visits with William and Beth had had the misfortune of visiting a doctor on a few occasions.

"Hello! How are you?" said Beth.

"We're all fine. We haven't seen you for a long time," said the receptionist.

"Yes, lucky you!" said Beth. "I wanted to have a word with Dr Langford about my Dad. Will he be free for a moment this afternoon?"

"If you won't be long with him, I'll squeeze you in."

"Probably thirty seconds!" said Beth. "I'll wait just outside here." Beth waited on the veranda. She avoided doctor's waiting rooms like the plague believing they were bug ridden from coughing, spluttering patients.

Beth waited about ten minutes when she was called in. "Hi Doc. I'm probably wasting your time and mine, but I wanted to speak to you about my Dad."

"Sure, sit down," said Dr Langford.

"I know his death certificate mentioned heart failure but was there anything specific that was wrong with him?" asked Beth. She didn't know why she was bothering to ask him.

"He was in his eighties and he was just old," said Dr Langford.

"Yeah, but there's always something that causes ones demise!"

"His heart was weak and he couldn't cope."

Beth sighed. "He saw a urologist a few times and you mentioned at one time that he had a high white blood count. Could he have had cancer?"

"As I said, he was just old."

Beth knew it was a futile exercise. "I just thought you could throw some light on it for me."

"I know it's hard to come to terms with these things."

Beth couldn't wait to leave the surgery. "I knew it. I shouldn't have asked," said Beth to herself as she walked outside. She got in the pickup, turned the ignition key and the diesel engine kicked into life. "Farting against bloody thunder."

"Hi Roe-Roe," Beth's voice rang out in the passage. Her visits were becoming such routine now but she enjoyed seeing Jill. She knocked on her bedroom door and walked in.

Jilly was lying propped up on her bed with the proverbial cigarette burning away in the ashtray next to her bed. The operation for the growth was on her left leg and she'd had the surgery for the break on her right leg and lying on either side was too painful for her.

"I'm surprised you don't get bed sores."

Jill held up her skinny arm and felt her biceps and mimed 'strong.'

"Wise guy hey. You think you're as strong as an ox. That's why you're a Taurus. A mad bloody bull," said Beth. "You're Roe-Roe the rodent, remember?" They were off again with their nonsensical waffle. "Are they still going to Maleme Dam tomorrow?" Beth wanted to know if Nora and Emily's camping weekend was still on.

Jill threw one arm in the air and mumbled something and Beth barely picked up one word.

"You mean they can fuck off?" Beth spoke for Jill.

Jill nodded and reached for her notepaper and pencil, wrote a note and handed it to Beth. 'Emily going to UK in a few months.'

"For how long?" asked Beth.

Jill shrugged her shoulders and wrote on another piece of paper. 'She can stay there.'

"Is she still screaming like a fish wife? Following in my footsteps I guess," said Beth.

As Jill nodded Nora came in the room.

"Emily and I are going to Maleme tomorrow for two nights and Liz said she'd spend two nights with Jill," said Nora.

"That's good. I'd like to help but I can't leave the house unattended," said Beth, "but I'll spend extra time here. Jill says Emily is going to the UK?"

"Yes," said Nora, a little breathless. "We don't know if it's for good or what her plans are." She looked agitated. The phone rang and she went to answer it.

"Oh, I forgot to tell you. That house sitter came around yesterday but she said the place was too big and she wouldn't have felt comfortable. So it's back to the drawing board. Would you prefer a nurse aide for those two nights? I'll pay," said Beth.

Jill shook her head and mumbled 'no' and started a coughing fit barely able to catch her breath.

Beth sighed. "We're all in a mess. The folks gone, the business on hold and you've got a way to go before you get better. The wheels are falling off hey?"

Jill flicked her hand towards the floor.

"What's that supposed to mean?"

Jill pointed to herself this time and flicked her hand towards the floor again.

"You're going to fall off your perch?" asked Beth.

Jill nodded and grinned.

"Don't you bloody dare pop off on me. I want you up and about again."

Jill started coughing again and shook her head. Her throat was thick and she mumbled "die," as though quite unperturbed.

"Don't talk like that you arse," said Beth seriously. "By the way, some more macabre news, which will please you no doubt. I've decided to have a headstone made for Pa; we've all agreed on the epitaph and I'll have the ashes laid before I go overseas. It's a ghastly chore but it must be done."

Jill wrote a note for Beth. 'When are you going?'

"Is this a quiz?" joked Beth. "*When* I find a suitable house-sitter *darling*." Beth spoke with a sarcastic tone but Jill knew it was intended with affection.

Jill rubbed the tips of her fingers against her thumb as she had done on other occasions, indicating she needed money.

"Bloody hell Jill. I've *told* you there's nothing I can do at the moment. I'm *not* using company funds to finance you, the lawyers don't want me to give you an advance on your share of Pa's estate and we're not selling the bloody house, as we've agreed *and* I don't see why I should pay you out for the share of the house you gave to me. One, I can't afford it right now and two, Margaret and I won't be benefiting financially seeing we're not selling it. This is driving me up the wall. I've told you I'll help out when I can. *Shit.* I must go. I'll see you tomorrow," said Beth and kissed Jill on the head. " All right Roe-Roe?" Beth felt guilty having read the riot act to her.

Jill looked at Beth her innocent eyes open wide and she nodded and waved.

Beth hadn't been able to bring herself to finalise the resting of William's ashes and the funeral parlour was holding them for safekeeping. She knew she had to go overseas for a month or so and decided to lay them to rest before she went. It was well over a year since William had died but she knew she would still find it difficult.

Diana never specifically requested what she wanted done with *her* ashes, although Beth did recall her comment when she was so very ill in hospital and expressed 'you can tie me with a ribbon and throw me in the deep blue sea.' William and Beth were undecided at the time what to do with them and they were too devastated to make any arrangements, until several months after her passing they decided to place her ashes on her mother's grave. They knew Diana had been close to Dorothy and they thought it appropriate.

William and Beth had had difficulty in locating Dorothy's grave in the Bulawayo cemetery but they found it eventually and, although in a relatively good state of repair, a huge tree root was growing dangerously near to the grave and Beth managed to axe the root to prevent further growth. They had a beautifully worded epitaph for Diana's headstone and they held a small graveside service when they laid the ashes, bringing back heart-wrenching memories. William had indicated to Beth on more than one occasion that he would like his ashes on the grave with his beloved Diana.

Beth took the bull by the horns and visited the monumental works and ordered a headstone for William having already worded the epitaph and had it approved by Margaret and Jill. With that in the pipeline Beth wanted to visit Dorothy and Diana's grave to ensure everything was

It's All Just Nuts

in order before the monumental works company laid the stone.

It was a hot sunny afternoon, so typical of Bulawayo's magnificent weather and Beth drove her 4x4 into the cemetery and stopped. There were three or four roads that crossed the cemetery from one side to the other and they all looked the same to her. It had been too painful for her to visit Diana's grave again and it was a number of years since she was there for the service. She thought William had been back a few times on days when he felt so alone, probably during the times her tongue had unleashed vulgarity at him. Beth sat quietly in the pickup, the diesel engine purring, reflecting on those days and she still hated herself venomously for the grief she caused her father and how she knew she had let down her beloved mother. She had loved them so much and she knew she'd never forgive herself.

Beth slipped into first gear and slowly released her foot from the clutch and drove down the dusty access road. They all look the bloody same she thought, even the trees. She just couldn't remember where the grave was. It was only the distance from a hedge that gave her an indication where to start looking. She stopped the truck on the road, got out and armed the vehicle with the remote control that bleeped loudly. "Quite a din in a deathly quiet cemetery." Beth was talking to herself again. "I suppose it would be *deathly* quiet, you dork."

She headed towards a row of trees where she thought the grave might be but she was wrong. A few headstones were lying on the ground and it appeared two had been removed, with distinct weathered marks at the head of the graves, which struck her as odd. The grass was knee high in places and sticky burrs had stuck to her legs. She carried on towards the next row of trees leaving the pickup at least two hundred yards away. She inadvertently walked into a metal number plate in the long grass demarcating a grave, and in so doing, sliced open the skin on her lower leg. Blood flowed down her leg and under her foot onto the leather sandal. "Bugger it," Beth said outloud. She had nothing to put on the wound and left it to bleed, feeling the sticky warm blood under her foot. "There it is," said Beth. She recognised Dorothy's headstone and stepped cautiously through the long grass until she reached the grave.

"I don't believe it. Shit and damnation." Beth stood at the grave in disbelief. Diana's headstone had gone as well as the box of ashes that had been encased under the stone. "I just don't believe this." She stood with her hands on her hips gazing at the grave, Dorothy's stone still intact. She started looking in the grass in the vicinity of the grave, hopeful of retrieving the missing items. There were at least two hours of good daylight left and she decided she'd search until dark.

She thought that if someone was to steal from the cemetery they'd head towards the main road and she concentrated her search between the grave and the road. Beth found the box of ashes just fifteen yards from the grave in a clearing of short grass. The box was unopened and intact. "Thank God for that." Beth spoke quietly to herself. She picked up the box and knelt at the graveside and placed it gently on the ground still with agonising thoughts of Diana's illness and so grieving her loss, but after years of deep meditation had some comfort that their separation although real, was only temporary. Beth was deep in thought for that moment and jumped when she heard a voice behind her.

"Good afternoon."

She stood up and felt the congealed blood had dried and stuck her sandal to her foot. A man stood behind her in a pair of council overalls. "Hello, good afternoon," said Beth.

"You've had something stolen?" asked the man.

"Yes. I'm bloody mad about it. My mother's headstone is missing from this grave."

"We've had a lot of thefts and vandalism here recently but no arrests," explained the man.

"I'm still looking for the stone. I'm going to search this area now," said Beth pointing towards the main road.

"I'll help you."

"Thank you!" said Beth, "two pairs of eyes are better than one."

It was a fairly easy exercise pacing the rows of graves and an abandoned stone would be easily visible. Beth knew the chances of recovery were slim but she knew she had to look for it. They reached the edge of the cemetery without any success but there was a five-yard strip of bush between the last row of graves and the road and the council man and Beth agreed they'd have time to search a reasonably large area before dark.

Beth's feet were brown with dust and small pieces of dry bush grass and dust had settled on the congealed blood on her wound. It was part and parcel of Africa and she wasn't bothered. "We'll never find it," she said to herself as she plodded through the grass, avoiding young acacia trees and thorn bushes with their sharp white two-inch thorns.

"Hello." Beth heard the man calling and she ran over to him, scratching her arms and legs on the thorns she'd avoided so carefully until now.

"Have you found it?"

"This might be it," said the man pointing to a headstone in the grass near the low wire fence surrounding the cemetery.

It was lying face up. "Great, that's it!" said Beth, Diana's name clearly visible, "and it's in one piece. Well done, you were very observant!"

It was bigger and heavier than Beth had remembered and she was grateful for the assistance. They went back via the grave, collected Diana's ashes and it was almost dark by the time they put them in the vehicle. She sat quietly in the pickup for several minutes enjoying the breeze through the open door of the cab, deliberating with immense sadness what to do with Diana's ashes and headstone. It was a nightmare, not something any of them would have envisaged.

The silver shimmer in the western sky was fading in the dusty evening haze as she slammed the cab door and turned the ignition key. Venus had pierced the heavens now, the link to infinity, the life beyond and Beth believed Diana and William were there, guiding and advising her.

The atmosphere at Jill's house deteriorated over the following weeks with Emily's moods and tantrums upsetting Jill and Nora, with Jill hinting to Beth on numerous occasions that she needed money, Beth repeatedly explaining that she intended working overseas for a few months that would enable her to assist Jill but Beth still needed to find a suitable house sitter.

Jill's condition was worsening, her cancer, the mild stroke and the emphysema all taking their toll on Jilly's strength. She was in a lot of pain, her morphine prescription required updating but because Jill refused to be attended to by a doctor the morphine stopped and she relied on a strong codeine-based painkiller which had her in a doped state much of the time with consequential falls in the night. Beth pleaded with her to be admitted to hospital, as did Nora and Emily, even for temporary assistance but Jill refused to go.

Beth wanted to avoid the turmoil in the household and her visits to Jill became less frequent. Over one period she stayed away for a few weeks but phoned Nora for updates on Jill's condition. During one telephone conversation Nora told Beth that Emily was leaving to live overseas and when she did eventually leave she didn't contact Beth to bid farewell.

When Beth visited Jill after Emily's departure, Jill indicated she was pleased to see her go but Beth often wondered if she had said that to cover up her heart ache at Emily's sudden departure in such an awkward time in Jill's life.

Nora was notably agitated and although it wasn't discussed she was clearly concerned that a substantial salary was no longer contributing to their budget and they were relying on Nora's relatively small income. Jill's request for money intensified and she was obviously being pushed to do so by Nora and Nora wasn't sleeping properly having to assist Jill to the bathroom at night.

Beth was at home one evening over a month after Emily's departure when Nora phoned which surprised Beth as calls from Nora were very rare. Nora spoke slowly and quietly but she made a vicious, vile attack on Beth.

"*You*," she emphasised quietly and venomously, "you are sitting there with *all that money*," she continued in a vile venomous tone, "and you won't help your sister. *You* are *despicable*...." Nora's sickening wicked tone continued and Beth wasn't going to listen to any more.

"Nora, will you *stop it* for heaven's sake. *What* is wrong with you?" asked Beth, aware Nora's attack was so out of character.

Nora tried to continue her vile attack, slowly and wickedly but Beth interrupted again not prepared to listen to her rudeness.

"Just *stop it* Nora, *stop it* for heaven's sake." Beth couldn't understand her ghastly tone. "Calm down and phone me when you're more civil," said Beth and she put the phone down.

Seconds later the phone rang again and Nora resumed her attack but Beth replaced the receiver and she didn't phone again.

"Bloody hell," said Beth to herself but she knew Nora was in a state over their finances with Emily's exit from their lives. She wondered why Nora hadn't asked for assistance from her two brothers, one of which ran a successful business. Beth had her own problems and she knew she had to do some temporary work overseas to assist Jill and herself.

Beth was so angry at Nora's outburst that she didn't go near them for a few weeks but continued her hunt for a house sitter and she had contacted someone who sounded promising. She wanted to tell Jill about it and the prospects of a temporary job so Beth eventually bit the bullet and went to Jill's house. Nora appeared on the veranda as Beth drove in the garden, which only raised her blood pressure. She *really* didn't want to see or talk to Nora. She had come to visit Jill.

"I don't want to see you." Beth spoke sternly to Nora.

"Well I don't want to see *you*," her tone still venomous but not as vile.

"*Get out of my sight then.*" Beth lost it and had shouted at Nora that fuelled a slanging match between the two, unfortunately right outside Jill's bedroom window.

A loud verbal noise, sounding like an elongated 'no' came from Jill's room.

Beth was concerned that she had upset Jill but despite her concern the heated language continued between her and Nora and Jill again protested from her room. Beth walked passed Nora, into the house and into Jill's room.

Beth knew she had done the wrong thing by upsetting Jill and she was ready to face the consequences. She stood silently at the foot of Jill's bed like a schoolgirl before the headmistress, willing to accept anything her big sister might throw at her.

"Hello," said Beth quietly.

Jill frowned at Beth and looked cross. "Stop it," said poor Jilly with an effort, her words almost clear but her throat still thick.

"Yeah," said Beth and sat on her folded leg at the end of Jill's bed, "but she was the cause of it." She sounded remorseful and spoke like a school kid. "Anyway she made me bloody cross, she was damn rude and I want an apology before I speak to her again." Beth's anger from outside a few minutes earlier was bubbling up again.

"Stop it!" gurgled Jill.

"Yeah, but tell her she'll have to apologise," said Beth wanting the last word. "Anyway, I've got some news," said Beth. Jill was reading a piece of paper in her hand and appeared to be ignoring Beth but she knew Jill was listening. "I've made comms. with another potential house sitter and she's coming around on Saturday. *And*, do you remember some old friends of mine, Alan and Les Greenwood?" asked Beth.

Jill shook her head.

"*Anyway*, they know a couple who own a small hotel in Cannes in France. Apparently they had a busy summer and want to get away for a few months. Les mentioned my predicament to them and apparently they want *me* to manage the hotel while they're away. They said anyone who's friends with the Greenwoods would be acceptable to them. It'll be autumn there and fairly quiet. So, what do you think?"

"Good," gurgled Jill. Beth deeply regretted upsetting her.

"I've got their e-mail address and I'll contact them when I've seen this potential house sitter at the weekend. Hopefully things are moving at long last. Enough about me. How have you been?" asked Beth.

Poor Jilly shrugged her shoulders. She was propped up on the bed, lying on top of the blankets, her short mousy-coloured hair sticking up at the crown, with her short fringe scattered on her forehead. Her left leg was permanently bent at the knee and she was no longer able to straighten it. She took her scraps of paper and pencil from her bedside table. 'Watch TV until 3am,' wrote Jill and handed it to Beth.

"Good, excellent! I'm really pleased you're doing that. Aren't you poop scared of falling between the sitting room and your room?" asked Beth.

Jill wrote another note for Beth. 'Gardener works 6pm-6am and helps me.'

"We spoke about that months ago and no one was interested in implementing the idea. Good, about time. Presume she's happy about it?" asked Beth again.

Jill nodded and reached for her cigarettes and offered one to Beth.

"I'll have a weak cooked one," said Beth.

Jill pointed to the front of the box. She rotated her cigarettes in the box, the front ones having been subjected to the menthol crystals for a lesser time than the back ones. Jill put a cigarette between her lips using her thumb and forefinger and Beth lit it for her, then lit hers and sat at the open window. She told Jill of her visit to the cemetery, the vandalism and desecration and her reluctance now to have their parents' headstones and ashes laid there in the event of further desecration or theft. She explained to Jill she had given Diana's ashes to the funeral parlour for safekeeping, together with William's ashes, Beth unable to bear the mental anguish of keeping them at home.

The gate bell buzzed and Beth spoke on the intercom. "Hello!"

"Hi, it's Mrs Stacy-Jones," came the voice from the gate intercom and Beth activated the button to open the gate for her.

Mrs Stacy-Jones was elderly and semi-retired, a tall strong woman, happy to housesit and look after Choo-Choo, Beth's most treasured asset and Beth was satisfied she could manage everything.

Mrs Stacy-Jones and Beth were talking on the patio when Choo-Choo joined them from the garden.

"Hello Choo-Choo," said Beth, picked her up and cradled her backside in one hand, the other hand holding her upright under her forelegs so her face was level with Mrs Stacy-Jones. "Say hello to Mrs Stacy-Jones. She's going to look after you."

"Hello Choo-Choo," said Mrs Stacy-Jones. "She's got lovely yellow eyes."

What Beth saw in the following moments was incredible and confirmed her belief that animals have a far greater intelligence than most would believe. Choo-Choo's eyes were level with Mrs Stacy-Jones' eyes and Choo-Choo stared incessantly and steadily at her face for over thirty seconds and Beth was convinced Choo-Choo believed she was looking at Diana, Mrs Stacy-Jones being of similar age and stature to Diana at the time of her passing.

Everything fell into place and within a fortnight Beth was running a little hotel in Cannes on the Mediterranean, pleased that Jill had perked up a little before she went away and was enjoying the cricket tournaments on television. She phoned Mrs Stacy-Jones a few times and everything was fine at home and she was delighted to hear that Choo-Choo would curl up on the floor in the evenings next to Mrs Stacy-Jones' chair. Diana never liked Choo-Choo on her lap and she would often lie curled up at Diana's feet like a dog, but then she thought she *was* a dog.

It's All Just Nuts

Beth returned home nearly three months later. It was late November and the rainy season had started in southern Africa, the bush transformed from a dusty brown landscape with leafless trees, their bare twiggy branches stretching motionless towards endless blue skies to tufts of greenery mixed with dry elephant grass and the predominant acacia trees bursting into life with their delicate green leaves.

Diana and William's perpetual haven was equally as beautiful, Beth still regarding it as their garden. The massive jacaranda shade trees were laden with their elongated bell-shaped mauve flowers, the flamboyant trees competing in the floral race with their silky red and yellow scalloped blooms. The lawns were green and finely trimmed, enhancing the containers of colourful flora. Beth was happy to be home and back in Africa.

She was nervous about seeing Jill, concerned about what she would look like after nearly three months. Beth drove to Jill's house the day after her return home and was pleased, at long last, that she had an envelope full of money for her. She had decided to give her an amount each month and not one lump sum for safety reasons.

"Hi Roe-Roe." Beth gave her usual greeting from the passage, disguising her concern about seeing Jill and popped her head around her bedroom door. "Hello!"

Jill waved at her and smiled and Beth gave a sigh of relief. Jill was thinner, if that was possible, her bare arms and legs like sticks but still tanned from years of sunshine. But her face was gaunt and pale, her eyes deeper in their sockets. She was lying propped up on her back in the same position as she was three months earlier, content in her shorts and airy T-shirt ventilated by self-inflicted cigarette burns.

Beth gave her a long noisy kiss on her head. "Hi Roe-Roe, I'm glad you smiled. How are you?"

Jill gave a thumbs-down sign and started a coughing fit, taking shallow intakes of air unable to catch her breath.

"Is the gardener still coming in at night?"

Jill nodded.

"And has she been any help to you?"

Jill nodded again.

"So she's taking you to and from the sitting room and are you watching the cricket?" Beth was hoping for a positive answer again.

Jill nodded and lent over to get her notepaper and pencil and wrote a note. 'There's a one day match tonight. SA v India. How was your trip?'

"Excellent, I'm really really pleased you're watching the cricket. The trip was OK but I'm glad to be home. This place has a magical pull; there's something special about Zimbabwe."

Jill nodded in agreement. She was as passionate about the country as Beth.

"Anyway, the work wasn't as complicated as I thought. The owners worked with me for a week and showed me the ropes then they went off on their holiday. They holidayed around the Caribbean and apparently they've got a timeshare there as well. I had accommodation in the hotel, so yes, it was good. Oh, and I've got some bucks for you." Beth took an envelope out of her pocket and gave it to Jill. "Sorry it's been so long in coming."

Jill help up her arms to embrace Beth and Beth bent down to kiss Jill. "OK Roe-Roe."

Beth left late because she wanted to see Jill ensconced in the sitting room before the start of the cricket match. She used a walking frame and it took her fifteen minutes to walk fifteen yards, her right leg at least three inches shorter than the left and her left leg shaped like a boomerang, the left knee stiff, almost seized in one position. Jill wouldn't use a wheel chair, indicating she wouldn't be seen dead in one. It was a painful sight for Beth seeing her once buoyant, vibrant sister struggling to walk, her head hung low as she concentrated on every move. Beth walked behind her ready to catch her if she lost her balance.

"I'm going to sell you to the supermarkets with a label around your neck. 'Guaranteed fat free,' said Beth. She knew Jill wouldn't mind her dry sense of humour.

Jill stopped and stood still for a few seconds, resting on her right foot, Beth still behind her. She lifted her right hand and gave Beth two fingers.

"That's the spirit! Did you know two fingers are politer than one?" said Beth.

Jilly looked so tiny and frail in the chair and Beth wished she would get well.

"I'd love to watch with you but I must get home. I promise I'll watch with you next week. Are you still watching those late night macabre murder movies?" asked Beth.

Jill nodded and gave a weak smile but there was such sadness in her eyes depicting her utter despair with her illness.

"You're a horror." Beth knew she had to be strong for Jill but it was heart wrenching and difficult.

Christmas was around the corner and Beth wanted it to come and go as a normal day. She told Jill she would visit in the afternoon on Christmas Day, having had an invite for lunch and Jill seemed satisfied with the arrangement. Nora had invited her to be with them on Christmas Day but Beth took up the other invitation, a foolish and ill-judged decision she'd later regret.

Beth left her lunch invitation later than anticipated and only got to Jill's house at 5 o'clock on Christmas Day. She walked into Jill's room and stood looking at her like a disobedient child. "Sorry I'm late," said Beth.

Jill lay on top of the bed and looked at Beth. Jill's lips stretched in grief and her eyes closed in her screwed up face as tears ran down her cheeks. As she lay on her bed, she must have had time to reflect on the many happy Christmas Days spent with the family.

"Oh Jilly man." Beth bent down and hugged her big sister. "Happy Christmas." Beth put a wrapped gift on her bed. "Sorry there's only one. Not like the old days eh?"

"Have you been on the bed all day?"

Jill nodded. She had stopped crying.

"I see Nora has a few friends around. That's good."

She stayed with Jill for a few hours and she perked up a little but Beth knew how weak Jill really was and her speech had deteriorated, virtually non-existent now and all Jill's communicating was done by writing.

The following weeks were more difficult for Jill and just walking to the en suite bathroom was becoming too exhausting. Beth had a commode made but her design wasn't suited to Jill's needs and they eventually managed to borrow one from a friend. Jill would sit on the edge of her bed in the early evenings and read her bible with the gardener's young daughter, both engrossed in it together and Beth would talk to Nora so not to disturb them. Days later Jill indicated she didn't want to watch the cricket and they knew Jill's strength was waning, yet a few days later it was Beth's birthday and she was thrilled to get a phone call from Nora indicating she was phoning on Jill's behalf to wish her a happy birthday. Jilly was an accountant, her mind active and methodical and despite the afflictions that wore down her leathery frame she kept abreast of daily events.

It was a warm sunny afternoon and Beth was driving home from town, Jill constantly on her mind. She had seen Jill two days earlier and she was much the same and Beth was undecided whether she should visit her. She stopped at the traffic lights at a major intersection intending to go straight across and home but she knew a friend lived down the road. The lights changed to green and in a split second put on her indicator and turned right and decided to visit her friend. She drove two hundred yards down the road and something made her change her mind and in a flash she did a 'U' turn in the road and drove straight home, her actions sufficient to convince any observer she'd escaped from a lunatic asylum.

She didn't dilly dally in the garden as she so often did and when she was on the patio she heard the phone ringing and flew inside to answer it.

"Hello!" she said cheerfully.

She heard Nora's voice, "come quickly," and the receiver was replaced.

"What's going on," said Beth to herself. She didn't wait a moment and went straight out to the car. What could it be she thought as the drove down the long driveway, aware it needed mowing again. Jill was much the same a couple of days ago, weak yes, but nothing dramatically different. Maybe Nora had phoned about something else.

Beth didn't call out to Jill in the passage as she normally did; the house was quiet and she knew something was different but she was sure Jill was all right. She stood in the passage at Jill's bedroom door cautious about entering, yet she knew she had no alternative. She should have been accustomed to facing agonising realities, sometimes having to push herself beyond an acceptable level of emotional trauma. She heard Nora sob and her mind switched over to auto mode, her head commanding her involuntarily entry into the room.

Jill was lying on the bed and her breathing was laboured as she gave shallow gasps through her mouth, fixed open like a little fish. Her eyes were wide with that tell-tale faraway look, lifeless and glazed and once more Beth felt a deep hollow in her gut and chest, Nora confirming her worst thoughts with the dreadful words 'she's going.'

Nora was standing at Jill's bedside, beside herself and weeping, repeatedly pleading to her, "Jilly don't go, come back, please come back. Don't go Jilly. Don't leave me." Jill had her right arm extended over the edge of the bed as though reaching for something and Nora and Beth were asking her "What is it Jill, what do you want?"

They knew it was futile questioning but they were devastated, wanting to help Jill in any way they could but they knew she couldn't answer. They felt helpless as Jill's gasps became slower and weaker and they watched her gently slip away, Nora still pleading to Jill to come back.

Beth couldn't take anymore. Her mind had been on autopilot for so long now, escaping the trauma of Diana and William's departure to the after life. Beth lent against the bathroom doorframe, her hands in her shorts' pockets, her head down. She couldn't cry, she didn't want to cry, she couldn't enact the ritual stereotype bedside death scene either. It was all taking place inside her soul, her very being, churning and biting and liquidizing her heart.

Beth tried to close Jill's mouth but it wouldn't budge, rigor mortis had taken its grip, her system having closed down before her last breath, protracted and hanging on, wanting to oblige Nora's pleas. That swirling liquidizer in Beth's chest couldn't turn off, having to attend further to Jill as she exerted pressure on her boomerang shaped left leg to straighten it as best she could. She found a piece of paper lying on the bed next to Jill with one word written on it. 'Die.'

"You bugger Jill. You always had a macabre sense of humour," Beth told Jill. "I bet you're watching me now and having a damn good laugh."

Jill was brought up an Anglican and attended the Baptist church during her life but Nora told Beth over a cup of tea that Jill said she wanted a Catholic service. Beth drove down to the Catholic Church and found the Father in Bulawayo who accompanied Beth back to the house to perform the final rites.

The Father was horrified at Jill's gaping mouth and wrapped a crepe bandage around her head and under the chin with little success. The resultant image was like a grotesquely gruesome vision from the grave, unquestionably to the delight of Jilly's grisly sense of humour.

Beth was more than willing, and grateful, that she could afford to fund the funerals for Diana, William and

Jill and although she wasn't familiar with funeral services in the Catholic Church she was told Jilly was afforded a full Mass. Nora and Beth were undecided what to do with the ashes and those too were held for safekeeping by the funeral parlour.

CHAPTER 14

Choo-Choo was rolling in the dust, one side then the other, squirming so as to get as much dust into her black fur as she could, then she rubbed her black cheeks and ears in it, revelling in the warmth of the winter sun high in the crisp blue sky. Beth was cleaning the pickup and kept an eye on the filthy cat, ready to chase her if she dared to venture indoors. Choo-Choo got up from her dust bath and strolled casually across the lawn towards Beth. Her silky sleek black coat was covered in brown dust, her head, cheeks and ears powdery brown but her face around her eyes and nose escaped the dust and remained black, the perfect image of a black-faced monkey.

Beth took her eyes off her and minutes later she rubbed up against her legs.

"Go on you dirty little bugger. Push off," and Beth pushed her gently away with her leg. Seconds later she was back. "Will you piss off. Go, buzz off." Beth flicked a dry cloth over her body and clouds of dust flew into the air. Choo-Choo was nearly thirteen now, accustomed to Beth and had no objection to the cleaning ritual as she rolled on her back trying to catch the cloth, wishing it was a flapping bird flying into her clutches. She had a huge garden to herself and enjoyed hunting lizards and birds, and at night the odd tiny shrew but the tastiest catch of all would be a

It's All Just Nuts

young gecko. Most catches required skill and were usually played with and seldom consumed, all making a welcome break from the strenuous routine of sleeping in a sunny spot, or sleeping under a shady bush *or* sleeping on Beth's bed.

It was late at night and Beth was sitting on the patio, as she did on so many evenings. It was nearly five months now since Jilly left them and she was frustrated with her situation and concerned that her finances were dwindling. A million things were churning over in her muddled mind. She knew that if Diana and William were still with her she would have dreamt up another business plan but things had changed now; nothing was the same. She had hundreds of acquaintances but a few friends and they had their lives to live and she couldn't live in their pockets. The political turmoil in the country had forced many of her friends to depart to other pastures, not necessarily greener either. For the first time in her life she felt alone, not lonely, just alone.

  Beth knew in her heart she had to change her circumstances and once she had that sort of gut feeling nothing would change it. The problem was; how where and when. She loved her country and its people with a passion. She had travelled to many countries and met many people from all walks of life but she felt happiest when her 'plane touched down at Bulawayo airport. There was a special magical captivating air about the country and its people, so hospitable, courteous, amenable and hard working and she cherished every aspect of it.

"What are we going to do Choo-Choo?" Beth spoke out loud to her friend. "If I go away for a while, what am I going to do with you? Put your head in a bucket of water, hey?"

Choo-Choo was lying like a guard dog on the edge of the patio, her head upright, diligent and alert, staring into the darkness beyond the extremities of the glare of the security lights, her ears cocked. Beth didn't need a dog thanks to Choo-Choo's vigilance and sharp ears and if anything uninvited was lurking around she'd scuttle indoors with the hair on her body at ninety degrees and her tail like a loo-brush, Beth fully aware that action speaks louder than barks.

It was a mild winters night and the ebony celestial dome was packed, bursting with brilliant stars, Beth consciously aware it was one of the many charismatic beauties that captivated her love of Africa. Chirping crickets and the occasional squawk from a nightjar somehow accentuated the tranquillity of the night and Choo-Choo gave a momentary twitch when an owl hooted in a nearby tree. She knew owls and was wary of them having had a brief encounter with one that had stood some fifteen inches high in a tree. They had watched one other for half an hour until it swooped down with its massive wingspan, terrifying the small black cat into defence mode, up on her hind legs, forelegs reaching to the sky avoiding the clutch of its claws.

Beth went inside to get her cigarettes and came outside again and sat down and put her socked feet up on the chair, her thighs against her chest. She sighed deeply and lit her cigarette, blowing the smoke high in the air, her thoughts still circulating in a mangled mess. Life had been so good, now everything had fallen apart. Her guilt over her disrespect towards William and her violation of Diana's desire that she respected him, still haunted her yet she knew they wouldn't want her to torture herself with such anguish and pain.

Jill had gone now. No one had mentioned Jill's will and Beth had no idea what was in it. She knew she would pay Jill's quarter share to her beneficiary, whoever it was. She had to. She had a moral obligation to Jill despite the lawyer advising her against it. It was financially feasible now owing to the devaluation of the currency but she couldn't help that. It wouldn't be the true value but it was better than nothing she thought. The house wasn't to be sold and she hoped her decision would fulfil the wishes of Jill and Diana and William.

She was sorry she hadn't spent more time with Jilly on their last Christmas Day and read her Bible with her but Jill had looked happy reading it with the gardeners daughter, so that was all right she thought. She grinned when she thought how wiry Jill really was; she was an old warrior. Beth recalled how Nora had given Jill those anti-cancer subcutaneous injections for weeks on end and poor Jilly was like a dartboard and punctured from all sides, not to mention big Nora's mental anguish each time she stabbed her lifelong friend.

Beth threw her cigarette on the lawn near the pool and Choo-Choo watched unperturbed as its smoking head glowed, accustomed to Beth's disgusting habit. She'd smoked too much that night but had thrown all her cigarette ends in a confined area on the lawn making it easier to pick them up in the morning.

Emily was a disappointment. She knew Jill hadn't long to go and she left her friend of twenty odd years on her deathbed and that was beyond Beth's comprehension. And Margaret, Beth often thought about her big sister but she was lucky; she never had to see any of her family when they were so ill but she had kept in close contact with the family on the phone and she was always devastated each time she received the news. She had come up from South Africa for Diana's funeral and the graveside services. Margaret was in England now and she kept asking Beth to go over there, but Beth always perished the thought of being so far from her beloved continent. She was in love with and umbilically attached to Africa and she knew her spirit would die if that cord was severed.

Beth knew her thoughts were drifting, rudderless, but had they seen land, had she deliberated into submission she thought. Yes, she would travel. She had to break her cycle of routine. She'd find a house sitter and escape on a working holiday but what about Choo-Choo? Mrs Stacy-Jones was renting a house now and she knew she'd never find another Mrs S-J and furthermore, Beth didn't want to leave her fury friend with a total stranger. A bucket of water was out of the question so she had no alternative; she would take her feline pal with her and spend time in England.

Choo-Choo joined the jet-set weeks later and flew to Johannesburg for her connecting flight to London and from there she flew on to Manchester to be met by a lady who owned a quarantine kennel in the Yorkshire dales. The precious girl had to spend six months in quarantine. Beth was worried stupid and concerned how she would tolerate the journey, keeping in close contact with all concerned. There were sighs of relief when she learnt her friend was in one piece and ensconced in the quarantine kennel in Yorkshire.

Friends took Beth to the airport, hot on Choo-Choo's trail. Beth didn't want to go now but she had already sent her pal ahead of her and now she had no choice. She had a window seat on the 'plane and once more found herself gazing at that balcony where Diana and William had stood so many many times before. Their usual spot was deserted now and that feeling of emptiness, that huge vacuum engulfed her. The engine revs gained momentum and they taxied off the apron and down to the bottom of the runway for takeoff. She was in a vortex now, a situation she was so against and torn from her beloved Africa, her mingling emotions churning like a maelstrom, incessant, veering towards eternity.

The aircraft banked south and gained altitude. There it was, the beautiful city of Bulawayo, aptly named the 'City of Kings' after two legendary Ndebele Kings, sprawling for miles over scenic bush, high on a plateau away from the turmoil and pollution of industry and the first world. There lay her memories, her life, and she knew she belonged there.